BELOVED SON

A Story of the Jesus Cults

Books by Steve Allen

BELOVED SON

A Story of the Jesus Cults

Steve Allen

The Bobbs-Merrill Company, Inc.
INDIANAPOLIS/NEW YORK

To Brian, David, Steve and Bill,
who are equally loved

Acknowledgments

I am indebted to a number of people, some of whom prefer to remain anonymous, for their assistance in providing me with information and literature—pro and con—about various of the new religious groups studied in the preparation of this manuscript.

For permission to use material belonging to them, I thank the following: Mrs. Kenneth M. Campbell, CBS News, Jackie Junso, Mr. and Mrs. Thomas McKnight, Jr., Terrence O'Flaherty, Mrs. Elizabeth Painter, The Safety Training and Research Association of Washington, and Wes Uhlman.

I also thank Synanon, the Love Family, and the Hare Krishna organization for providing information and literature about their views and activities; Mrs. Henrietta Crampton of the Citizens' Freedom Foundation for copies of that organization's anti-cult bulletin, and Kathy Crampton, for an expression of her views. I am also indebted to Steve Hassan, founder of the Ex-Moon organization, for his help, and to Rameswara Swami and Mukunda Das of the Hare Krishna religion, and Vicky Sinunu and Larry Israel for helping with the preparation of this public account by making themselves available for tape-recorded interviews.

I also wish to thank Jeffry Freundlich, of my office staff, for his research, editing and help in organizing repeated drafts of the manuscript; Maureen Earl for her assistance in research and the submission of some first-draft materials on religious groups; and Karol Greene, who, although she joined our staff near the end of the process, nevertheless provided important aid in research and editorial advice.

Lastly I owe an enormous debt to Stefanie Tashjian Woodbridge for her wise and incisive editorial assistance.

Table of Contents

Introduction

I sometimes think through a problem best if I write about it. When my son Brian suddenly—unexpectedly—joined a religious commune called the Love Family in 1971, I confronted not only a family crisis but an emerging social problem—that of "cults"—which continues to affect our nation ten years later. I felt I had to make sense of it for myself, and so, as I explain in the following pages, embarked on a personal study of the subject. This book represents a layman's modest effort to examine at least a few of the new sects and cults, to position the debate about them within a larger context that makes it somewhat more comprehensible, and to suggest that the issue is not a simple matter of right vs. wrong. The book is also concerned with the effects of the new religions not only on the young men and women who join them, but on their parents, brothers, sisters, other relatives and friends.

Before I proceed, a word about words: in discussing Brian's case and the large movement of which it is a part, I shall have to employ the nouns *religion, church, sect* and *cult,* even in reference to one particular group. No particular onus attaches to *religion, church* or *sect*—except perhaps in the minds of atheists—but *cult* has somehow grown hair. My intention is to use it in a simple, factual sense.

One of the most poignant human discoveries, and one which many never grasp, is that part of the troublesome drama of life results not from a flat conflict between good and evil but from clashes between various forms of good. Ours would be a far simpler universe if virtues contradicted only vices. In fact, however, virtues themselves are sometimes in contradiction.

One reason for the difficulty of understanding the controversy surrounding the newly proliferated sects is that the history of religion itself is an account of long centuries of precisely such conflicts. The unknown authors of the Old Testament described hundreds of violent physical confrontations between, on the one hand, members of what they perceived as the One True Faith; and, on the other, not atheists or agnostics, but people who perceived religious truth in other forms, who "worshipped other gods." On the limited canvas of American religious experience, too, we have seen endless conflict, disagreement, persecution, and occasionally violent confrontation among religious believers.

We can be thankful that the angry dialogue among participants in the latest religious controversy is at least not so heated or so physically destructive as the long centuries of actual military confrontation between Catholics and Protestants which continues even to the present moment in Ireland. Nor should it be supposed that it was only the Protestant Reformation that gave rise to such tragedies and atrocities; for the long pre-Protestant centuries of Christian experience, going back to the time of Christ Himself, have been characterized by endless angry diatribes, denunciations, excommunications, purges, armed battles, and bloody executions by sword, axe, pressing with weights, hanging, boiling in oil, and burning alive.

Charity may be the greatest of the Christian virtues, but in the context of the historical record, humility is equally important.

In getting the religious cults into focus, therefore—a necessary preliminary to rationally evaluating them—the observer ought not to assume an either/or sort of structure with "traditional religion" on the one hand, perceived as a generally peaceable, rational, dignified and socially responsible entity, and "the cults" on the other, perceived as radical and dangerous departures from ages-old religious norms.

We must realize that religion means different things not only to Catholics, Protestants and Jews, but to the numerous separate sects and subdivisions within those three large categories—and, for that matter, to the millions within the separate denominations.

It has long been my own opinion that no two individuals, even if, for example, they both call themselves Methodists, share precisely the same religious beliefs. The reason is not only that a human being is, by nature, an incredibly complex creature, but that a religion, too, may have literally thousands of components. Therefore it is inevitable that religion on planet Earth will continue to be what it has always been, a phenomenon taking not one but thousands of forms.

The story that follows begins with my son's decision. Why did he make it? In attempting to provide at least a partial answer, I shall portray him almost as if he were a character in a novel. In doing so I shall have to describe the family and social background from which he emerged. Despite the fact that popular television entertainers receive extensive coverage in the media, it is surprising how little even our admirers know of our actual personal circumstances. I suppose it is a matter of fairly common knowledge that I do comedy, created the "Tonight Show," appeared as clarinetist Benny Goodman in the film version of Goodman's life, have written a number of books and popular songs, and am married to actress Jayne Meadows. While these factors had much to do with the circumstances of Brian's early life, it was not in my capacity as entertainer, musician or author that I influenced him, but in my role as his father and the husband of his mother.

Writing this story has served me well. I hope reading it will serve others equally.

Steve Allen

*To Brian**

Brinie, you were a poet at six
Middle-child, with the imp-green eyes,
Sent to produce laughter if not always to share it.

Remember the birds on the meadow?
The seeming thousands of blackbirds swarming cloudlike
    in the dusk?
Stevie said there must be a million of them,
And you said there are more,
There are ninety-eight million and pigeon-jumpy thirty!
I said what is pigeon-jumpy?
And you said that's a number so high a pigeon
        can't even jump off it.

Remember the Mexican fried beans simmering in the
        black iron pan, pastily?
You'd never seen fried beans before, but you knew
        what to call them with the poet's sense.
You sniffed and looked and said, Oh, boy, chocolate
        mashed potatoes!

And then you went outside that summer and played
        at the channel's edge,
Striking your little red tin shovel flatly along
        the water
And at the skipping of the shovel's blade, you said,
The water feels like jello.

---

*From *Wry on the Rocks* (Henry Holt & Co.).

CHAPTER 1

My Son Brian: The Child

One day in 1971 I received a letter from my son Brian, who was then twenty-four. He explained that he was turning his back on the world; had joined a religious commune based in Seattle, Washington; had changed his name, and would neither write to us nor—apparently—see us thereafter.

"Dear Dad," the letter read,

> I have joined the Church of Armageddon here in Seattle. We are a church and a family.
>
> Our only book is the Holy Bible, King James version.
>
> The head of the church is our Lord, Jesus Christ.
>
> *Love* Israel represents Christ and God as the final word in all matters concerning the church, by the total consent of all church members.
>
> I have given up my old name and all that went with it. My new name is *Logic* Israel. I do not expect to be returning to Los Angeles.
>
> This will be my last letter.
>
> I have found my true home and I am happy. Now I can be what I am, a son of God.
>
> Please see that all of the members of the family read this letter.
>
> I love you all very much.
>
> Our address here is:
>> Love Family
>> 818 W. Armour St.
>> Seattle, Washington
>
>> With all my love,
>>
>> *Logic* Israel

To all of us who loved Brian—his mother, my first wife, Dorothy; his stepmother, Jayne; his three brothers, Steve, Jr., David and Bill—the

3

letter came as a bombshell. We were hurt and stunned. Brian had never struck any of us as a particularly religious person. I would have sworn he was literally incapable of religious zeal. We did not know what to think. Questions flooded our minds. Who was *Love* Israel? What was the Church of Armageddon? What experience had led Brian to such a dramatic and unexpected decision? Most of all, why? Why—especially in the light of the love we knew he felt for us all, stated twice in the letter—why had he chosen to turn his back on us, his family, his old friends in Los Angeles and, in a sense, the entire outside world?

Although we had never heard of the Church of Armageddon, we immediately assumed that it was one of the new cults or small churches that had begun to spring up in many parts of the country. By 1971, of course, the whole nation had heard the shocking story of the Manson Family, which, though it was certainly not a religious group, was nevertheless an experiment in communal living, characterized by mindless submission to a dominating authority figure. I knew that once Manson's followers had surrendered to him their capacity for rational, self-willing behavior, they had placed themselves in grave danger, a danger later dramatized when Family members committed the series of murders that brought them to national attention.

We were somewhat reassured by the word "church" and also by Brian's references to Christ as "head of the church," which suggested that the intentions of the Armageddon group—whoever they might turn out to be—were virtuous. But I knew that although the two thousand years of Christian experience encompassed the high-mindedness and spirituality of the saints, the fanaticism and murderous hatred of the Inquisition and the religious wars were also part of it.

At that time all we had to go on was conjecture. I was then doing a comedy-and-talk television show five days a week, which tied me to the Hollywood area; I could not simply take off to Seattle to investigate. And even if I had been free, I felt I would have been intruding on Brian's privacy. He was an adult. He had a right to live his own life. So we hoped for the best. And worried. And wondered.

I knew one thing: I did not want to lose my son.

From infancy Brian was an unusually lovable fellow, blond, with blue-green eyes and a smiling face. So far as I know, he has never had an enemy in the world; he was always loved or at least liked; even strangers took to him. On his second-grade report card his teacher praised his schoolwork and added, "We all enjoy your happy and pleasant personality." Four years later his sixth-grade teacher wrote, "You will always be well-liked, I'm sure, because of your happy disposition."

Adults always found Brian charming, and very often amusing as well. Actress and TV panelist Betsy Palmer, an old friend from "I've Got a Secret," reminded me in 1980, for instance, that Brian had once informed Jayne that it was Betsy Palmer who made the first American flag.

Many children's malapropisms and mispronunciations entertain their parents. Brian's were delightful. One day he said to his stepfather, "Gosh, Andy, you sure comb my hair fast. You do it in a fracture of a second." Perhaps I thought that since both my mother and I performed comedy professionally, Brian was somehow gifted with the same tendency.

He was also known to announce that his favorite part of a steak was the "tenderbine," and that his favorite television show was "Ozziet and Harriet."

One day Dorothy was playing a game with the three boys which involved her reciting portions of poems that the children were supposed to finish. She said to Brian, "Little Miss Muffet—" to which he responded, "—went to the cupboard."

During the ensuing laughter he said with great spirit, "Yes she *did,* Mama, and it was bare."

My favorite line of Brian's came during the following conversation between him and his older brother Stevie:

Brian: Look, Stevie, there's a big crow out on the front lawn. Let's get our bows and arrows and shoot it.

Stevie: Don't be silly, Brian. What do you want to shoot crows for?

Brian: Because they're a menace to worms.

On another occasion Dorothy was telling a friend that her sister Mildred was to be married the following Saturday and that someone named Bob was going to be the best man.

"Can I be the best boy?" Brian asked.

Another time, when Brian, Stevie and I were driving to the Los Angeles Airport, Brinie suddenly pointed off to the right of the road and said, "I don't remember that old building. It must be new."

In the summer of 1958 I took Stevie and Brian by boat to Europe. Stevie reminded me, as we got ready for our voyage, that Brian—then ten years old—was not to be trusted alone on deck, having almost jumped overboard on a boat trip some years before.

"Brinie," I said, "I know how we can solve the problem. I'll put a large ball and chain around your leg."

"Good," he said impishly. "That way I'll sink faster!"

The afternoon of our first day at sea Brian was gazing out the window.

"Look, Stevie," he said, "we're in a fog-storm."

The entries in Brian's daily travel journal from that trip have always made me laugh. His opening notations for Thursday, July 10, were as follows:

We had a party on the boat. People took pictures. I was on the radio.

Jayne and Audrey [Meadows] waved good-bye as the boat left the harbor.

The waiter we had said "My God" at everything we said.

Part of his entry for Friday, July 11:

Today I got up late and went outside. I watched some other children play games like deck tennis, table tennis and deck golf.

Then I went to the movies. . . .

After the movies I had cocktails with the [John] Hammonds. I didn't have anything to drink; I just had candy and nuts. . . .

I played Bingo in the cocktail lounge. I almost won $95.

A few minutes later Miss Rita Hayworth played Bingo with us.

Then I went back to my stateroom and did this.

On Monday, August 4, by which time we were at the Lido Hotel on an island off Venice, there occurred The Adventure of the Cuttlebone. Brian's entry:

I got up late, and just as I was getting up Dad was coming in from swimming.

Then I went down to the beach. I found a cuttlebone and brought it up to the room. And I washed it off, and when the water touched the cuttlebone it made a terrible smell so that I thought that if I washed it for a long time it wouldn't smell.

But as the time went on the smell got worse, so I came out of the bathroom and put our diving mask over my face. That way I could not smell it.

When I came out of the bathroom I asked Dad to smell my hands.

He said to go get his after-shave lotion. That helped, but you could still smell it.

The smell, actually, was horrible. I'm not sure whether there is any military or industrial application of this fact, but our family does know now that monstrous fumes can be produced by putting a piece of cuttlebone into hot water.

Certain cities through which we passed advertised themselves as the something-or-other "capital of the world." Dijon, for example, was said to have been the Mustard Capital of the World. Another community was the Nougat Capital of the World. This was not lost on Brian. His entry for Wednesday, August 6, referring to our having just left Venice:

> We put the luggage in the car and started out. We went through two cities, Ferrara and Bologna. We ate lunch in Bologna, which is the bologna capital of the world.

On Friday, August 15, we had dinner at one of the famous restaurants of Rome. Brian made the following observations:

> Jayne was over-tired and went to sleep early, but Dad, Steve and I went out to dinner with Sid Caesar and [comedian] Cliff Norton and their wives. We met them at the Hassler Hotel and then we all got in Sid's hired limousine and went to dinner. We ate at Alfredo's. This is the restaurant where they feature a solid gold fork and spoon given to the owner years ago by Douglas Fairbanks and Mary Pickford.

I'm sure that what Sid remembers about that evening—because he has told me so—is not so much the famous pasta or the solid gold fork and spoon of distinguished parentage, but rather the fact that Brian did a good part of the talking. Some children have a blithe confidence which leads them to believe that all adults they meet will be utterly fascinated by their every word. For my own part, my children have never been able to talk too much for me, since I am intrigued by everything they say. I am, of course, somewhat less intrigued by what other people's children say. But in this case Brian began to tell Sid and the rest of us about how much he enjoyed a film he had seen a few days earlier. He had enjoyed it so much, it turned out, that he related the entire plot, which took, as I recall, about twenty minutes. Sid responded with the kind of facial reactions for which he is famous, pretending interest in what Brian was saying, frowning as if in serious concentration, rolling his eyes as if to say, "Is this ever going to stop?" and all in all putting on a show in which Brian was his unwitting straight man. It's hard to say whether Sid or Brian enjoyed the experience more. I know the rest of us were delighted.

Brinie was always an attractive child. By the time he was of high school age his blond hair had darkened and his eyes had turned hazel; he bore some resemblance to Elvis Presley. He was in the audience of one of my television shows one night. Shortly thereafter I received the following letter:

Dear Steve,

Recently I was watching your show. Your son Brian was shown several times. You are always having contests and I have a great idea. Why don't you have a contest to give away Brian for a few weeks?

I'm sure that many girls all over the nation would write in. You could call it, "Why I want Brian Allen for my very own." You would probably get quite a response, especially from the girls in Grove City.

Thank you.

Sincerely,

Dawn McGinnis
143 States Street
Grove City, PN.

In the days that followed the arrival of Brian's letter I discussed the situation with Jayne, who dearly loves her three stepsons. Finally I sent a letter back to Brian.

My Dear Son,

As a Christian I was naturally pleased to learn, from your recent letter, that your new church affiliation has brought you a sense of peace, love and happiness. Since these are the three supreme human goals, you are fortunate indeed to have achieved them. As I'm sure your good mind has already made you aware, it is apparently impossible to sustain an immediate grasp of these noble ideals throughout every minute of one's life, but even so your feelings of security and comfort in your new environment gladden my heart.

I am pleased, too, to know that your new friends are not only members of a Church but of a *Family*. No doubt it was Christ's original intention that all members of His flock should regard one another as members of one human family. It is sad that so often these ideals of brotherhood and closeness are lost sight of, not only by members of Christian churches but also by members of families. But in each case the ideal is there and its appeal is strong,

It is interesting that the members of the Church of Armageddon take new names when they make their new profession of faith, apparently in the same way that many American blacks take new names when they join the Islamic brotherhood. The two components of your new name, "Logic" and "Israel," are certainly two of the most important words in the record of human experience. *Logic* is but another word for the exercise of man's greatest faculty, *Reason*, which distinguishes him from the lower animals. Most all the important work of man down through the countless generations of human history has been done by applying the power of reason, of logic, to the mysteries that surround us. One by one they have opened to minds bent on the reasonable approach to Truth.

Reason, of course, has its limits. The greatest Christian philosophers and saints have conceded that it can take us only so far in our journey in quest of Truth. It takes us, fortunately, most of the way, but at last we come to a chasm across which it seems possible to pass only on the bridge of Faith.

This, indeed, has been the message of all sacred scriptures—the Christian, the Moslem, the Oriental, and those of the people of Israel, without whose historic testimony there would have been no basis on which to construct the edifice of Christianity.

It is interesting that during these recent days, when you have been making your decision to depend so utterly on the wisdom of the Bible, I have been engaged in two writing projects that brought me to a study of the Old and New Testaments as well as other Christian sources. As we know from the testimony of countless scholars over the centuries, and can perceive on our own, there is much wisdom in the Scriptures. Honest Christians differ, of course, on the meanings of Biblical passages, and that is why I am pleased that you have made the word "Logic" part of your new name, since without the application of the God-given power of Reason to the complex record of the Scriptures one would have difficulty in knowing what to believe. Reason aims always at *consistency* and therefore protects us against the accumulation of mutually contradictory views which, in the long run, cause us discomfort.

The news that it may be a long time before you return to Los Angeles naturally saddens us, but this initial response is, of course, a selfish one. What we want more than anything in the world is *your happiness;* and, although I love you deeply, I would gladly give up the sight of you for the rest of my life if that simple decision were all it took to ensure your personal contentment. Life, alas, is not so simple as that, but I do want to emphasize that you need feel no guilt whatever about your decision to leave behind you the scene of so much unhappiness for you over the years. My feeling in regard to this matter, I suppose, is much like that of those parents whose children decide to enter one of the contemplative orders of the Catholic Church, to become a monk or a nun secluded from the world and to devote their lives to prayer in relative solitude. Here again, selfishly speaking, the parents' hearts ache at the knowledge that they will henceforth be deprived of the sight of those they love. But if they share their children's faith, their sorrow is balanced by a sense of happiness that the children are doing what brings *them* a sense of spiritual satisfaction.

In any event, you have entered no such secluded environment. The world is small today, and grows smaller daily. None of us can perceive the future except dimly, and each day brings its share of surprises and decisions that might not have been anticipated.

For my own part, I should like to visit you and your friends of the Love Family in Seattle sometime, as I have in the past visited you in San Francisco and Steamboat Springs. I will naturally not make such a trip soon, since I would not wish to intrude on your new life until you feel there might be some benefit in my seeing you again and having the pleasure of meeting your new friends.

As I write these few thoughts to you my eyes go back again and again to your letter. How my heart is warmed by your expressions of love, and I know I speak here for your mother, for Jayne, for Steve, David and Bill, as well as Robin [Dorothy's child by a later marriage]. . . . All of us are made happy by your words, "I love you all very much" and "With all my love."

I know we are all pleased, too, by your sense of having found a true home. One of the thousand-and-one reasons why our planet is described as a Vale of Tears is that, even in the best and happiest of homes, the simple passage of time brings about an evolution of parent-child relationships characterized, at the end, by a growing apart of two who were at first so close. All the world's mothers start by holding an infant within their bodies, then at last in their arms. And then, in the end, the new being grows, matures, and walks away on his own path of life. . . .

Till we see you again you will be daily in our thoughts. Our home is filled with reminders of you. Not only your pictures but the fine works of art you have created. . . . I know that you will turn these artistic capabilities as well as your many other gifts to the benefit of your new friends. Whoever they are, they are fortunate indeed to have such a fine young man as yourself among their circle.

Take care of yourself, Son. We will write to you, but do not trouble yourself about the question as to whether you should respond. That decision will emerge as the circumstances of your future unfold.

I love you with all my heart.

Dad

CHAPTER 2

Brian the Adult

We had known for some time that Brian, like many other young people of the 1960s generation, was having trouble finding his proper niche in life. He had worked for a while in the construction trade but seemed to have no precise professional or personal goal. He was certainly bright enough, successful in school when he wanted to be, and—most notably—an artist of considerable gifts. Like William Blake he had learned to create his pictures in the form of engravings, though he also drew and painted. He had studied silk screening as well, and his work was professional. Some of his things were displayed in our home, some at my television studio.

His most remarkable artistic creation unfortunately no longer exists. It was a life-sized human figure in three dimensions, constructed entirely of matchsticks set into the form of small squares. Into each of these squares were glued papers of various colors, chiefly reds and blues. It was a dazzling object which, since it was rendered in the seated position, could be displayed on any chair. Brian presented it to his older brother, Steve, as a gift, and it was exhibited in Steve's home for some time. But it was delicate, and when one day a pet cat attacked it, it was destroyed.

But Brian's art did not, apparently, satisfy or nourish him. When I offered him the assignment of designing the covers for my record albums, a job which would have brought him several hundred dollars per cover, he declined, saying he had little interest in making money. I still wish he had accepted the offer, simply as a way of gaining experience and confidence as an artist.

Brian almost seemed to lack the mysterious inner ballast that secures most of us to reality and our places in it. Even as a child he had a side often found in people who have artistic or creative gifts—a tendency to daydream, to march to the sound of a different drummer. The sixth-grade teacher who had commented on his happy disposition had also written, "I hope the people in that 'other world of daydreaming' that you visit so often are as fond of you as we are. May they do you justice in the end."

Brian graduated from Birmingham High School in Los Angeles in the summer of 1965. That fall, Steve, Jr. and I accompanied him to Steamboat Springs, Colorado, a ski town in the mountains, where he was to attend Yampa Valley College, a new school offering individual attention to its small student body. Brian's younger brother, David, also elected to go to Yampa Valley later on.

Brian wrote us enthusiastic letters during his freshman year, describing his classes, the mountains, the snow, and the active outdoor student life. He particularly liked his roommate, an African student from Kenya named Munga Githenguri, dubbed "Stanley" by European missionaries. Stanley, said Brian, was considerate, funny, smart—"the perfect roommate."

All of us maintained close touch with Brian. Although to get to Steamboat Springs I had to fly to Denver, rent a car and drive for about six hours, I had wonderful visits with him there. The college was having serious financial difficulties at the time, and on one occasion I did a benefit performance on campus to raise money. On another, Steve, Jr. came along, too. The three of us went mountain climbing, and I was so touched by the experience that I wrote the following poem.

VISITING MY SON

Visiting my son, at school in Colorado:
    Steamboat Springs, we share each
    other and the mountain air, the
father-son embarrassment and love,
    the brash and tumbling creek he
takes me to, high in the hills.

He is an eighteen-year-old collie-dog,
This fine young man of honey and of bone, he
    and an older brother—we, strung together by
    invisible
ropes of love, move up the mountainside.

Bushes tremble, boulders split in the screaming
    silence of the rocky mountain Spring.
We who elsewhere see, smell, feel the brusque
assaulting
    sea that crashes on a pliant coast
assume that this is water's chiefest power.

But truly it is found on inland hills and crags
   where melting snows and clouds, out of
   their gentle softness,
work a fearful force that budges,
   cracks and heaves the mightiest wood and stone.

A lovely chaos blinds and then re-opens eyes afresh
   where water works some Oriental forms out of
   this occidental mass.

At day's end: darkness comes?
   The hell it does. Light goes.
What comes is verbal symbol for the negative.
We sense little but in relation to its opposite. It
   takes hard stone to make us tingle to soft flesh, a
   desert
   to delineate the water, and hatred to make clear
   how rich is love.

There was one unhappy incident that winter, a town-gown conflict, Colorado-style. In late March Brian and some of his college friends were accosted by a group of local toughs, cowboys who had been drinking and were looking for trouble. Many of the students at the Yampa Valley State College came from distant urban areas; there had already been some friction between them and local ranchhands.

As soon as I heard about the incident I fired off the following telegram to Colorado's Governor John Love, whom I knew:

Dear Governor Love:

I request an immediate investigation by Colorado's Attorney General of an outrageous attack by four intoxicated bullies upon a group of young college boys last Wednesday in Steamboat Springs, Colorado. One of the boys is still in the hospital; another has a badly injured arm. I am informed that a local police officer not only stood by and watched part of the fight, but actually refused to arrest the attackers. As if this were not intolerable enough, the local police that same evening arrested a college boy for blowing a bugle.

My son Brian was attacked by an adult bully who prides himself on being a bull-dogging rodeo champion.

Before writing of this matter in my syndicated newspaper column, I would like to be informed as to whether meaningful law prevails in Steamboat Springs so that the students of Yampa Valley College, some of whom are from other parts of the world, can be fully protected against assaults by local plug-uglies.

Sincerely yours,
Steve Allen

Although the college students were the victims of the incident, they were nevertheless—if you can believe it—put on trial. The court session was scheduled for May 2. Steve, Jr. and I flew in to be on hand since I have always had strong feelings about any incident in which bullying is involved. Perhaps because of the interest shown by Governor Love, common sense set in, and the cowboys were eventually fined for their attack on the students.

As a student Brian tended to do well in subjects he liked and to apply himself less rigorously to material that did not, for whatever reason, catch his fancy. Since this had been my own pattern in school, I could at least understand uneven academic performance. But perhaps he worried more about such small failures than I had done at his age. My own father had died when I was an infant, so I never had a father to compete against or measure up to. Brian was perhaps too concerned with what I would think about his marks or other achievements. Another complication, I believe, was that his older brother, Steve, was always a crackerjack student. Steve is today a doctor and, in a sense, has always had a doctor's personality —bright, methodical, calm, in control. So Brian, I suspect, may have felt that he could not successfully compete with Steve either. It is easy for the rest of us to say that he should not have suffered from such insecurities, but much human behavior is not directly subject to rational self-analysis, much less control.

After two years in Steamboat Springs, Brian, still restless, decided to leave Yampa Valley. In the summer of 1967 he moved to Hayward in the San Francisco–Oakland area of California. He rented modest quarters, decided to attend a local college, and in a letter to us said, "I don't look forward to registering. Competing with six thousand other students who already know the system for classes is going to be a frustrating drag."

At the time, he was keeping company with a young Los Angeles woman named Susan, of whom Jayne, Dorothy and I were very fond. She was a very sweet, quiet, ladylike sort of person—pretty, retiring, and quite in contrast with the more strikingly good-looking but somewhat neurotic girls Brian had dated during the few years previous.

He came down to visit Susan and the family in November of that year. But even earlier it became clear to us that Brian was not applying himself at school, that he was bored and really did not know what to do with himself.

Brian himself assessed his attitude realistically. He didn't feel any motivation to study, he said; he didn't seem to be getting anything out of his courses. All that his education was doing was keeping him out of Vietnam. Over the winter of 1968 he repeatedly conveyed the message to all who loved him that he was at loose ends. None of us could understand why he therefore chose to live in a distant city. We wanted him to move back to the Los Angeles area where we could be with him and help him. In Los Angeles, I reasoned, he could also be of some help to his mother, Dorothy, and to Dorothy's daughter, Robin; and feeling useful would be good for him.

I finally wrote Brian the only stern letter I have ever sent him, assessing the situation and recommending that he move to Los Angeles and undertake some form of professional help with his problems, at my expense. Besides, if he were in Los Angeles, I said, I could have the pleasure of seeing him.

But it may be that when we are in trouble, we are inclined to hide from those who love us, as if we feel that by having problems we are failing them. So Brian seemed to feel. Instead of coming to Southern California, he left Hayward for San Francisco.

He did come down to visit us early in May of 1968, and he, Steve and I spent some time together discussing more openly than usual the emotional tensions among the three of us. Such exchanges, of course, do not concentrate on the problems of just one of the participants but touch on those of all three.

I was prepared, by that time, to go into the painful subject of the long-past divorce between Dorothy and me, though I was still reluctant to give my sons the full details. But I did take up with them the guilt I felt about my separation from them when they were so young. I told them that I quite understood the moments of resentment toward me that they must have inevitably experienced, whether they could bring themselves to face it or not. I also discussed with them tensions between them and Jayne, their stepmother. Jayne is such a wise and compassionate person that by and large she was a very good stepmother indeed. But because she has the nervous system of a hummingbird and remarkably high intelligence, she is sometimes impatient with those who do not instantly perceive the wisdom of whatever she might be saying. I suffer from the same character fault myself, but of course those who are criticized by the quick thinker at moments of confrontation are unable to take so detached a view. They are simply hurt and, when such instances are repeated, invariably resentful to a degree.

I recall one instance in which Jayne had personally planned and organized a wonderful birthday party for Brian, then about fifteen. She had hired striped-jacketed men from Will Wright's, a local ice cream emporium; had arranged for balloons, cake, flowers and all the trimmings; and had fixed up the house in a festive manner. On the day of the party she had worked on the preparations and the general housecleaning from early morning until party time. When Brian arrived a few minutes early bringing with him two of his school chums, Jayne was still wearing an old robe, not yet having had time to dress or make up for the occasion. "Brian," she called through the front door, "could you and your friends go around to the back kitchen door, dear?"

Unfortunately Brian had no idea why he and his companions were not welcomed at the front door, and this later led to some static. (The party itself was a great success. Among Brian's Birmingham High School classmates who attended were the now-famous actresses Cindy Williams and Sally Field.)

The boys were spared one of the classic reasons for resenting their stepmother, because they were well aware that I met Jayne quite some time after I had separated from Dorothy; they knew that Jayne had nothing whatever to do with the separation and the divorce that followed it.

Dorothy's second husband, Andy, had died by this time, and that too was a traumatic blow for the three boys. They had been abruptly separated from a second father. A later complication was that they were not nearly so fond of Dorothy's third husband as they had been of Andy.

Although some of the discussion was pretty rough going—as I wrote Brian afterwards—I was pleased we had undertaken it. We opened a few doors, and we saw that we could walk together through areas we had avoided before. Some of our opinions differed, to be sure, but the differences were offset by the desire to understand one another and to be closer.

That autumn Brian's fortunes took a decided turn for the better when he decided to resume his education at Steamboat Springs. We were all sorry that he would be so far away from us, but pleased that his life seemed to be getting back on a more productive track.

His letters now had a different, more sober tone. "Dear Dad," he wrote in November,

> It has taken a long while to get settled. "Dropping in" has been much more turbulent than "dropping out." To blend idealism with realism is a frustrating chore.
>
> School is going very well. In each of my classes (World Affairs, Spanish, Literature, and Design) I have an "A" or "B" average.

I spend more time studying now than three years ago, yet I do so with much less effort.

My house is over near the Lumber Mill we visited one day. It is an old, small one-bedroom house. For some extra spending money I am helping the owner add on two more bedrooms and a bathroom. Until now the house had no plumbing.

I keep "warm" by burning wood and coal in a small furnace in the living room. So far I have been chopping my own wood and even mining my own coal. . . .

Actually I enjoy all the work around the house. It keeps me busy.

I am taking mountain climbing again. Last week we climbed a 1,000-foot vertical wall in Wyoming. . . .

"It was great to hear from you, Son," I wrote back.

I am glad that you've finally adjusted to the "dropping in" process. Actually, I never had any fears that you would not succeed at it. Congratulations on the marks you are achieving. Keep up the good work.

Although the house near the lumber mill must be pretty damn cold when the temperature drops, it also sounds—at least from this distance—rather romantic and adventurous.

It's great that you are doing that construction work with the owner, too. I wish somebody had shown me how to combine a hammer and a nail when I was your age.

Does the place have electricity? If it does, I can send you some kind of electric heater. . . .

When Brian came to Los Angeles for Christmas, he had achieved a 3.50-point average for the fall quarter and had made the Dean's List. We were all encouraged that school was proving more "relevant" and rewarding than it had seemed during his earlier bleak year.

Yet at the end of that school year, despite his successes, Brian once again left Yampa Valley College behind, returning to California. Nineteen-seventy was another somewhat aimless time for him. He settled into San Francisco's Haight-Ashbury section, a crossroads of the beat and hippie cultures. I was doing another comedy-and-talk show at the time but kept in touch with him by letter, phone calls and occasional visits.

Brian and I spent one marvelous weekend together during this period. I was then doing daily crazy comedy routines and stunts on my TV show. That Friday I went out on Vine Street in front of our theater wearing an invisible wireless microphone and began to hitchhike, waving at passing cars. I could not be recognized as Steve Allen because I was dressed as the hippie of all time—in Levis, sandals, a long black wig, Tarzan headband, dark glasses and an Attila-the-Hun mustache. When a driver would stop for me I'd jump into his car and say, "Thanks, man." He, of course, would ask the traditional "How far ya goin'?" "Oh, just to the corner," I'd answer, to the amusement of the studio audience back in the theater and the consternation of the good Samaritan who had picked me up.

Since I was scheduled to fly to San Francisco that night to visit Brian, I decided to keep the costume and use it as an aid to privacy while walking about the Haight-Ashbury neighborhood with him. He was living at the time with a group of other young people, all of whom broke up when they saw how I was dressed. The next morning Brian and I went for a walk. Almost at once a girl of about fourteen ran up, stood next to us for a moment, and then ran away.

"What was that for?" I asked.

"She just had her picture taken with two hippies," Brian explained, pointing across the street to the girl's mother, her camera still focused on us.

Later in the day, at the Sausalito waterfront, a busload of tourists suddenly aimed a dozen or so movie and still cameras at us. To amuse Brian I went into a shuffle-off-to-Buffalo step, keeping up with the bus as it moved slowly along the street. To this day there are people showing home movies of their trip to San Francisco who will have had no way of knowing, unless they read this, that the tall hippie dancing for them was a well-known television comedian.

There were creative, artistic people in Haight-Ashbury, but there were also losers, loners and drug people. My son was in his twenties, had yet to take advantage of his various gifts, and was drifting.

It was during this period that Brian met a young man named Paul Erdman with whom he discussed the idea of forming a religious commune. Erdman went to the Yucatan area of Mexico to explore the possibility of settling there. Brian remained in San Francisco. But we knew nothing of this until *Logic* entered our lives.

CHAPTER 3

The Painful Background

Brian didn't answer my long letter to *Logic* Israel, but I hadn't expected that he would. In the now lengthening silence I began to wonder how I was responsible for his decision—my version of the classic parent's question, "Where did I go wrong?" That line gets laughs from TV audiences because it has become a cliché. But most comedy is about tragedy; and there is nothing funny in the possibility that you have hurt your child.

I reasoned that if my marriage to Dorothy had not failed, Brian, Steve and David would have been spared the suffering all children of divorce know. Brian's problems were caused in part by my imperfections. When I married his mother, for instance, I was not really prepared for the roles of husband and father.

My father died, as I've said, when I was eighteen months old, so I had no male role model. My vaudeville comedienne mother, though a good soul in many ways, was one of those people who never should have gotten married and who, once she did, should almost have been forbidden by law to become a mother. Her own family background had been so chaotic that she was not at all good casting for the roles of wife and mother. But I have written of my early life in an autobiography, *Mark It and Strike It,* and in fiction. I choose to start here with the year 1942, at which time I was twenty years old.

That year I made up my mind to marry a girl I had been introduced to at Arizona State Teachers College the year before: a tall, pretty, dark-haired, green-eyed Phoenician named Dorothy Goodman. Dorothy was eighteen.

She and I were really in love with love first and with each other second. We would not have conceded anything of the sort at the time, of course, but the statement is accurate. Oh, we displayed all of love's normal symptoms. We wanted to be with each other every minute and were unhappy when separated. But we were very young and consequently terribly eager to fall in love, with anybody. In fact, not long after we had decided to Go Steady, Dorothy met a young Air Corps lieutenant stationed in Phoenix who fell in love with her at first sight and almost induced her to marry him on the spot. It might have happened the other way around, too, for Dorothy and I were simply a rather average, unrealistic young couple. We were unconsciously determined to be in love, and almost any presentable person of the opposite sex would have filled the bill. Or would have seemed to.

From the first we realized that one problem would cause awkward moments. We were not of the same religion—I was Catholic and Dorothy's people were Methodists—and both our parents were opposed to the marriage on this ground as well as others. Moreover, 1942 was wartime. I was soon to be drafted into the infantry; the asthma that had driven me from Chicago to Arizona had cleared up in the state's clean, warm air, and there was no longer any apparent reason for the Army not to induct me. Naturally the knowledge that we might soon be separated, perhaps forever, made our moments together seem the more precious. With the blindness of the immature and love-struck, we pretended to ignore the matter of my impending induction. And, like many other young couples, we eventually decided to get married, come what may.

Within a few months I was indeed in the service, going through basic training at Camp Roberts, California, the sprawling Infantry Replacement Training Center hidden away in the dry, lion-flank central California hills. The camp was situated a few miles from the tiny town of Paso Robles. Although it was made rudely clear to all incoming soldiers that there was literally no place for any newcomers to live in the town—no rooms to rent, no vacancies of any kind—I nevertheless blundered ahead, told my mother and Dorothy to come to Paso Robles, and made arrangements for the ceremony in one of the camp chapels. One makes such mistakes at twenty-one.

Somehow our simple physical determination—or dumb luck—brought it all off. Mother found rundown living quarters in a rebuilt chicken shack in the poorest section of town, and Dorothy and I rented an ancient room—also poor—a few blocks away. As thousands of ex-infantrymen will recall, Paso Robles was unbelievably overcrowded in those days. On weekends the soldiers, who greatly outnumbered the townspeople, swarmed through the streets like ants, standing in line at the few ıestaurants and bars, milling around the pool halls and USO quarters, shouting, laughing, swearing, getting drunk and into fights.

The wedding service itself is something of a blur in my mind, like many of the other events of that stifling summer. I was with the rest of my company on the machine gun range when the time came. Moving as if in a dream, I reported to an officer as previously arranged, was excused, ran to the barracks, showered, dressed, ran to meet Dorothy, her parents and my mother at the Catholic chapel, entered, and went through a brief service. Both Dorothy and I were pitifully nervous. I recall her stuttering and saying, "For richer, for p-poorer," during the ceremony. Then somehow it was all over and we were standing out in the hot California sun again, blinking, feeling no different at all and yet now *married*.

In a daze our party drove into town for a small "celebration" at the Paso Robles Inn, made possible by the generosity of my mother (who must have spent her last cent). Then—and after thirty-five years I cannot remember—I either had to go right back to camp or else we said good-bye to everyone after lunch and repaired at once to our "honeymoon" suite at the Taylor Hotel, an ancient and none-too-tidy establishment in the heart of this sleepy western town. Nor can I remember much else that occurred during the next few weeks. The heavy weapons infantry training itself kept my fellow trainees and me exhausted. But at every opportunity I would jump on the Paso Robles bus in the evening and race into town to be with Dot. Or if I couldn't get a pass she would come out to camp and we would walk around the grounds at night, holding hands, going to the PX for a cold beer or a thick malted milk, still trying not to think of the fact that within a few weeks I would be shipped off with the other members of my company to—depending on which rumor one preferred—North Africa or the South Pacific.

During the last few weeks of infantry training the men naturally speculated more and more as to where we would be sent to fight. In our naïveté many of us had assumed that the action would take place in Europe, as it eventually did. But at that time millions of young Americans from high school, college, drugstore counters, gas stations and shops were being sent either to the Pacific islands or to the deserts of North Africa. Our company had, in fact, been given special training in what was called water discipline, because of the possibility that we might see service in Africa.

But I was never to see overseas service—or, for that matter, much more stateside service. Soon the business of running up steep hills in the morning dampness carrying a machine gun or mortar led to the recurrence of my asthma. After a few weeks the company doctors got tired of hearing my wheezing and sent me home. Dorothy and I returned to Phoenix. I took my old job back at radio station KOY, and we rented a little house and settled down to typical Arizona life.

It was 1943. At about this time I began to create some comedy-character voices and use them as part of a morning disc-jockey show I was doing. One of these characters was called, for want of a better name, Claude

Horribly. He was more or less an imitation of Edgar Bergen's Mortimer Snerd. Critics who today observe that my specialty is sophisticated, satirical or ad-lib comedy may be surprised to learn that I started from quite another direction. A fellow announcer on the KOY staff, Wendell Noble, heard my various characters and came up with an idea.

"Listen," he said, "you do crazy voices and so do I. You play the piano and I sing. Maybe we could do some sort of an act together and pick up a little loot around town."

We did exactly that.

Several months later Wendell left Phoenix and moved to Hollywood, where in short order he found a job as announcer with station KHJ, the Mutual Broadcasting System outlet for the Los Angeles area. In those days announcers in the West usually broke into the business in South Overshoe, Montana; learned the tricks of the trade; then, if they had some special ability, moved to a medium-sized city like Phoenix or Denver; and finally, after three or four years of further training, made the big step to Los Angeles. In the Midwest the goal, of course, was Chicago, and in the East, New York. The more fortunate announcers would strike it rich in the big city and eventually get into network radio; others might settle in at one of the local independent stations and in a few cases eventually become wealthy disc jockeys. I realized that in due time the moment would come to make the move from the desert to the Coast. I saw, too, that I would never be able to save enough money to make this jump on my KOY salary, which was something like eighty dollars a week at its highest. So I took a night job in addition to my daily duties, working as singer and piano player at a popular Phoenix night spot called The Steak House. As a saloon pianist I picked up ninety dollars a week, most of which I was able to put right into the bank.

But now I had another reason to increase my earnings; within a year after our marriage Dorothy and I had our first child, a beautiful boy whom we named Stephen, Junior. The day he was born I was so rattled that, without even letting anyone know that I was taking off, I wandered away from the radio station about ten minutes before I was due to introduce an important program. It was Dorothy at the hospital who told me I was supposed to be on the air and sent me back to work. Fortunately my employers, taking the reason into consideration, overlooked my mistake.

Little Steve was an angelic child from the first, and I have always regretted that during the first few months of his life I was so busy working night and day at the station and the restaurant that it wasn't possible for me to spend as much time with him as I wanted to.

I played with him and carried him about when I was home, however, and invented a sort of Indian dance with a chant that I performed holding him in my arms that would invariably make him stop crying.

Dorothy did not share my eagerness to save enough money to enable us to move to Los Angeles. She was quite content with life in Phoenix, and thereby hangs one of the several tangled tales of our later difficulty. It was at about this point in our relationship that an observer might have predicted eventual conflict, although neither Dorothy nor I would have entertained such an idea in those days.

A woman who knows Dorothy and me well and is fond of both of us said to me, "As individuals I like you both, but I couldn't imagine a more unlikely husband-and-wife combination." What she meant, in part, was that Dorothy had always been cut out to be a small-town homemaker. Her interests (and wonderful All-American interests they are) were recipes, her family's affairs, back-fence gossip, movie and women's magazines, and the same decent activities that millions of other women in this country are involved in. I was simply not the best sort of husband for such a woman. Born in a trunk, having always led a gypsy life, having from the first known excitement and emotional insecurity and music and laughter and poetry and drama, I was poor casting indeed for the role of small-town husband and father. Actually, at that early age I don't think I would have made a truly good husband for any woman, but for someone like Dorothy in particular I was not a satisfactory partner.

There were many pleasant memories in our relationship, of course, but like the smiles that may be part of an unhappy childhood, they were counterpoint to the main theme and not an essential part of it. Since on religious principles I would not even admit the possibility of a divorce, I did not recognize certain storm signals. If a man foresees a clear danger that his marriage may founder and end in divorce, he will take careful measures, when trouble arises, to improve the situation. But when divorce is simply out of the question, he may close his eyes to his problems. "We are going to stay together come what may," he may think to himself, "so what is the point of worrying about details?" For some men this careless approach may result in a measure of success if not real happiness. For me it ended in failure.

But in 1944 such failure was unimagined. After working several months at The Steak House, I had been able to put exactly one thousand dollars into the bank. At the time it seemed to represent a great deal of security. Dorothy knew that I was determined to move to Los Angeles and make the attempt to better myself professionally. My plan was to leave her and Stevie in Phoenix, go ahead to the Coast alone, quickly get a job, find an apartment, and then send for her and little Steve as soon as possible. Somehow I had the idea that I could achieve all of this in a few days. In fact, I realized, I would have to accomplish it promptly because after I quit my two jobs in Phoenix there would be no means of support for Dorothy, the baby, my mother, and myself except our thousand-dollar nest egg.

Part of my confidence in my ability to turn the trick was based not on any great regard for my talents but rather on the fact that during the war many of the regular Los Angeles announcers were in the service. It had been widely reported in the trade that jobs were open to any qualified 4-Fs or veterans who might apply. Unfortunately I found Hollywood swarming with 4-Fs and veterans.

I made the trip from Phoenix in a battered 1932 dark blue Model-A Ford coupe, one window of which was broken. Driving immediately to the heart of Hollywood, I found cheap lodging in a decrepit house called the Cahuenga Rooms, the superintendent of which was a young Swede who played recorded symphonies, concertos and operas at earsplitting volume during all hours of the day and many of the night. The sidewalk in front of this establishment was cracked, and I have always suspected that the fissures were caused by my host's high-powered Victrola.

Having checked in early in the evening, I went out for a walk to case the new neighborhood I now proposed to call home ground. Hollywood Boulevard was two blocks away. Keeping an eye out for Lana Turner or Clark Gable, I strolled about, drinking in the excitement of the town. Although not nearly so glamorous as outlanders have been led to believe, Los Angeles nevertheless has a certain excitement—at least to those who come to it from smaller communities. After a couple of hours of walking and gawking, I ate a large dinner, bought the evening newspapers, and returned to my room.

Opening the papers to the radio page, I copied the names of all the local stations onto the back of an envelope. The next morning, after a breakfast of scrambled eggs and bitter orange juice at a drugstore across the street (I soon decided that California sent most of its best oranges to the East and left the worst to the natives), I began making the rounds.

At each station the manager was cordial but discouraging. "There's just nothing open right now," was the general idea, "but if you'd like to audition and leave your name, we can call you." Within a week I had auditioned, to no avail, for an announcer's job at almost every station in town. Wendell, who had a good job at station KHJ, helped me to obtain a hearing there, but since there were no openings, nothing resulted from the contact.

By the time another seven days had passed, my thousand-dollar bankroll was dwindling fast. I stopped eating three square restaurant meals a day and instead took to eating sparingly in drugstores. At night I would stop at the Mayflower coffee-and-doughnut shop on Hollywood Boulevard and pick up a bag of chocolate-covered doughnuts to take back to my room. I would put these on the chair next to my bed and in the morning eat them for breakfast before getting up.

At the drugstore lending library I had picked up a copy of the novel *Studs Lonigan* and now read chapters of it each night before turning out the light. Since my own background had been similar to that of the characters in the book, it fascinated me and instilled in me the desire to write something of a generally similar nature. Almost twenty years later I did, in a novel and play called *The Wake.*

After a few nights of staying awake till dawn hungrily reading *Studs Lonigan,* then sleeping till two in the afternoon and eating four doughnuts for "breakfast," I began to sag somewhat in both spirit and body. Having exhausted the networks and the stations, I now began to approach the advertising agencies, starting with the big ones. Here, too, I met with no success. Then one morning I stuck my head into the hole-in-the-wall office of an advertising agency so small I had never even heard of it. There was no secretary on duty, but a kindly gentleman of about sixty greeted me.

"Looking for a job, you say?" he asked.

"Yes. I've had a great deal of experience in writing radio copy, and I was wondering if you might have anything open along that line."

"Well," the man said, "come in and sit down."

I have never learned whether he extended this invitation because I looked forlorn or whether he was lonely himself and just wanted company, but in any event we struck up a pleasant conversation, and after a few minutes he invited me to lunch at a restaurant down the street. He told me that at present he had but one account and that his only activity was to produce a fifteen-minute radio travelogue for a small bus company. Somehow, in my now-desperate circumstances, this project sounded extremely attractive. I felt that I might be able to make an important contribution toward its continued success, and I got up from the table with the impression that I had a job with this gentleman's agency. In any event, I was quite certain he had offered me the use of his business premises for an indefinite period, so for the next several days I reported to his office, hung up my jacket, sat down at a typewriter, and wrote God knows what. Actually, I was afraid to ask the man point-blank if I had clearly understood him for fear my dream would evaporate. I realize now that had I said, "Look here, am I on salary or not?" he would have said something like, "My goodness, no, young man. I simply want you to feel free to use these premises until you get professionally located, and I wish you the best of luck." But for some crazy reason I kept putting off this moment of reckoning. I wanted a job so desperately that I talked myself into believing I had one.

To make matters worse, I now called Dorothy and said, "Guess what? I've got a job with an agency over here. You and the baby can come right along." I took a train to Phoenix, and we closed down the house and left for Los Angeles. Wartime transportation being what it was, Stevie, who was just a year old, caught a bad cold on the way over and arrived in Los Angeles with such a hoarse throat that he was unable to cry; that is, he was able to cry but unable to make a sound in so doing. I shall never forget the pitiful mutelike sounds he made as he opened his little mouth, contorted his face, and tried to give voice to the wail of a normal infant.

When we arrived at the rundown Cahuenga Rooms, Dorothy was naturally disappointed. "Couldn't you find an apartment?" she asked.

"No. I've looked high and low, but there's nothing to be had—nothing we could afford, anyway. But don't worry; we're bound to find something eventually."

Those who lived in Los Angeles during the war will recall the desperate housing shortage that prevailed. Dorothy, Stevie and I now occupied one room, a cubicle so small that when I put up the baby's bed next to ours there was literally no room left to walk on the floor.

Fortunately within a few days I was able to find an apartment, and even though it was to-hell-and-gone down at a beach community known as Playa del Rey, we did not hesitate to move in. Our new quarters were cold, drafty, immorally expensive, and generally unattractive, but after a week spent in the Cahuenga Rooms they seemed like Buckingham Palace.

During that week I had been forced to face the reality that I did not have a job at all, a fact which naturally did not sit too well with Dorothy. While I was kicking myself for having gotten her and Stevie into such a predicament, I was suddenly granted one of those breaks that have made my professional life such a relatively smooth passage. Within the space of one week three of the radio stations at which I had auditioned called up and offered me work. I accepted the job that paid the most money and started work as a staff announcer at station KFAC on Wilshire Boulevard.

A problem soon emerged, however. The salary I was making at KFAC just wasn't enough. For the last few days before payday we frequently lived on meatless spaghetti or cereal-filled meatloaf. On one occasion we were down to our last dollar and nineteen cents; in fact, we were completely broke until we found a glass piggy bank of Stevie's that gave up that amount. On the spur of the moment we took the money, and the three of us went to the old rundown amusement park at Venice, where we played penny machines in the arcade, ate popcorn, and went on various slides and rides. Perhaps because we were doing it all on our last cent, we got more fun out of it than anything we had done for ages. We lived a simple, innocent life in those days. It's sad that it could not continue.

All in all, however, the year and a half at Playa del Rey was not the happiest time of our lives by a considerable margin. The part of the community that nestled on top of the steep oceanfront cliffs was a comfortable neighborhood, but we lived down in the "slum" section on the flat land across the main road. Instead of palm trees, bathing beauties, or sunny beaches, our view included rusty oil-pumping equipment, black canals, oil-covered pools and puddles, cracked sidewalks, dusty unpaved streets, and ancient, unpainted, weatherbeaten bungalows. The area resembled one of those rundown sections you see in old movies based on novels by James Cain in which Alan Ladd gets shot at while trailing a killer.

Toward the end of our stay there, however, we could see slightly better days ahead. After working a few months at KFAC, I received a phone call from the program manager at KMTR. I had auditioned for him some time previously, and since he now had an opening for an experienced man, he offered me the job. When I found out that it paid ten dollars more per week than I was making at KFAC I took it at once. The new job also had the attraction that its home base was Hollywood. KFAC had been located down in Los Angeles, and this seemed, psychologically at least, like a move in the right direction.

I remember few details of my months at KMTR except that for a time I served as announcer to a young radio "gossip columnist" named Irwin Allen who years later became a famous and successful producer of disaster films. The year was 1945, and I was twenty-three years old—a fact which now seems to me fantastic and unreal. I can clearly remember the feeling of being five years old or twelve or sixteen. I remember what it felt like to be nineteen or to reach thirty or forty. But I have no firm recollection of ever having been twenty-three.

What a pathetic, naïve age it seems. I was my present size, had a wife and a baby and a job as a radio announcer in a big city. My voice must have been heard daily by hundreds of thousands of people—yet I was really a child masquerading as an adult. Being now in my fifties, I would like to bless all people of twenty-three, all the poor, dumb, sweet young people who think they have grown up and who smoke and drink and mate and have children and read popular magazines and haven't the vaguest idea of their pathetic ignorance or immaturity. I imagine a tremendous number of twenty-three-year-old soldiers get killed in wars. It is a terrible age.

I got over it, naturally. One thing I particularly regret is that I had to be poor little Steve's father at such an absurd age. I loved him dearly, but what was I? What did I know about mature love or being a responsible father? I see pictures of him now, taken during that year at Playa del Rey. He was about two, wide-eyed, always looking up sweetly at the ignorant giants around him. He had almost no one to play with in the neighborhood and, ah, God, how I wish the now-growing-old me could somehow, by magic, be rushed back through time to be his father when he was two.

Now, damn it, Steve is a doctor, nearing forty, living in Elmira, New York, married himself and the father of two beautiful children, Danny and Julie; and although we have a good relationship, it's too late for me to carry him on my back or tell him how much I love him or take him to get haircuts or buy him toys. Ah, well.

CHAPTER 4

The Collapse of My Marriage

In 1946 Wendell and I had a stroke of luck. Having noticed that a number of the fifteen-minute radio programs carried on the Mutual Network were—well, the word lousy comes to mind, it occurred to us that though we were very far indeed from being a threat to Laurel and Hardy or Abbott and Costello, we could nevertheless do better than much of what we were hearing on the radio. When we communicated this simple point to Tony LaFrano, head of programming for the Mutual Radio Network's western division, he surprised us by telling us to put together whatever sort of show we had in mind. Accordingly we prepared two fifteen-minute pilot shows which we recorded a few days later at the Mutual-KHJ Studios on Melrose Avenue. One of them, called "Wendell and Steve," depended chiefly on Wendell's pleasant baritone voice and my abilities as pianist. The other show, which we called "Smile Time," also included music, but its primary ingredient was comedy. Mutual bought the comedy version and put us on the air almost at once. After a few weeks the budget was increased, which enabled us to hire a third cast member, a clever young woman named June Foray, who specialized in providing voices for cartoons. This meant that neither Wendell nor I any longer had to play women's roles. Within six months the program had become successful enough that our employers decided to carry it on the full network, coast to coast. They also further enlarged the budget so that we were able to add a guitar player, Earl Colbert, and a full-time accompanist, Eddie Truman—and later, Skitch Henderson, who had just gotten out of the service. Years later I would call on Skitch again, to serve as conductor on the "Tonight Show."

In 1947 Dorothy gave birth to our second child, a naturally cheerful blue-eyed, blond-haired pixie who seemed very happy to have arrived on planet Earth. We named him Brian.

The better salary I was earning from the "Smile Time" show enabled Dorothy and me to buy a little house at 2318 Luella Avenue in Venice. We set to work painting, putting up wallpaper, getting to know our neighbors and playing with the children.

But when, after two tremendously instructive years, the "Smile Time" show was suddenly dropped by the Mutual Network, Wendell and I were undecided about our course of action. Although we let it be known about town that we were available, there were no takers. After a few weeks it became apparent that since we could find no work together we would have to fend for ourselves individually. Accordingly Wendell accepted an assignment as a late-evening record spinner for his parent-station KHJ and did other radio work in his capacity as singer, while I gratefully acknowledged an offer from the local CBS outlet, station KNX, to do a nightly thirty-minute records-and-talk program. At the time I considered this move as decidedly in the wrong direction, but took the job because, like most Americans, I had little or no savings and was supporting a wife and two children. The moral is that we often do not recognize our greatest opportunities. Far from being the end of my career as a comedian, the move to KNX opened entirely new fields. By virtue of accident and necessity it called forth abilities I might never have developed had I stuck to the format of scripted comedy.

When I went to work for KNX in 1948 my instructions were simple, but I made it my business to disobey them at the earliest opportunity. "Just play records," my new employers told me, "and in between do a little light chatter. We don't want a straight announcer or disc jockey for this assignment. We'd like somebody who'll handle the show with a humorous approach."

Perceiving at once that by playing a great many records I would be performing an inestimable service for Bing Crosby, Frank Sinatra, Dinah Shore, et al, but doing very little for myself, I decided to make music on the new program secondary in importance. Therefore I wrote a seven- or eight-page script each evening, read it in an offhand conversational manner to create the impression that I was speaking extemporaneously, and played a bit less music than instructed.

The reaction from listeners was immediate and encouraging. Within a very few nights the program had attracted a group of avid fans. Cheered by their reaction, I took to talking more and playing even fewer records. This continued for about two months, until one day I received a memo from a member of the KNX program department. "We hired you to play records," the directive said in substance, "not to do a comedy program."

Here was a formidable obstacle to my plans, vague as they were. Although a number of my friends had made announcing a lucrative profession, to me, as an entertainer, becoming a standard-model disc jockey was a fate worse than death. I solved the dilemma by reading the memo on the air. As I had expected, listeners came at once to the rescue. In the following two days I received over four hundred letters, all of which stated the case precisely as I perceived it myself. "If we want to hear music," was the general idea, "there are a dozen other stations in Los Angeles playing it night and day. The reason we listen to this particular program is that it offers us something different."

The following day, carrying a large box full of mail, I walked into the office of Hal Hudson, the man who had written the memo. "I think you'll be interested in these letters," I said.

It was gratifying that after he had sampled the contents of the box he at once reversed his former position. "Well," he said, "you win. Go ahead and talk. But play a *little* music, okay?"

I assured him I would, but by the time another eighteen months had passed, there were no records played on the program at all. A few days after I had been given free rein in producing the program, people in the business—actors, writers, musicians, song-pluggers—began dropping into the tiny studio in which I worked. If anything happened to strike them funny, they laughed. People listening at home heard the laughter and began writing in to request permission to visit the studio.

"Since ours is not the sort of program that has an actual audience," I wrote in reply, "there are no tickets I can send you. But if you care to drop in on a catch-as-catch-can basis, we can probably put you up."

Within a few days we had an audience of ten or twelve at each program—although I could not understand why they wanted to watch a man in his shirt sleeves sit at a table and read from a script, now and then introducing a recording. Feeling that I ought to give the visitors a little more for their money, I replaced the table with a piano. At first I did no solos, however; I used the instrument solely as a means of gracefully dissolving from a recording into speech and then back into another record.

Twelve people laughing in a small room sounds like a larger number. The studio audience now began to snowball in size. The station soon offered me a larger studio, one that could accommodate about fifty people, and also requested that I lengthen the program to fifty-five minutes. Unfortunately, they offered no increase in salary. A little embittered by this, I decided not to spend additional hours writing comedy material but instead to fill the extra time by interviewing guest singers and musicians. It was this decision that led by a fluke to my doing ad-lib comedy and that consequently opened an entirely new line of work for me.

Within a few months our studio audience had swelled to over a hundred. Considering that our broadcast time was eleven o'clock at night—in an early-to-bed town like Hollywood—this was regarded as phenomenal. One night my scheduled guest was Doris Day. Fortunately she never showed up. I say "fortunately" because if she had I might still be doing that same radio program. The press agent who had promised that Doris would appear had evidently neglected to tell her where and when, and at 11:30 on this particular evening I was suddenly faced with twenty-five minutes of dead air. I had used up all the prepared script, had played the available records, and was frankly at a complete loss. The solution: I interviewed people in the studio audience and got bigger laughs than I had been getting with prepared material. Within a few nights the ad-lib forays down into what I called the Snake Pit had become the most important element in the show, which became even more popular. I learned that people like Ethel Barrymore, Fannie Brice, Al Jolson and Phil Silvers were regular listeners.

But the very factor of professional success created a danger to my marriage, though I was unaware of it at the time. My work took a great deal of concentration and energy. Another problem was that I was on the air late at night five nights a week and did not get home until one o'clock. Dorothy would sometimes be waiting up for me, having listened to the radio show, but by the time I had a bite to eat and got to sleep it was usually two o'clock in the morning.

This meant I was not awake early to play with the children, although I loved having them awaken me. Stevie used to climb on the bed, wake me up, and then, in his own words, "smuggle under the cubbers." To this day the phrase is one of the family's private jokes. I had become interested in stereo-realist 3-D color photography by this time and delighted in taking endless series of pictures of Stevie and Brian. Soon there was a third little fellow to take pictures of, a boy we named David. Like his two older brothers, he was a strikingly beautiful child. But despite the joys of fatherhood, five nights a week after dinner I would drive in to station KNX, since I had to write several pages of comedy material before going on the air at 11:00.

One night in 1950, in the CBS radio studio from which the nightly program was broadcast, something happened that shattered my life in every sense, something I could not possibly have anticipated and for which I was therefore totally unprepared. From the first I viewed it as—in part—a disaster, the sort of sensational or tragic experience that happens only to others. What I am talking about is that I fell in love with, as the saying goes, Another Woman. I do not mean to be in the least facetious about this; there was nothing amusing in the entire drama as it was subsequently played out. Not only was I married to Dorothy, but ours was a Catholic marriage and I was the father of three beautiful children. I was not a philanderer and was in fact emotionally quite naïve and inexperienced. Had my views on the subject of adultery been consulted three minutes before I met the woman who was to change my life, I would have gone on record as taking a very dim view of it. For that matter, I still do—not simply because Catholic moral philosophy opposes extramarital affairs, but because they harm the marriage relationship, particularly one in which children are involved.

Nevertheless, the tragic thing happened. That night a friend—my agent at the time, Jules Green—was in the company of a young woman we will call Betty Harrington. He introduced her to me, quite casually, when I had finished the program. There were the usual eight or ten people milling about on the stage, exchanging pleasantries. My disturbing, immediate reaction to her cannot possibly be explained solely on the grounds that she was beautiful. The world is full of beautiful women, and the percentage of them is higher in Hollywood than in any other city in the world. I had met any number of them, some quite famous, in my few years in the Los Angeles radio and film community, and had felt nothing more shattering than the common male response to a pretty face or ankle, as our grandfathers used to put it.

Thinking back now, thirty years later, and not having seen the woman for a very long time, I'm reminded of the verb *to fall,* as in "to fall in love," "I fell in love," "They fell in love with each other." The word is used figuratively, but in a sense it is strikingly apt. I did indeed seem to *fall* into this other person, almost as one would fall into a pool, or over a precipice. There was not the slightest calculation to any of it. Indeed, as soon as I was able to collect my wits, my calculations were all directed toward extricating myself. Betty herself was not only attractive but charming, witty, intelligent; I basked in her company. It did not help matters that she loved me, too. But I always perceived the beautiful, romantic aspects of the relationship through a filter of horror and guilt. Today, at the age of fifty-nine, considerably more experienced and more calloused by life's buffetings and adventures, I am not, for better or for worse, the same man I was at the tender age of twenty-eight. I now realize that largely because of my naïveté I was literally defenseless when the moment of crisis came.

It was not until several tortured years later, with the help of psychoanalysis, that I realized why only Betty, among the great number of beautiful women I had met, affected me in this way. As the sophisticated reader may already have assumed, it was because certain facets of her totality reminded me of my mother. Not, obviously, my middle-aged, bitter, saddened mother of that year—1950—but the beautiful, idealized woman of my infancy, the mother who was warm, physically comforting, young, vibrant, entertaining; the mother who kept disappearing, who—with a maddening combination of the best of intentions, financial desperation, and maternal irresponsibility—not only abandoned me but did so repeatedly.

Betty had the same tortured, expressive blue eyes, the same witty, knowing smile, the same free spirit, the same warm flesh, the same throaty, worldly-wise voice. I recognized none of this at the moment of our meeting; it was a puzzle pieced together long afterwards. But the result was that immediately this woman seemed not a new but a very old friend. She had a rich sense of humor; she loved poetry, music; she was bright—one of those women who make good wives for authors, composers, creative men. Any computer match-up would have printed out that we were well suited to each other. I feel even today that Betty and I could have had a happy lifelong relationship had we been single when we met. But neither of us had the slightest right to the otherwise happy relationship that an accident of fate had suddenly presented to us.

As I've said, although I was uncomfortably conscious that my marriage to Dorothy was considerably less than ideal, the idea of divorce had never entered my mind. I was a Catholic. Besides, while Dorothy was not perfect—who is?—she was by no means without virtues. She too was pretty, enjoyed laughter, had a sweet, amiable side to her nature, and was generally a relaxed, cheerful person. If Dorothy and I ever had any serious arguments, I cannot remember them. On the other hand, there was never any sense in which I could share my work with her, whether it was comedy, acting, writing or music. But that, too, is true of millions of marriage relationships. And Stevie, Brian and David were three such incredibly beautiful and appealing children that I loved them passionately.

There were problems in my marriage, yes; but they did not seem to me at any time severe. To the extent that events forced me to be conscious of them at all, I tended, no doubt unwisely, to put them out of my mind: I was going to stay married to Dorothy no matter what, and there was not much sense in complaining about a state of affairs in which I was sure to remain.

But then, as I've said, I met Betty Harrington, and my life changed.

Oddly enough, my very determination, from the first, to give Betty up, To Do the Right Thing, only fanned the emotional flames, giving every moment with her the kind of poignancy we usually experience only when we say good-bye to a loved one going away to war, to another part of the world, or perhaps to death. If a supply of something is running out, even if that something is a human being, one's powers of appreciation become incredibly heightened.

The next couple of years were sheer hell. At the same time, by dramatic coincidence, CBS executives advised me that they would like me to move from radio into the new medium of television. They wanted me, in fact, to do a daily program for them, along the lines of the late-night KNX show. This in itself would not have been such a dramatic change, but I had to go to New York to take advantage of the opportunity. In those days there was no transcontinental TV cable, and New York was a more important television center than Los Angeles. So there I was, on the threshold of professional success beyond my wildest expectations, and I was walking forward into it emotionally shattered.

Totally unable to conduct ourselves as we both felt we ought to, Betty and I simply gave in to each other for the time being and—because I had to report for work on January 1, 1951—left Los Angeles on my birthday, the day after Christmas, and drove together to New York.

There is certainly no good time, God damn it, to walk out on a wife and three wonderful children, but the holiday season is definitely the worst time of all. I seriously considered suicide on more than one occasion in those days, but it was always the thought of the children more than anything else that stayed my hand. Why that same thought could not have driven me firmly away from Betty is a good question, the answer to which is that one day it did, but for a long time I was simply unable to give her up, though I tried repeatedly.

In any event, despite my repeated attempts to do the virtuous thing, my marriage was eventually shattered. Upon finally—correctly—perceiving that I was not about to return to her, Dorothy gave up on me.

By that time we had moved into a new house in a former peach orchard in Van Nuys. On moving day a friendly neighbor introduced himself and offered to help unload furniture and other belongings from our rented U-Haul trailer. He was Gus Bivona, a gifted clarinetist who had played with the orchestras of Tommy Dorsey, Harry James, Bunny Berrigan and other bandleaders of the 1940s and was now a member of the MGM studio orchestra. Gus and his wife, Ruth—a sister of famed lyricist Leo Robin—have been dear friends ever since.

They were sympathetic to both Dorothy and me during our ordeal. Later, through them, Dorothy met a wonderful fellow named Andy Young, a saxophonist who played in the MGM orchestra. A couple of years later Dorothy and Andy were married, and to this day I feel that his death not long thereafter was a greater tragedy for her than my leaving her.

Andy was one of those relaxed, likable, husbandly and fatherly fellows who must have come as a godsend into her life at the moment. Too, he was something of a father figure to her, partly because he was some fifteen years older.

But before she met Andy, I had rented a house from actress Gene Tierney's mother in Westport, Connecticut, had again said good-bye to Betty, and had brought Dorothy and the children East.

The experience turned into a nightmare.

CHAPTER 5

A Time of Torment

In a zombielike state, I got the car out of the garage and drove out to the airport to meet my family.

The plane came in on time.

I felt a strange surge of something like happiness and hope as I watched the passengers filing out of the airliner, and when at last I saw two familiar small figures hopping down the steps, my heart leaped up and I walked quickly forward.

"Daddy! Daddy!" Steve and Brian screamed, running toward me at top speed. As they leaped up into my arms, I caught them both and swung them around and laughed and then put them down and picked them up one at a time and kissed them; and then I saw Dorothy approaching, carrying little David.

She looked pretty.

"Hi," she said, smiling tiredly.

"Hello, honey," I said, kissing her on the mouth clumsily. "How was the trip?"

"Oh, awful," she said, laughing. "This one is quite a problem child."

"Here," I said, "let me take him." I lifted David from her arms and kissed him on both cheeks and said, "How is Daddy's big boy, huh? How is Daddy's big old boy?"

He smiled shyly and took my hat off and held it against his little face.

As we drove back through the city, picking up the parkway drive to Westport, it almost seemed like one of the Sunday afternoon drives of days gone by. We were all together in the car; all talking rapidly, joking; making small talk, family talk. It felt good.

We entered the children in school, but the boys seemed to sense the bitterness that stood between us. Steve took sick and Brian wouldn't eat. And then one day we awakened to find that heavy snow had fallen all during the night; I couldn't get the car out of the driveway, and we were trapped in the house. Finally we just sat, the five of us like wolves trapped in a cave, now and then snapping at one another, waiting for some sort of deliverance.

I was now half demented from frustration and remorse at the evil or at least stupid thing I had done in bringing them all East. Again, in trying to do what was right, I had done what was wrong. My self-contempt knew no bounds, and I became angrier and more desperate by the hour.

The house had fireplaces and central heating, but it seemed impossible in the wintertime ever to completely banish the chill that crept in through cracks and crevices or filtered in some mysterious way even through solid surfaces, through glass and wood and stone; it settled in sofas and rugs and drapes, found warm flesh and made it shudder, and seemed to pass through it, too, as easily as it had passed through everything else, and to settle in the bone. We lighted bright fires and turned the furnace up high; but in certain corners of the room, at certain low levels near the floor, lurking between the sheets, the chill lay in wait, ever in wait, drawing its own cruel strength from the snow piled outside, from the winds that congregated high in the bare skeletons of trees and rattled windowpanes not violently but gently and relentlessly.

If it had been a happy house for us, if it had been a house of love, the cold would not have brought such an air of loneliness and desolation with it; but while there was love in the house, it could not flow freely then between any of us, could not unite in one spiritual blaze to warm our hearts and souls, but rather flickered weakly, seeking a ground, then dissipated itself in the air, leaving us uncomforted, insecure, and cold.

The children went out again and again, bundled up with leggings and scarfs, to play in the snow, the first they had ever seen, but even their play seemed subdued, their squeals of wonder and surprise muffled, like the cries of lost birds, free but starving birds trapped in the North.

I walked with them in the snow, looking at them the way a man who knows he is soon to die must look at his children, trying to crystallize certain moments and sights and sounds and preserve them in his memory. I saw their red cheeks and uplifted smiles, watched them struggle through snowdrifts on little legs, looking like lost explorers on a strange planet; and because I knew, or at least was afraid, that something might take them away from me again (for, yes, they had been taken away from me by something, even though I had performed the act of leaving, even though I had removed my body from the presence of theirs in the West), I stared at them hungrily as they rolled and fell and recovered with piping cries and wandered in the snow; stared at their faces the way men stare at the forms of loved ones through prison bars, the way the condemned stare at the sun and sky before the black bag is lowered over their heads, the way God must stare at the souls in Hell (if there is a Hell), and the way those souls must stare at God (if there is a God).

I wanted to kneel before them and say—oh, say what? The only words that occurred, and dimly, vaguely, at that, would have been incomprehensible to them as well as embarrassing. I wanted to say absurd things like: Oh, you little tiny human beings, you toy people whom I love so much, with your little toy noses and your ridiculous adorable voices and sweet trusting little hearts, how I wish it were possible for those of us who are members of the giant race that rules the planet to kneel on the floor and in the snow and in fields of flowers with you and get into your world, somehow, rather than dragging you into ours, to kneel with you and look very closely into your faces and say how is it in there and we are sorry, truly stricken, that we ever hurt you.

But of course it was all nonsense, the whole idea, and I knew it; so all I could do was look at them as the days passed, look at them as they climbed panting up the rolling white hills and slid down, as they built snowmen and wandered through the stand of trees that surrounded the house, look at them as they walked gnomelike under the cold winter sun and under the sharp, crisp glittering stars of early evening. All I could do was watch them and think: God, what a supreme joke! I, who would be tempted to kill anyone else who hurt you, am hurting you more than anyone else ever has. And you will probably never understand; and how could I expect you to, when I myself do not understand?

Ah, well, someday you will know, and perhaps you know already in some very basic way, that my love for you exists, that it exists whether you are on my lap or thousands of miles away under other stars.

Or is there any good in that? Is love, for a child, nonexistent if the one who loves is not present? Oh, enough! Enough and too much of this endless looking at you and loving you and wondering, trying to piece together a puzzle that now can never be put together because some of the pieces are missing, having been lost or burned or pushed over the edge of the universe, gone, ever gone. There is only the present, doled out to us second by second, and at least you are here, now, at this moment, and that is something to be thankful for. I love you now, here in this cold forest, here in this quiet house, here in this lonely Connecticut lane, and you are here to know of my love, so that is what I will have to settle for now. Tomorrow can take care of itself. It is idle to dream of freezing time in the now, sticking to one point of time, stopping all motion the way it is stopped by a photograph or a flash of lightning. I will pick you up now and kiss you and take you into the house and make you hot Ovaltine. Not to coin a phrase, my beloved children, we will eat, drink, and be merry, for tomorrow we die.

Dorothy did not have the time or the inclination to make any friends in Westport, and after the first few days, after she tired of the scenery, tired of the trees and the snow and the clean, still country air, she had nothing to occupy her mind but her misery.

"Why in the name of God did you drag us back here?" she would shout. "Why didn't you leave us alone? This was your idea, not mine!"

The period is largely a blur in my mind in which certain moments, certain scenes stand out as they do in dreams. At one point, stunned by the realization that I could not put the pieces of my marriage back together, I hurried into the room where the children were playing, half-watching a TV set. The boys had always been able to make me laugh heartily, and I loved to talk with them, because it fascinated me to watch their minds function.

When Stevie was only four years old he had gone through a period where he had trouble with his *r*'s and his *l*'s. "I wike Wichard," he would say; or "I've been wunning." We had thought it was cute, but one day I decided to explain to Steve that such pronunciations were faulty and might be improved upon.

"I want some waymuns," Stevie said. He meant raisins.

"You want what?" I asked.

"Waymuns."

"You mean raisins."

"Yes."

"But that's not the way to say it. Say it slowly now. Rais-ins . . . "

"Waymuns."

"Here, now. Break the word up into two parts. First say raise."

"Raise," Stevie said, carefully.

"That's fine," I said, lifting him to my lap. "Now say ins."

"Ins."

"Wonderful. You're a very smart boy. Now slowly say raise—ins."

"Raise—ins," said Stevie, concentrating.

"That's perfect. Now say it fast. Raisins!"

"Waymuns!"

Their three faces, turned now toward the television screen, made my heart leap. They were going to be taken away from me again, although I accepted all the blame for what was about to happen. After a moment Steve looked up with what I thought was a measure of apprehension.

"You kids getting hungry?" I asked in a casual tone.

"Not me," Brian said.

"If anybody's hungry," I said, "I can bring you some waymuns."

They all laughed.

"Hey," I said, "anybody want to go with me to get the mail?"

"It's too cold," David said, and they laughed again.

I left them there, put on a jacket, went outside and walked down the drive to the mailbox at the side of the road. Inside were three advertisements for the former tenants and an envelope from my mother. Standing there in the snowy cold I opened the envelope with stiff fingers and read her letter.

My Darling Son:

After all your kindness and thoughtfulness to me what must you think of me allowing so much time to pass without writing to you? It's constantly in my mind, but I don't do it. I wonder what is in a person that causes them to do things they don't want to do and leave things undone that they want to do.

Thanks, for sending me those magazines. I enjoyed reading them and I guess if it wasn't for the reading and the radio and the television I don't know what I would do sometimes. The set you bought me is still working just fine although I had to have the man replace a tube the other day. I am so grateful to God for the great gift of a good child. Our Lord said the good (meaning the ones that loved Him) would suffer much and carry a heavy cross. He said He came to bring them a cross and not a crown. God help the ones that don't believe in another life beyond the grave. How can they stand their troubles here? And everyone has them sometime, sooner or later in their life, whether they bring on their own troubles or not.

Little Brian has a birthday sometime in March. I lost the dates of all their birthdays so I can't remember just what day it is but I wanted to remind you so you could get him something. He loves you so much.

Oh, Steve, by the way, thanks so much for the picture of the children and me. I wish sometimes that when you're moving around in important circles back there that you could meet Fulton J. Sheen. I know you meet a lot of important people and I'm sure he could comfort you a great deal. I wouldn't miss his Sunday broadcasts for worlds. Such a speaker.

Honey, thanks for sending me the book *Show Folks*. It wasn't bad but it seems to be just an ad for *Variety* and Joe Bernie. It is far from being a really complete picture of what was going on in vaudeville, believe me. I really didn't expect them to mention my name but, hell, in all fairness, I did originate a style of comedy that a lot of people he mentions stole, imitated, or profited by . . .

I slowly folded the letter and put it into the inner pocket of my coat as I walked back to the house. It was so typical of my mother. The rambling thoughts; the sharp, sensitive but teeming, undisciplined brain, alternately bitter and loving. It was difficult for me to sit alone at home for more than an hour, and often at such times I would reflect that my mother spent most of her time alone in her apartment, watching television, or crocheting as she sat in the big chair by the window, and I would wonder how she could possibly stand it. Would I ever become like her, able to sit alone day after day, as one day perhaps I must?

A long time later I realized that I had only a vague memory of the next few days, although they were hardly more painful than countless other days, and I was getting almost accustomed to misery. For some reason my mind had tried to blot out the period during which Dorothy made plans to leave Westport and return to California.

It was, I at last concluded, something about the look on the faces of the children that drove special knives of torture into my heart. They had thought they had me back, and now they discovered that they had been misled. The truth was withheld from them, of course; it had been a lovely winter vacation, they were told, and now they were going back to their nice, familiar home in sunny Southern California; and just as soon as Daddy could arrange it, he would come out again and have a wonderful visit with them. Externally, they accepted it all, but their eyes revealed their sensitivity to the emotional realities of the situation.

I spent two days closing down the now tomblike house, deliberately working myself to the point of exhaustion. When the job was done I moved back into my apartment on Park Avenue, which itself seemed deserted and sepulchral.

CHAPTER 6

Taking a Look Within

As if all this were not confusing enough, at one point, in desperation and panic, I reasoned as follows: I am unable to give Betty up, partly because of my powerful physical attraction to her. Perhaps, therefore, if I deliberately involve myself with another attractive woman, something like the same process that separated me from Dorothy will occur, and I can use that process as a sort of lever to pry myself loose from Betty.

Now it is easy to see how mistaken I was, but a drowning man rarely reasons well. The only practical result of my making overtures to a young woman of my acquaintance in New York, of course, was that Betty was shocked and puzzled by my behavior. So in the end I had alienated and hurt five people.

Another man, from another childhood, might have been less jolted by this whole experience. But the chaotic nature of my early years had made me wary of emotionality, almost allergic to it. My mother was a violent person; my whole family, the Donahues, were a wild bunch. They were fascinating, witty, lively, charitable and entertaining. Less interesting people gathered around them for their vivacity. But at home they were sometimes violent, not with clubs but with words, with emotion. When my mother was in a good mood, she was great company. But when she was not, her heights of irrationality were spectacular. No one could live with her then. Now, an adult who couldn't live with her could say, "Well, to hell with you, too!" and walk out of the house; but a three-year-old son couldn't. Instead, he—I—was simply crushed.

Consequently leery of emotion, I learned to protect myself to a degree by relying on logic. To this day I prefer things to be stated sensibly and analyzed reasonably. When emotions are appropriate, I let them flow as they should. But I tend to be at least somewhat legalistic and rationalistic. Human affairs are not run that way, of course, but to abandon reason altogether is to plunge into chaos.

During this difficult time, trying to analyze my way through problems

43

as I had always done, I was doubly disturbed to discover that pure reason did not offer any solution to my predicament. Or, when reason told me what I ought to do, I found I was totally incapable of acting on its wise advice.

One especially painful aspect of the experience, which has persisted to the present and will, in fact, to my dying day, is that whereas I could stop loving Dorothy and, once she had happily remarried, even stop feeling a sense of obligation to her, I obviously would never stop loving my three sons. I loved them even more fiercely, in fact, because I was separated from them, and also because of guilt for what I had done to them. There could never be the slightest possibility of fully explaining any of that to them in the days during which it was happening, nor have I been able to offer them an adequate explanation since, except in one instance when, a few years ago, Steve, Jr. and I discussed the matter in a somewhat awkward manner. Tragedies of almost all other kinds can be discussed with children. If a father is dying of cancer, his sons or daughters can be taken into the family's confidence; if a father is going away to war, or has been killed in battle or in an accident, all of this—however painful and tragic—can be taken up with children. They will weep and suffer, God knows, but eventually they can get some sort of philosophical grasp of the reality that has caused their pain. But when their father has Abandoned Them, and for Another Woman at that, then they will simply wander in the dark, confused, totally uncomprehending why that man, that big, tall, strong, loving figure who kissed them good-night and tucked them in, who played with them and tickled them in the morning, who carried them on his back around the house, who took them to the circus, who bought them toys, who took them Christmas shopping, who was in a sense the God in their lives, simply kissed them very tenderly good-bye one night, stared at them fiercely for a reason they could never have suspected, muttered something ineffectual and confusing to their mother, and then put on his hat and coat and walked out into the California night.

To the children that night was not the worst part of the whole damnable experience. The worst for them would be doled out day by day, like a slow numbing poison, by the seemingly endless, continued absence of that man to whom they could no longer daily run to complain that a neighborhood bully had threatened or beaten them, that they had hurt themselves—that man whose every former affectionate act now echoed through their minds in the hideous form of its absence.

I was not gone forever, of course. During the nine years' residence in New York required by my television duties I flew back to Los Angeles every few weeks to spend time with the boys. Only those parents who have suffered through this kind of relationship with their children—and there are now, God help us, many millions of them—can know the peculiar mixture of pain and pleasure in such fleeting hours. It is something like the emotional process involved with separation from a mate or a lover. The very shortness of the hours, of the minutes, makes each the sweeter and yet the more painful. At the deepest moments of joy, holding a little one on your lap, you know that tomorrow, or the next day, or the next week you won't be able to hold him. I was in those days in a situation remarkably similar to the predicament of the laboratory animal in a maze, except that there was no one solution which was proper; there was merely a choice of a limited number of alternatives, all tragic.

Although it is difficult to explain, the collapse of my marriage and my self-image proved to be a point of important transition in my life intellectually as well as personally. Before the tragedy brought me face to face with reality, I had somewhat smugly assumed that the world was what I believed it to be and that people whose picture of life differed from my own were simply wrong. I believed that I was fairly well educated and that I understood myself and my fellowman reasonably well. I was happy in my work, enjoyed my home life in many particulars, and thought I was a responsible adult and citizen of the world.

It took three solid years of misery to make me realize that my lifelong picture of myself and my universe had been badly out of focus. Until the age of thirty I had been "a writer," but I had written nothing of consequence. When the question occurred to me at all, I thought of myself as perhaps a bit more virtuous than the average, but that was only because like many Irishmen I related virtue almost exclusively to sex. I wasn't conscious that I had inherited the family failings: a short temper, unease with certain strangers, and a feeling of intellectual superiority for which there was not the slightest justification. Fate finally rubbed my nose in the fact that I was not a man at all, only a boy in adult's clothing. Because of my quick wit I had in a short time risen to a position of prominence. But my off-the-air self was not then equipped to handle the role.

When the marriage ended, I began to read seriously and to discuss my problems with others, to challenge all the opinions and ideas I'd taken for granted for so long. I tried to pray, but I finally realized that, at least in my case, prayer was somehow a retreat from reality. It certainly did nothing to remove my crushing sense of guilt.

In praying I was asking God to solve problems that were, in a factual sense, incapable of solution.

Alone in New York—Betty having returned to Los Angeles—I wrestled with my problems month after month. During this time I had to go on the air five days a week and be funny. CBS put me on at 7:30 in the evening, then at noon, then at 3:30 in the afternoon. The programs were well received, but somehow they weren't as good as the old late-night Hollywood show had been. Frankly, I wasn't giving my work nearly the attention it deserved. Much of my energy was going into arguments, depressions, and storms of guilt brought on by my personal difficulties. At the office I was often distracted and listless, edgy with friends and uneasy with strangers. All my life I had been regarded as good-natured; now I began to read in newspapers that I was "moody," "cold," and "withdrawn." Today people who interview me often say they are surprised. "I'd read that you were distant, hard to talk to." The explanation, of course, is that for the first two or three years I worked in New York I was aloof and ill at ease. Today my life is happier and more productive. I've learned again to enjoy social contacts. But those old press clippings are still in the files.

Life has become an exciting adventure, and I am thrilled by every day of it. My mind is closed to few possibilities. I am continually impressed by the earnest goodwill of people whose opinions seem to me to be completely unwise, and I have learned that there are at least scraps of truth in every intellectual camp. And while my historical outlook has become in some respects pessimistic, I feel more compassionate and sympathetic toward others than I ever did in the old days.

The intellectual awakening that I have described was not a sudden explosion but a long, slow, painful process that often left me confused and frightened as well as exhilarated. Now that the storm is over, so to speak, I have found reassurance and new strength, but the first half of the 1950s was a time of fearful emotional rearrangement.

I went through periods when atheism seemed, if not a comforting philosophy, at least a rational and methodical one. I carefully studied the arguments for and against the existence of God and learned that atheists are not evil, bearded devils in human form as I had been led to believe as a child. Often they are highly intelligent, and frequently they are people of high ethical standards. Of course the fact that in our time atheism has been equated in the minds of many with communism has dreadfully obscured the issue. Actually there have always been atheists, but communism is a relatively modern phenomenon. If and when communism ever passes from the earth, atheism will still be a philosophy that will appeal to a number of people. Through reading the works of various atheists, heretics, agnostics, rationalists, and secular humanists, I realized at last that it is not hardness of heart or evil passions that move certain men to atheism or agnosticism but a sort of overly scrupulous intellectual honesty. Although I think he is essentially right, the average believer rarely subjects his beliefs to a calm, critical examination; he might not even know how to do so. Although I think he is essentially wrong, the average atheist has usually arrived at his intellectual position through a long, tough-minded consideration of philosophical questions. In fact it seems to me that the average atheist is more interested in religion than is the average Christian. Some theologians argue that an atheist who leads a good life and is honestly convinced of the correctness of his views will at death be received cordially into God's presence, whereas a confirmed believer who leads an immoral life is likely to spend eternity in Hell.

My present position as to the existence of God is that though it seems utterly fantastic, I accept it because the alternative seems even more fantastic. All so-called proofs of God's being, however, seem to me indications and not proofs at all, in the strictest scientific sense. The difficulty arises from the fact that the only two means that man has of measuring his experience—time and space—are both completely mysterious in essence.

Consider, first, space. Either it has a limit, a boundary line (which is absurd, because one could always go to that point and then reach out a little farther), or else it has no limit (which is equally absurd to the mind of man). The ignorant sometimes say they have no trouble in imagining infinite space, but to the intelligent man the concept is beyond understanding.

There is the same difficulty with the idea of time. Either it had a beginning (which sounds ridiculous, since we are able to think of the day before time started), or else it had no beginning (which sounds even more absurd). To consider the problem at its other end, either time will one day stop (which is inconceivable because we can think of the day after time stopped), or else it will never stop (which is also unthinkable).

Against this background we may begin to see that when we deal with such classic proofs of God's existence as the First Cause, we are dealing not with simple, reasonable, and irrefutable concepts but with mysteries that the mind of man cannot ultimately fathom. It is known, of course, that philosophers have set forth various explanations of such fundamental questions, but the fact that the explanations are various speaks for itself. The nonbeliever says, "If everything must have a cause, then God must have a cause. But if there is anything that can exist without a cause, it might just as well be the Universe as God." Probably it is speculations such as this that have led to the creation of those philosophies that suggest that the Universe is God.

I will not discuss here such things as the Argument from Natural Law, the Argument from Design, and so forth. Let the interested reader refer to Thomas Aquinas, Spencer, Spinoza, Bertrand Russell and company for a thorough examination of these issues. My point in introducing the matter here was to observe that it came as a shock to me that atheism was a philosophy that might be entertained by honorable and intelligent men. Having been conditioned by a Catholic education, I had perceived the very word atheism as evil, taboo. Unfortunately, such a fate befalls many words, and whenever it does it renders them (to some degree) unsuitable for purposes of rational discourse.

I had no way of knowing in those days that Brian would one day wrestle with some of the same philosophical problems and come up with his own answers, some of them dramatically different from my own.

CHAPTER 7

A New Wife and Stepmother

In July of 1952 something happened that helped me begin to put my life back together.

I met Jayne Meadows.

In the flesh, that is. I'd seen her in motion pictures and on television, and she has told me that in the old days in California she used to lie in bed at night and fall asleep listening to my night-owl radio program. But we were only celebrities to each other, not people, until the night of July 3, 1952, when Jayne made her first appearance as a panelist on the "I've Got a Secret" show.

She was unwinding after the excitement of doing the program, and since I had nothing much to do, I accepted the invitation of mutual friends to join their group. It included Jayne and her sister, Audrey, whom I had already met.

Coming into contact with Jayne Meadows for the first time is like being exposed to the Statue of Liberty or the Grand Canyon for the first time; one is apt to just stand and look. Like these other natural wonders, she is big and beautiful and a bit overwhelming. You are suddenly confronted by a barrage of red hair and earrings and perfume and eyelashes and a generous red and white and pink mouth that keeps talking and smiling and gasping and laughing, and—well, you've seen her. Press agents have applied the adjective "glamorous" to practically every female in pictures this side of Lassie and Marjorie Main. In reality few of today's actresses have glamour, although many are beautiful. Jayne has it.

From what she has told me about her early years it is difficult to believe that the neurotic, unsettled Jayne of, say, twenty-two could have grown into the insightful and maternal woman of today. She had concluded a brilliant series of turns on Broadway by going to Hollywood at the suggestion of producer Pandro Berman. There she had appeared in a number of motion pictures—*Undercurrent,* with Robert Taylor and Katharine Hepburn; *Lady in the Lake,* with Robert Montgomery;

Enchantment, with David Niven; *Luck of the Irish,* with Tyrone Power, and several others. In all of her roles she had turned in electric performances. Hollywood considered her the most gifted young actress in the business, in terms of sheer original dramatic talent. She had one exciting professional opportunity after another, and yet some inner insecurity made her temperamental and difficult for producers to handle. In the end she began turning down pictures her studios wanted her to do. Finally in 1952 she abandoned Hollywood altogether and returned to New York to live with her sister, Audrey. This not only was a gesture of defiance; it represented a break in her marriage to screenwriter Milton Krims as well as in her career. Now she was just beginning to come out of the darkness and to take firmer control of her destiny. When we met that summer we were two lost souls who in time were able to give each other strength.

Despite Jayne's glamour, beauty and charm, however, we did not fall in love at first sight. On that sultry summer night when we met, each of us was in the process of surveying the wreck of a first marriage. Certainly neither of us was looking for a new life partner that evening, nor were we looking for someone to love. We were just at loose ends, wondering what was to become of us. We enjoyed each other's company, once I got over my initial shyness, but we didn't see each other again for over two weeks, and even then we met accidentally.

Shortly thereafter I took Jayne out on our first real date. Instead of going to a nightclub or theater, I thought it would be fun as well as educational to take in the show at the Hayden Planetarium, which included a surprisingly realistic simulation of a rocket flight to the moon. As we were leaving the auditorium at the conclusion of the program, I said, "Other men may have taken you to the Stork Club or Twenty-One, but I'll bet I'm the first to take you to the moon."

During the early stages of our relationship we did not limit ourselves exclusively to each other's company, but little by little Jayne's maternal, wise, and feminine qualities led me to gravitate toward her. We found that we were able to discuss our problems with each other, and during these conversations I was always impressed by her intelligence. Although I have a reputation for being a quiet, meditative sort, the truth is I love to talk. (I do not particularly relish talking about myself, however, which is what sometimes misleads people who interview me. Also, I cannot think of much to say to certain people. To open up I must first pick up some sort of emanation from another's mind; if I find you stimulating, I will talk your ears off. That's how it is when I'm with Jayne.) After the first few minutes we started a long-playing conversation that has been running steadily now for some twenty-nine years. We have been able to mature together, to study together, to openly discuss our innermost secrets, longings and fears; and we have both benefited greatly.

Two psychoanalysts have told me that Jayne has such great sensitivity to others that it is a pity she did not train to practice counseling herself. But it had taken a long, painful analytical exploration of her past to bring her to her current state of productive adjustment. Her experience in the field stimulated my own interest; I too found that consultation was extremely beneficial.

Although Jayne has not been able to acquire the formal knowledge that the analyst must have, she nonetheless serves as mother-advisor to many of her friends, who seem to perceive in her an earthy, inborn wisdom. Jayne is, to put it in the simplest words, a Woman. *San Francisco Chronicle* television critic Terrence O'Flaherty captured her perfectly in a story he did for *TV Week* in late May of 1981.

The word *interview* suggests a dialogue between two people. An interview with Jayne Meadows is a monologue. You simply introduce yourself, ask one simple question, sit down, and listen. She does the rest, and it's a fascinating experience—similar to watching a performance of the monologists of the recent past—Cornelia Otis Skinner and Ruth Draper—women of charm, poise, humor, and above all theatricality.

Miss Meadows adds another quality. At first look (and listen) she seems dizzy—by which I mean pleasantly exuberant and possibly a little scatterbrained. But after a while it becomes apparent that this is misleading. She is intelligent and fun and just a tiny bit dizzy. Most of all she is an actress and a good one. And God knows she can talk.

She has done everything from theater and TV to game shows and being married to Steve Allen, which must be a career in itself. . . .

She has led an interesting life. She was born in China, where her parents were missionaries. She was successful on the stage from the start—a tall beauty with an elegant figure, big eyes and good legs. She was brought from Broadway to Hollywood to play with Katharine Hepburn in *Undercurrent* and recently was a big hit in *Once in a Lifetime* in New York.

With all this behind her, what is Jayne Meadows herself really like? That was my first question.

"When I was playing the role of a young woman opposite Walter Slezak, he took me aside and said, 'Jayne, you're too much of a character actress. You must take a part and bend it to your personality. No matter what they've written, bend it.'

"That made me realize that I could play anything, but it was very hard for me to be ME. Art Carney has the same difficulty. I went to a psychiatrist for years just to learn how to walk into a room and be ME. It was easier to hide behind a role—a character, someone else. When I was young, I'd write plays and make my sister Audrey—who was hopeless and always crying—the princess and I'd be the witch because it was the best role. . . . But anyway . . . Let's see, I've lost my train of thought here. Everytime I do it, I have to wind myself back. . . . Oh, yes . . . When I was a small girl in China, a British naval officer gave me a present—a doll with seven heads. One was Chinese, one Indian—all different nationalities. You screwed on the right head and put on the appropriate doll clothes. It took a psychiatrist to make me realize that I identified with that doll. Change heads and put on different clothes. ACTING!"

That's only part of O'Flaherty's story, but it gives the gist of Jayne better than anything I've ever read on her.

Well, in time this vital, colorful, warm woman met Steve, Brian and David and loved them at once. David was only about four when Jayne met him, so, as "the baby," he was especially dear to her. And she and Brian fell in love at once, too. Jayne responded to his cheerful, impish personality and loved to laugh at and with him. She loved Steve too, but he was the oldest and therefore had in clearer focus the fact of my having separated from his mother. He was a quieter, more thoughtful child than the others. Though Jayne's heart went out to him from the first, it took a bit longer to build a relationship between them.

When Jayne gave birth to Bill a few years later, in 1957, Brian, David and Steve must have had some feelings of loss or jealousy; his arrival must have been, at least in one way, one more source of sadness for them. He lived with me and they did not—because Dorothy had been given their custody—although we saw each other frequently. But from the first time they met little Bill they were fond of him, as they are to this day.

Jayne did more for Steve, Brian and David during those early years than they will ever know. She helped me become a better father. She was meticulous about their birthdays, made plans to care for them when they came East, in many ways devoted herself to their care. And she sensed from the first the special problems they had, simply as children of a prominent man.

Children of celebrities face unusual circumstances. When a father— and in this case the stepmother as well—is well known, it means that the parent is more than just a parent. All of us experience the fact that our parents loom very importantly in our eyes. But when society emphasizes that importance daily, the situation becomes more complex.

There is a degree to which it is natural, even necessary, for a child to rebel against the parent—especially when the child is right and the parent wrong on a point of disagreement. But the parent's combined celebrity and natural authority may lead to the repression of the child's rebellion. Or the rebellion may be more explosive and painful if it does occur; or it may seek a substitute target.

Furthermore, there is great competition for such a parent's time. The famous person—whether he is an entertainer, politician, athlete or business leader—generally works more than the traditional eight-hour day. His duties may require him to be absent from the home, sometimes for relatively long periods. He may have to work at times in other parts of the country or world. Also, people who become successful often do so because they have a certain measure of ambition, a personal drive that will inevitably have egocentric elements. To the degree, then, that the parent is concentrating on himself, he may be less than adequately sensitive to the needs of his children. There are more than enough instances of this sort of problem in American society in the separate families of the Kennedys, in Ronald Reagan's family, Bing Crosby's, etc. Indeed the incidence of such cases is probably higher when the parents are politicians or actors than in any other professions. So this, too, contributed to the difficulties faced by Steve, Brian and David.

There are, of course, advantages to being the child of a prominent person. During the summer of 1964 Jayne and I took Brian, who was seventeen at the time; David, fourteen; and Bill, six, on a tour of the Orient that included stops in Tokyo, Bangkok, Calcutta, New Delhi, Hong Kong and—for Brian and David—Saigon. The most fascinating part of the trip came by chance in Hiroshima, a city in which we found ourselves on the anniversary of the American atomic bomb attack. When I discovered that visitors from various parts of the world were staying at our hotel, I engaged them in conversation and somehow arranged for a visit to the final rally of the Japanese Peace Conference Against Atomic and Hydrogen Bombs, which was held in a large athletic stadium. The tenor of the meeting was, perhaps understandably, anti-American, although we personally were kindly treated. But even in the best of circumstances children pay a price—for instance, in the envy of school and neighborhood peers.

The negative effects were less noticeable in the case of my youngest son, Bill. This is interesting, because his mother too is a famous personage. And since he spent the first twenty years of his life in our home, he was daily exposed to evidence of our celebrityhood. In his case, however, we were well aware of the problem, as well as the entire spectrum of parent-child difficulties, and worked very hard in our roles as parents. I expressed this insight some years ago in a poem:

MY SONS

I fished for souls in the deep can-be void of time
    and drew up singly three, clothed them in flesh,
    prized them, boasted of them, practiced love
        upon them.

But while my back was turned they swam away;
not hopelessly beyond my sight, 'tis true, but
    always slipping, after that, the tattered nets of love.

They still splash close but own themselves.
I readily concede their right to freedom
    but feel their loss as much as if it could
        have been prevented.
When the fourth appeared I looked away the less
    and smiled the more into the waters.

CHAPTER 8

Some Aspects of the Larger Problem

Back to 1971. Although at first we viewed Brian's decision only personally, we soon realized that what had happened in our family, with our son, was happening in thousands of families in all parts of the country. In a sense, Brian's withdrawal from the world introduced me to an emerging social problem, one that affected not only the young people who joined some kind of new religious sect, but their parents, their brothers, sisters, friends, everyone who loved them and was concerned for their well-being. In the classic way, I had not recognized the dimensions of the national situation until it hit home. Once I considered the larger problem, I was able to look at our situation in a fresh light. And this new perspective was some comfort—not because "misery loves company," but because my emotions were now guided by the challenge of understanding a social phenomenon. I continued to ask myself why my son had joined the Church of Armageddon, but now I began to ask why so many young people were joining any such group.

When a subject interests me, I collect information about it, at first almost without planning to. I read, start a file. I follow up tips about articles in magazines, talk to friends and interview strangers, tape-record thoughts that come to mind as I'm driving. So without consciously intending it, I found myself reacting to Brian's situation by studying the new movement of which his story was one small part.

Fueled by my emotion, my need to understand launched what became a formal research project. Knowledge is power, and Brian's decision had made me feel helpless. What were the different groups like? I wondered. Was there a particular kind of young person who was attracted to a religious sect? What were the common experiences within the groups? With time, in fact, I became a kind of self-appointed investigative reporter.

Because I am known chiefly as a comedian, perhaps I should explain that of my twenty-five published books, very few have been in the category of humor. Besides two volumes of short stories, two volumes of poetry, and two novels, I have done seriously intended books on the farm labor controversy, political conservatism, white-collar crime and corruption, and the People's Republic of China. Secondly, I am a student of religion and its history, prepared to consider new religious developments within the context of the past. As I have described, part of the difficult period I had gone through was spent reassessing the religious background I had taken for granted. A positive result of that period is an increased familiarity with the Bible, with theological and philosophical issues, with religious history.

Also, I had already written about religion. In 1958, for instance, *Look* magazine asked me to prepare an autobiographical article, and I set down a few ideas on a number of philosophical questions, including the nature of prayer. My experience had convinced me that there were limits to the power of prayer, that it was not a solution to all problems. As skeptics had pointed out—I observed—no one had scientifically tested the influence of prayer in human affairs in the same way that the power of medicines is tested. If two groups were checked over a specified period, one praying for certain things, the other not praying for the same things, the group that did not pray might find just as many lost articles, get just as many desired jobs, win just as many football games. This would only confirm that the most meaningful form of prayer is the prayer of thanksgiving, the prayer for grace, the prayer that we may be given strength to improve our spiritual selves.

If Christ came to preach spiritual values and deemphasize involvement with the tangible, why should we constantly pray for material things? God helps those who help themselves. If our wills are strong enough, we usually can secure our material needs for ourselves. We should pray rather for wisdom, for a love of peace, for an increase in charity. This is the sort of prayer that is answered in the very moment of its utterance; it is the sort of prayer that would be answered even if there were no God.

I had also pondered the essence of Christianity. Faced with Brian's desire to lead a Christian life, I could view it with a sense of what such a choice really meant. I recalled Chesterton's remark that Christianity had not been tried and found wanting, but that it had been found difficult and so rarely tried. Jesus, Brian's new lodestar, issued the hardest challenges for us: Give up what you have and follow Me. Turn the other cheek. Love your enemy. To follow such moral guidance requires extraordinary inner strength, a sense of self, perhaps, so strong and fundamental that it permits freedom from self to focus on others for their own sakes. How many of us are capable of that? I know people who are religious and good, religious and saintly, religious and generous; but I have never known one who practiced the complete Christian philosophy. A Catholic priest, one of several who wrote to me at length after I had published my articles in *Look* in the fifties, said he had known only two such people. Philosophers like Ayn Rand, heroine of American conservatives, say bluntly that the Christian ideal is wrong and certainly impossible of attainment for individuals, much less nations or groups, given man's instinct for self-preservation and his selfish expediency.

Other people say that all there is to Christianity is keeping the Ten Commandments. If this were truly the case, of course, there would be some question about the necessity for Christ's coming to earth at all; the Ten Commandments do not include the admonition to love one's neighbor (a fact that may be explained by the ferociously warlike history of the early tribes of the Old Testament).

Man has always done rather well when it came to the formalities of religion; he will willingly burn incense, sacrifice lambs, make pilgrimages, bow to Mecca, light candles, sing hymns, march in processions, mutter prayers—often without thought of their meaning—flagellate himself, make certain signs and gestures, tithe his salary, and all the rest of it, but he will usually be God damned (if you will pardon a play on words in this paradox) if he will love his neighbor.

Loving one's neighbor is the heart of the Christian message. After all, man had walked the earth for hundreds of thousands of years (as even theologians somewhat belatedly now agree) before hearing the message of Christ. In relative time Jesus walked among us almost yesterday. What made Christianity something special, even to those who see nothing divine in it, is that it contained the idea of brotherly love not as a vaguely admirable ideal (for Christ was not the very first to refer to it), but as a real, no exceptions, flesh and blood, everyday reality (for in this sense Christ did bring something new).

I knew some of what Brian must have felt: the yearning for a pure life, for dedication and truth. Even today, there are rare moments when I feel an urge to take to the streets as a preacher. I am still studying and creating, however; my philosophy is still a mixture of elements, so how can I preach? But I think there is another reason I don't do it: I lack the courage. It is a terrible irony that those who do have the courage, who literally give up what they have in order to follow in the Master's steps, are dismissed as Fools for Christ even by many who are sympathetic to their aims. Did Brian have that courage? I wondered. And would I prove to be one of the dismissers?

My credentials as investigative journalist also included experience with two other elements relevant to the new movement. One was a sense of the nonrational aspect of religion; the other was drugs.

I realized early on in our experience with Brian that one distressing factor in the new religions was their nonrational element. Almost all religion involves a nonrational aspect, of course. If there is a God, clearly He is beyond the power of reason alone to define. But the new religions seemed to me to be nonrational in a worrisome way. For a rationalist like me, that was the hard pill to swallow, the factor I most wanted to fathom, the one that seemed most likely to lead to trouble for the believers themselves. Where was the line between essentially reasonable faith on the one hand and fanaticism on the other?

As it happened, I had had two encounters with the nonrational in religion. They no doubt affected my thinking on the issue. One took place in 1957. During the years when I was serving as host of the "Tonight Show" I would occasionally make a philosophical observation or refer to a book that had captured my attention. In response I received a number of letters from people who wished to stimulate my interest in various issues, causes and schools of thought important to them. As part of the process of self-education I gave respectful attention to such letters, met some of my correspondents, and, during those early years in New York, learned a great deal more about the universe than I had known when I arrived during the winter of 1950–51. One invitation I accepted was to attend a meeting—called a *latihan*—of a new (to me, at least) religious group called Subud.

At the Subud headquarters, I joined a group of perhaps forty men—men and women were separated—in a large room, newly carpeted and ringed by wooden folding chairs. In the center a man sat at a card table, taking the names of those clustered around him. I joined this group, gave my name, received instructions concerning future lectures and *latihans,* and retired to a corner to await developments. During the next few minutes I observed those present and was impressed first of all by the fact that they seemed to defy consideration under one descriptive heading. None seemed to be younger than twenty, nor were any more than middle-aged, but they were a variety of types. Some looked intellectual, a few had beatnik beards, some were chatting amiably, others sat quietly. They looked, in other words, like a group of men assembled entirely at random.

After a few minutes, Mr. J. G. Bennett, an official of the group, came into the room, followed by the movement's leader himself, Pak Subuh. Bennett was a tall, distinguished-looking Englishman, Subuh a short Javanese of surprisingly unprepossessing appearance. Bennett instructed that all present remove their shoes, jackets, wristwatches, and eyeglasses. We were then asked to stand and distribute ourselves about the room, with the newcomers in the front. After we assumed a sort of loose version of the military open formation, Bennett made a few introductory remarks in which he suggested that during the exercises that were to follow, we keep our eyes closed. This, he explained, was to prevent our becoming interested in one another. If we put aside our curiosity and communed with our inner selves, he explained, we would be more likely to have a meaningful experience. There was really nothing to *do*, Bennett said. We were simply to relax, to think of nothing, insofar as that was possible, and to pay no mind to the doings of those around us.

Bennett then introduced Pak Subuh, who made several brief statements in his own language, each of which was translated by Bennett. After the last of these, with no particular preamble the spiritual exercises formally began. A light was turned off, throwing the room into semidarkness. Neither Bennett nor Subuh said another word. I stood with my eyes closed, head down. There was perhaps thirty seconds of silence; then a man somewhere behind me began to hum loudly. Almost immediately another man behind me began to breathe very deeply and audibly. Then a third started to sing softly in a foreign language I could not identify. For some reason these sudden manifestations of I-knew-not-what startled me, and I opened my eyes slightly, still looking at the floor. Slightly ahead and to the left a youngish blond man was weaving back and forth, swinging his arms around in a manner that faintly suggested shadowboxing. Suddenly the man directly to my left fell to the floor as if he had been struck by an axe! He remained spread-eagled, face up, without moving, for the rest of the period. Now in the back of the room another man began making strange animallike sounds deep in his throat, alternately growling and saying "Allah." The word changed from Allah to Mallah to Mother and then into a sort of babbling which was either in a strange language or else complete nonsense.

After a few minutes I became used to the atmosphere, closed my eyes once again, and attempted to throw myself into whatever psychic stream in which the others had apparently successfully immersed themselves. These efforts, I regret to say, were unsuccessful. I tried to concentrate very hard, and then I tried to think of nothing. At last I sat down on the floor and attempted, by resting my head on my knees, to fall into a normal sleep, all without result. Of the forty or so men in the room, I would guess that about ten were manifesting some sort of reaction. Whether the others were coming up as blank as I, I cannot say. After more than half an hour had passed, Bennett suddenly said "Finish!" and all manifestations ceased. The light was turned on, everyone quietly put on shoes and jacket, and the *latihan,* at least for the newcomers, was over.

There is a good deal more to the Subud religion, of course, than babbling incoherently and falling to the floor. Subud was by no means totally nonrational. Quite the contrary, some of its leaders and practitioners were eminently reasonable. But it is an Oriental denomination, and as such involves factors other than those immediately apprehended by the rational faculties. Nor should Christians feel the slightest superiority to believers in Oriental religious disciplines as regards such factors, since they have been part of Christian experience for many centuries. By the 1980s American interest in Oriental religions had become so common that such behavior no longer seemed as exotic as it had in the 1950s. But because statistically few Americans will have had such experiences, those experiences do bear mentioning in this report.

The nonrationalism of Eastern religions should be distinguished from the nonrationalism of Western religious sects closer to the apparent fundamentalism of new groups like Brian's. I had my first experience with the latter in 1940 when I was in high school. One night in Phoenix I was out walking when suddenly, from a point that seemed about a block away and off to my left, I heard a man screaming. At that distance I could make out no words and, at first, could make no sense of the situation. Drawn by nothing more than the same sort of morbid curiosity that makes people stop to study the scenes of accidents or other disasters, I moved toward the sound, my brain trying to make some sort of sense out of what I was hearing. Had a madman been let loose on the streets? A second hypothesis came to me a moment later: there was some sort of altercation in which one participant was violently denouncing the other. Then I began to distinguish occasional words: "Jesus," I heard, "God," and "eternal damnation." Whatever the reason for the outburst, it clearly had to do with religion.

Rounding the corner, I saw that the shouting was coming from a small church; and then, of course, I knew that I had stumbled on a Fundamentalist revival service. I had occasionally heard revival preachers on the radio, but although they were given to much higher pitches of enthusiasm than the Catholic priests I was familiar with, they still had seemed generally coherent, if somewhat embarrassingly emotional. But what I was now listening to was something very different indeed. I do not see how the man I was hearing was able to continue for so long a time shouting at what must have been the loudest volume of which he was capable. A second factor—puzzling because I had never previously encountered it—was that there was a sort of animal growl to certain of his words. There is one radio and television preacher of modern times who has that same angry rasp in his voice, a Reverend Scott, some of whose sermons are characterized by a remarkably undisguised aggressiveness and suspicion and who, if he ever has made reference to such traditional Christian virtues as gentleness, meekness, love, compassion and humility, has not done so during the occasions when I have listened to his broadcast outpourings.

Through a series of open side windows, I saw that the speaker was dark-haired and overweight. He had taken off his jacket and rolled up the sleeves of his white shirt. His collar and tie were loose, and he was totally bathed in perspiration. He did not stand in one place, as had the other Christian speakers I had previously heard, but prowled about the stage like a madman who could not contain his energy. At this point he held his arms straight out and up in a winglike pose and said something like, "Jeeeesus-uh, I am an angel, a *heavenly* angel," at which he slapped his arms like wings and seemed almost to attempt to elevate his body into the air. He still seemed to me more a madman than a minister of the Gospel, although I now realize this was due in large part to my ignorance of the fact that such a preaching style is one of long standing in rural American Fundamentalist Protestant communities.

I no longer remember what he was saying. I recall only the clear impression that if he had behaved in that way in any other sort of social context he would, quite literally, have been taken in hand and locked up, if only for his own protection. Even today society does not countenance such outbursts in any other context but the religious. When the subject matter is religion, however, we are disposed to tolerate bizarre modes of address.

But if religion has a nonrational component, how are we to distinguish legitimately between the "acceptable" nonrationality of the established denominations and the questionable nonrationality of new sects? That was just one of the questions I wanted to answer.

For the past quarter-century an important issue dividing the generations has been that of drug abuse. As a social problem the controversy about narcotics is incredibly complex. There is, therefore, no simple solution to it. The only societies that can "solve" such problems are totalitarian dictatorships. One of my primary social concerns is the ongoing and sadly all-too-demonstrable deterioration of the American intelligence. The widespread use of drugs is part of the general moral and intellectual collapse which, though fortunately far from total, nevertheless characterizes American life in the latter half of the twentieth century.

Generally speaking, many parents locate religion on one side of some moral dividing line and the use of drugs on the other. They are consequently confused, not to say shaken, when they encounter instances of chemical substances used in a religious context, for religious purposes. They are also startled to be told that certain drugs may actually induce feelings of religious exaltation and insight.

When confronted with such information, many parents simply reject it and assume that drug users are hypocritically trying to legitimize their dependency by wrapping it in the mantle of religion. No one familiar with religious history would make such a mistake. The ingestion of various substances, not to mention other appeals to the senses, has been part of religious experience—Christian and otherwise—since before the dawn of history. Religious believers have always felt that certain states of spiritual ecstasy were so important that almost any means of inducing them was acceptable. To achieve such transported states, believers have used music, the deliberately monotonous repetition of certain phrases, meditation, fasting, wine, mushrooms, marijuana, etc. The Love Family used the chemical toluene for such purposes.

Although I am strongly biased against the use of drugs, I feel it is important that the ancient connection between narcotics and religion be understood. Since most readers of this book will not be drug users, I refer in passing to my participation in responsible experiments in the effects of the drug LSD which were being conducted in the late 1950s and early 1960s by a number of scientific researchers.

It is fortunate that in our day formal research is being directed toward phenomena that till now were apparently arbitrarily assumed to be incapable of rational analysis.

Because much of the literature of mysticism has positioned it within the larger context of religion (almost all mystics have been religious people), there has been, down through the centuries, almost no consideration of the possibility that mystical phenomena might also occur outside the context of religion. Such speculation is of course frustrated by the fact that neither the word *religion* nor the word *mysticism* can be used with the slightest scientific precision. To simply "feel high," of course, is not the same as the hard-to-define sense of having been spiritually transported, but even in the respectable literature of drug research there is a great deal of material that establishes a cause-and-effect relationship between the use of certain chemical substances and altered states of consciousness and awareness accompanied by a sense of philosophical insight. I have had two experiences which involved the clear recognition of being in a state which, however it might best be properly described, was certainly not the same as that sense-of-self I view as normal for myself and therefore assume is normal for others.

In one instance a religious component was present; in the other it was not. Contrary to what many might hope, it was the religious experience that was drug-induced. Before sensation seekers leap to telephones and typewriters, I should explain that I am in no sense a drug user. My one experience of this sort took place within the context of a scientific research program. But of the two instances mentioned, it is this one that seems easier to understand.

I have viewed with dismay the heavy use and abuse of LSD-25 in the American youth culture during the last twenty-five years.

But some years ago—long before dropouts and flower-children heard of the substance—a small number of perfectly respectable individuals (the distinguished Jesuit theologian John Courtney Murray, for one) were experimenting to discover what its effects were. In 1962 I discussed his experience with Father Murray; he told me it had given him a kind of self-insight he had never before attained. I recall particularly his observation that the drug had revealed to him the existence of the thin shell of phony exterior with which most of us surround ourselves as a "protection" from the realities of social contact. He also said that the drug had enabled him for the first time to see that his inability to give up cigarette smoking was a character weakness, something he had previously hidden from himself.

Conservative leader Clare Boothe Luce also ingested the drug at this time, as part of the same sort of scientific research.

Another eminent man who had wide experience with the substance in the late fifties to early sixties was philosopher Gerald Heard, a friend of Aldous Huxley. It was Gerald who first told me about it, and it was at his home in Pacific Palisades, California, that I participated in a series of experiments then being conducted by Dr. Sydney Cohen of UCLA, who was administering LSD-25 to professionals in the arts to see what effect, if any, the substance might have on their creative potential.

The point is that intellectuals, artists, authors, educators, clergymen, composers, medical researchers and others—people of impeccable social credentials—were then taking the drug to study its effects, not for kicks or party entertainment.

On August 19, 1959, at 10:35 on a beautiful California morning I was given a 100-gamma dose by Dr. Cohen, in a cup of plain water. I am able to give a detailed account of the experience because I kept extensive handwritten notes throughout. I also have Gerald's notes and those of his secretary, Michael Barrie. My notes show that we sat and talked in Gerald's study till shortly after 11:00.

The first notation—made at 11:15—is as follows: *"The first possible symptom, an inability to pick a needed phrase out of the air."*

The next entry says, *"Origin of my humor, a secret delight of childhood."*

Between 11:15 and 11:20 I noticed—for the first time—the lines on Gerald's forehead. Formerly if I had looked at him I would have assumed I was looking at his face, or perhaps his entire head. But now my mind began to observe his face in its separate parts.

At 11:20 I said, "About five minutes ago I think I felt something." It had been a physical reaction; I felt a slight inclination to smile or laugh.

I recall holding my hand to my mouth and jaw while engaged in conversation with Gerald and Michael.

I attempted to make this a seemingly casual gesture, but my real motive was to hide the smile I felt beginning to form because I was embarrassed to be smiling for no apparent reason. There came at about that same time a slight feeling of apprehension, something a little like stage fright, that seemed localized in the chest. I have always felt sudden sharp fears in the chest rather than the head.

By this time I had excused myself, gone into another room and sat on a bed, to experience the sensations in privacy. I then wrote, "Deep, hearty laughter held back because of embarrassment."

Later: *"Beauty of petals on ground."* Some flower petals lay on the ground outside. I was deeply impressed with their separate beauty, even unattached to the flowers. They were not mere waste, nature's discards; they still had color, texture, importance.

"Tears for lost childhood"; *"for freshness."* I was overcome at that moment with a uniquely tender emotion. I not only *appreciated* the beauty of the flowers I was looking at; there was something that seemed strongly *reminiscent* about the sensation! It was not altogether mysterious and new. I recalled having felt the same way about flowers when I was four or five years old. I thought, Good Lord, I'm thirty-nine, and during all those long years, from five or six all the way up to thirty-nine, instead of improving, growing in all ways, I have *lost* something. There has been a gap, one never to be refilled. The realization was crushing to the point of tears. I felt a tenderness toward my lost innocent childhood self.

Weeping of this sort is, of course, common to everyone's experience. We weep not only at moments of sadness but also at moments of great joy—at weddings, graduation ceremonies, reconciliations with members of our families, the reunion with a lover. The emotion is so powerful at such times that it simply brims over, in the liquid, physical sense.

I must say a word here about *the appreciation of color,* apparently common to almost all LSD experiences. Let the reader recall the sight of a particularly beautiful rose, sunset, seascape, mountain view. Now suppose that a graph is made out, on a zero-to-100 scale. Let the most beautiful sight you ever saw—and your response, your appreciation of it—represent 100 on this graph. Most reactions to beautiful sights, alas, would probably register in the below-10 area. One way to describe the sense of beauty appreciated while under the influence of LSD would be—and I am attempting to be precise, to avoid exaggeration—that the chart would have to be extended far beyond its normal borders so that a rating of, say, 750 could be recorded!

And yet, as I have observed, the sensation was partially new and, apparently, partially *recalled.* I remembered one specific instance, in fact, when the beauty, the colors, of a natural scene had struck my heart in this same knifelike way. The year was 1950. I had been sitting for about an hour—with the woman herein called Betty Harrington—in midafternoon in a dim restaurant cocktail lounge on the beach at Malibu, California. My eyes had apparently adjusted to the small amount of light available. It is also relevant to recall, though the memory brings no pleasure, that this period of my life was one of great inner turmoil as described earlier.

I paid the bill, and Betty and I prepared to depart. As we stepped out into the brilliant light of the sun and suddenly felt the ocean breeze and saw the stretch of beach, the wild waves, the clouds and blue sky, the sandy cliffs across the ocean highway, the gulls overhead—I was literally *seized* with beauty. I could not recall ever having seen colors so dazzling. I stood as enthralled as a man who had just landed on a strange planet.

As I reread the preceding sentences I am aware that they utterly fail to convey the depth of the emotion that gripped me, controlled me, at that moment. *For the first time in my life I fully appreciated the beauty of the natural universe,* not in any abstract sense, as one might in a moment of dreamy evening reverie, in a comfortable chair, reading a poetic description of a lake or waterfall, but in an immediate sense, something like the sense in which a famished person appreciates a bite of food. Everything visible seemed appreciated, incredibly precious, very sharply focused, absolutely dazzling and fresh as if never seen before.

It seems clear that at least three factors had combined to create such a reaction to scenery that is, after all, familiar to anyone who lives in Southern California. One was the emotional pressure, the storm of mixed guilt and desperation by which I was being buffeted during that period. A second factor was Betty herself. The combination of her beauty, her love for me, and the crushing realization that I was not entitled to either had brought me to a moment of unusual sensitivity. The third factor must have been the long time spent in quiet conversation in the dimly lighted interior of the restaurant.

I am not the sort of person who is normally insensitive to the beauties of nature. On the contrary, from early childhood I have been enchanted by skies, clouds, stars; the moon, the sun and the planets; water in its natural state, green growing things, the odors of the countryside, etc. All the more remarkable, therefore, that in this instance I had an utterly clear impression that I had never before totally appreciated the glory of nature.

The fact that we can, then, experience these rare moments of appreciation suggests that the drug adds nothing, *but rather releases an inborn ability.* This would be consistent with the theory that LSD does not act directly on the brain (since its most powerful effects seem to take place after the drug has passed out of the body, which it does rather quickly, in the urine) but rather stimulates some other center in the body so that the center secretes the natural liquid or substance which is the direct cause of the powerful effects commonly reported.

One of the first thoughts that occurred to me a few days after the experience was that *the visions reported by religious mystics might be partly attributable to body-chemical substances naturally produced in the brain or elsewhere.* Some research tends to validate this hypothesis. Traditional religionists may recoil from the theory, but I see no reason why they should. Even if it were possible to establish that St. Francis of Assisi, St. Theresa of Avila, Blake, Swedenborg and other mystics were especially "chosen" to experience religious visions and ecstasies by having been born with unusual brain chemistry, nothing whatever that is important in Christian or other religious traditions would be contradicted.

Because of my 1959 hypothesis I was excited to learn that the human brain does manufacture its own hallucination-producing chemical, identical in every respect to that found in certain Latin-American plants long used by witch doctors. The substance, called serotonin, is produced in the *pineal gland,* a small structure at the center of the brain about which not a great deal is known. But it is possible, it seems to me, that even among normal people occasional irregular production of serotonin—perhaps triggered by emotional stress—may produce moments of creative insight in the artistic, philosophical or spiritual sphere.

When I arrived at home after my experience with LSD, a most unusual thing happened. My mother happened to be visiting us, and my children were in the house. I chose not to go in to talk to them immediately. When I stepped out of the car I was suddenly struck as never before by the incredible beauty of the shrubs, bushes and flowers around our home. I decided to stroll about our grounds for a while. For perhaps fifteen minutes I walked about the property, examining hedges, flowerbeds, and lawns, enraptured. But more importantly, I was consumed at this point by an immensely strong feeling of love and compassion for all of mankind, including those in my home. I thought, in a flash of understanding, "Aha, so this is what has motivated the saints. If I felt this every day I would have to devote my life to public service. I would have to work in a leper hospital perhaps, or take care of the poor, in the way that humble saints and seers have done." *Perhaps the strangest thing about this intense religious or spiritual experience is that God—as idea or reality—seemed in no way connected with it.* It was I who "so loved the world," its human creatures and its natural beauty.

I then went into the house.

My mother was sitting in the kitchen. As I have earlier explained, my relationship with my mother, from infancy, was a difficult one. On this night—*for the first time since I had been a small child*—I felt perfectly at ease in my mother's presence. I understood her and loved her deeply. I neither said nor did anything unusual, merely greeted her with a slight smile and made the usual small talk. But when I left the room a few minutes later my mother said to Jayne, "Steve looks as if he's heard some wonderful news."

Some religious people are unnerved by reports like this; others are pleased. Let us assume there is a physical seat of those emotions commonly described as religious. What would follow were such a thing to be established? Some might argue that all religion would finally be shown to be mere sham or self-delusion in that what had always been supposed to be a spiritual manifestation, a form of unearthly communication between God and man, was finally shown to be purely physical in nature, a phenomenon involving the chemical or electric stimulation of certain brain cells rather than one related to such concepts as sin, prayer, grace and faith.

But it could be at least as easily argued that God was so mindful of the necessity for a spiritual component in man that He contrived, by means of physical nature, to implant within the human mind a material capacity for certain types of emotional experience. Those long-recognized mental capacities for mathematical insight, musical composition, scientific speculation, artistic genius, etc., have been shown to be seated in specific areas of the brain. Would it therefore really be so surprising were the same thing to be true of religious emotion or creativity?

CHAPTER 9

My First Visit to the Love Family

In sad times the heart clutches at strange comforts. So it occurred to me that although Brian was now living far from us, his distance, in a sense, represented no change, for he had already left us and gone out into the world. But the perception afforded little reassurance. I began to do something similar to what I had done during the ten terrible years I lived apart from the children in New York. In those days I had focused attentively on young children who resembled my three sons. A television critic had mentioned, sometime during the 1950s, that I seemed to take a special interest in interviewing children in my studio audiences. Indeed I did, and do to this day. Before that time, oddly enough, I suppose my attitude toward the children of the world was that of most adults; I regarded them kindly, but took no special interest in them. Then, in the early 1950s, my interest had become special indeed. Every little face seemed somehow a reflection of the three I missed. The piping voices, the innocence in the eyes, the unintentionally comic mistakes of speech held such fascination for me that my interviews with the boys and girls whose parents brought them to our studios were more than the usual "Hello, where are you from?" interrogations designed to produce only straight lines for such jokes as I could create.

In early 1972 I conceived an idea for a short story—which I have yet to write—about a father who has lost a son, perhaps by death, perhaps in a war. Hurrying about his business in midtown New York one day he suddenly spies a young man walking in the opposite direction on the other side of Sixth Avenue. So striking is his resemblance to the missing son that the father stops in his tracks and stares at the young man for a moment. The hair, the height, the type of clothing, the manner of walking, the face—which he can only partly see—convince some part of him that the young man is in fact his son, although the more rational part of his nature

68

tells him that this is very unlikely. He follows the young man for several blocks, afraid to catch up with him and discover the truth. At 59th Street the young fellow crosses into Central Park, sits down on a bench, takes a paperback book out of his pocket and begins to read. The father stands not far from him, staring, knowing now that the young man is in fact a stranger, but still unable to turn away, so strong is the resemblance to the boy he has lost.

Those scholars who specialize in the study of creativity are aware that it is often impossible to identify the causative factors leading to the moment at which the idea for a short story, a novel, a screenplay, poem, painting or song occurs. But there are instances in which that particular mystery, at least, is easily penetrated. It is not difficult to see that because I missed Brian—and did, during this period, consider him lost to the rest of us in his family—the idea for this particular story came to me. And indeed it was, to a degree, acted out in reality, because during that time—in New York, Los Angeles and other parts of the country—I did see certain young fellows on the street, in passing cars, in crowds of people, who looked like Brian.

But all such reveries and reflections were rudely interrupted when, after months of silence, I saw in the paper one morning a story about the death of two young members of a religious commune in Seattle, Washington. With a shock I realized that the account concerned Brian's group.

On January 23, 1972, two members of the Love Family had been found dead after they had inhaled the fumes from a liquid substance as part of a religious ritual. The King County Medical Examiner's Office said the victims had taken part in the Church of Armageddon's rite which involved the use of the liquid substance toluene, placed in a plastic bag and held over their mouths.

Deputies reported that the Church of Armageddon believed that the men would revive in three days. At the request of church officials, an autopsy was postponed until the following Tuesday morning. The victims were identified as *Reverence* Israel, William Vand Brunt Eddy, twenty-six; and *Solidity* Israel, Gregory Lemaster, twenty-two.

I shared the news with Jayne and Dorothy. We were all depressed by it, not only out of sympathy with the two unfortunate young men who had died—and their families—but because of the reported belief of church members that the two dead men might come back to life. Since this is an obviously fanatical, superstitious belief, it cast a depressing light on an existence that we had been prepared to assume might have its attractive and productive aspects.

In response to the barrage of criticism that resulted, the church prepared and distributed a six-page statement which I quote in part.

This is to clarify some of the beliefs of the Church of Armageddon. The Church of Armageddon is dedicated to the creation of one pure, beautiful, and holy community where men are free to live in accordance with God's way—the way shown to us in the New Testament of Jesus Christ. We are the servants of God, and are here to help free mankind from the bonds of fear, loneliness, lust, sickness, and death. We are the representatives of God, here to show mankind the reality of God's Love.

As Christians, who understand that nothing in God can really die, we are free to offer our bodies to God, in the hope that He can use us to help free all of mankind. From our experience, we cannot deny that certain organic chemical substances taken in the right environment and with the right motivation can help people.

Our belief in Jesus Christ has freed us from the fears which, in the mind of the world, surround the use of these chemicals. We have seen that we have eternal life, that the God in us can never die. The fact that the world considers a substance harmful or deadly means little to us, since Christ said clearly that one of the signs of His believers is that "if they drink any deadly thing it shall not hurt them." (Mark 16:18) God is stronger than any chemical.

We see that we have nothing to lose, since the world we were born into believes that *all* human activity leads inevitably to death. Many of the most popular human activities are considered or "proven" deadly: smoking, driving, eating, drinking, exercise, etc. Yet man has not made these activities illegal, not even smoking, which is clearly a selfish, inconsiderate, and degrading habit, contributing nothing but guilt, pain, and pollution to our minds.

Fear, however, has resulted in laws preventing people from experiencing the effects of certain useful chemicals. Fear has been responsible for depriving mankind of the potential these chemicals have for bringing a man into a closer relationship to his brother and to God. People who use these chemicals illegally are subject to the fear of getting caught at doing something "wrong." This fear of authority, or paranoia, is one of the worst aspects of these experiences. Society's laws have made criminals out of people exercising their constitutional right to the pursuit of happiness and peace of mind.

It was largely in consideration of this paranoia that we chose to experiment with tell-u-all, a legal substance, rather than some of the more desirable and safer illegal chemicals such as LSD, peyote, or psilocybin. From our first experiences with the supervised inhalation of tell-u-all, in the spring of 1971, we discovered that this chemical had strong potential for helping people free themselves from the common lies of the world: belief in sickness such as colds or cancer, negative habits such as smoking and alcoholism, physical and mental disorders, and the fears of death.

A fundamental principle was discovered in these experiences in breathing: those who breathed from a motivation of giving or helping others were rewarded with a variety of positive experiences. Those who breathed selfishly or greedily experienced a variety of negative effects. A charitable attitude proved to be essential to a constructive use of these vapors, as did a solid foundation in the Truth of Jesus Christ. The breathing was done only on a voluntary basis, and many of the Church family were discouraged from breathing because of weakness in faith, tendencies toward disobedience, or wrong motivations. Some were asked not to breathe tell-u-all at all, because of their immaturity.

Reverence Israel, pronounced dead from "asphyxiation due to toluene intoxication," was one Church member who had been frequently advised not to breathe tell-u-all because of certain misguided attitudes and beliefs he maintained. The experience that led to his disembodiment was unsupervised. It may have been the result of misunderstanding; it may have been direct disobedience to the word of his minister and guide, *Love* Israel. We love *Reverence* and *Solidity* Israel; they are eternal members of our Family. We cannot mourn their loss, because we are clearly aware that their spirits are with us *now*, and that their disembodiment was the perfect will of God. The incident only helps to define the line we are drawing for all mankind—the line between the world and Jesus Christ, between death and eternal life. Some will condemn and hate us, some will seek to meet us and understand us. Every man will ultimately have to decide whether we are true patriots, supporting the ideals of freedom this country was founded on, or fools.

Our request that the bodies of *Solidity* and *Reverence* not be mutilated for three days was in keeping with our belief that it is unnatural to physically alter the body by cutting, puncturing, tattooing, etc. We wanted the worldly authorities to allow for the possibility that God might restore their spirits to the same bodies, as he has resurrected many in the past.

It is disheartening that the King County Medical Examiner's Office went back on its word to us and disrespected our belief by performing an autopsy long before the three-day waiting period was ended. It only indicates to us that it is impossible to deal reasonably with the existing system. We were unable to find one responsible final authority with whom we could reach a reliable agreement.

We are fully assured, however, that in due time God will give the spirits of *Reverence* and *Solidity* new bodies to dwell in. When this happens, many people's eyes will be opened.

There is no *need* for the use of chemicals within our Church. Our only need is for a totally dependent faith in God, our Father. We are not seeking to "get stoned." We are not seeking the Truth. We have already seen the Truth: that we are all one, that God is Love, that Jesus Christ *is real,* and that our Father's job for us is that we love people no matter what happens.

We do recognize, however, that the vast majority of mankind is still suffering from loneliness, misunderstanding, and limiting false beliefs. We are dedicated to helping these people in any way we can: through the Bible, meditation, chanting, chemicals, or any other means God reveals to us. How could a person know whether one of these avenues could help him until he tried it?

For now, we have discontinued the use of tell-u-all.

It was abused in our Family through disobedience and misunderstanding. . . .

However, we do maintain the right of any man to seek God through the use of any means as long as he does not infringe on the rights of his neighbors. And since all of our experience has shown us that environment is one key to a sound mind, we are dedicated to the creation of one holy, beautiful environment based on the New Testament where people can find peace of mind amid a troubled and confused world, a sanctuary hosted by loving and understanding servants of God.

In the meantime, we invite people everywhere to join us in our main Church "rite": our gathering together to eat our meals as the body and blood of our Lord Jesus Christ, in daily celebration of the Lord's Supper. Food taken in the spirit of this belief heals us and nourishes us unto everlasting life.

Disturbed by the tragedy, I hurried north for my first visit with Brian and his friends in Seattle. Brian was waiting for me at the airport; we exchanged an affectionate embrace. It was good to see him again. There was a slight initial stiffness between us, due in large part, I suppose, to his not knowing how I would adjust to his new role. His hair was longer, and he and his companions were wearing robes of ancient design. In such situations we are never able to withdraw and analyze. One simply moves forward through the scene, continuing conversation, establishing contact. There are immediate reactions, obviously, but they are filed away in our internal computers, as it were, to be withdrawn for later reflection, since the conscious mind is occupied with the combined immediate tasks of sensory perception and verbal communication.

The commune quarters, a group of old but beautifully restored, cleaned and painted homes in the hilly, attractive Queen Anne section of the city, was obviously no withdrawn rural retreat. I could see at once that the members of the Love Family freely interacted with neighbors, neighborhood merchants and visitors. Brian conducted a tour of the facilities and introduced me to *Love* Israel—formerly Paul Erdman—as well as to a few dozen of his fellow commune members. They all wore clothing of the sort seen in sketches of Christ and the Apostles. Brian particularly, with his longer hair and neat beard, looked much like certain pictorial renderings of Jesus. When a photographer for a Seattle newspaper took the particularly lovely full-page portrait of Brian shown in the insert following page 114, I had copies of it made and sent one to Jayne's mother, Ida Taylor Cotter, who at the time was living in the family hometown of Sharon, Connecticut, where she conducted a real estate business. A former missionary, Mrs. Cotter was a highly religious woman, and under the glass-topped desk in her office she had long displayed an artist's portrait of Christ. She later told us she removed the artist's version and replaced it with Brian's picture on the grounds that it looked more like Jesus than the one she had.

I met *Simplicity,* Brian's future wife. Brown-eyed, with brown hair, pretty, sweet, quiet, she seemed, in a way, an old-fashioned sort of woman, as did almost all the other women of the commune. They wear no makeup and look like nothing so much as pioneer women in old John Ford films about the American frontier. Indeed the many women of the late 1960s who adopted the look may have drawn their new image from such a source.

The women were subservient to the men, though apparently with perfect willingness. *Love* Israel turned out to be just a likable young fellow, not at all typical casting for the role of dynamic leader. Although he had been a successful salesman and, as some of his critics have alleged, something of a con man in his earlier life, he did not have the typical salesman's glib personality, nor the deadly serious air of the religious fanatic. He did dominate the members of his group, but his methods were subtle and much the same as those apparent in any social situation in which one individual must, to a degree, control the direction of his group.

In our conversations there were frequent references to Jesus, but after a few hours I began to get the impression that the image of Christ was somehow different here from what it is in more traditional Christian contexts.

Even now, almost ten years later, the figure of Jesus seems in fuzzier focus in their belief systems than it does in those of the traditional churches. During my Catholic childhood, for example, I heard far more about Christ than I did about God, although Catholics, of course, believe that Jesus *was* God, in the most literal sense. But in the new sects and cults the name of Jesus seems to be invoked more for its magical or perhaps even public-relations effects than in any clearly defined theological way. While the cult members do spend time—sometimes a great deal—in reading the Old and New Testaments, they are more given to quoting relatively obscure or philosophically perplexing passages. The Sermon on the Mount, for example, seems rarely referred to. Indeed it is typical of a certain form of Christian mentality that it would rather speculate on the most bizarre portion of the New Testament—Revelation—than on Gospel stories about the actual experiences and teachings of Jesus.

(In this study, by the way, I discuss the Scriptures largely in the context of traditional Christian assumptions about them—that they are divinely inspired and therefore factually reliable as history. There is a great deal of debate on these points even among theologians, but I exclude such considerations here.)

During my three days at the commune, Brian was completely open and affectionate, as always.

"I brought along a tape recorder," I said to him at one point. "Would you and *Love* and the others mind if I put a few questions to you and tape-recorded our conversation?"

"No," he said. "I'm sure that will be fine."

During my conversations with Brian there was a good deal of skirting around the emotional issues. I did not discuss with him the hurt all of us had felt, how we had missed him, worried about him. We rarely say all that we think in such situations. I did bring up the issue of the deaths of the two members. Brian and the others basically repeated the points stated in their formal comment on the case. The statement, I would think, must hardly have satisfied the families of the two victims.

It is notoriously difficult to preach to the recently converted, but I did say at one point, "I hope the tragedy at least dramatized for you the fact that such chemicals are dangerous. In this case they were poisonous."

Brian, then relatively new to the Family, deferred to *Serious* so far as responding to questions was concerned, although he had talked to me freely the day before about customs and beliefs within the Family.

The reader will note that it was not my intention during my talks with Family members to debate them or to antagonize them. I wanted to find our what *their* views were. My questions were unplanned and random.

S.A.: The Christian Scientists are generally socially conservative people. To what extent have they been open to you here?

Serious: They have a church right here on the corner. We've been trying to make contact with them by going to their church. They only have services twice a week, a service once on Sunday morning and one on Sunday night. They're very loving people. They accept us warmly in their church, but we haven't seen that much of them.

S.A.: What has been your contact with the Jehovah's Witnesses?

Serious: We have some friends in that group, too. We're very well received. A few of the businessmen who have offices up by ours are Jehovah's Witnesses. Their point of view toward us is that we're closest to their religion.

S.A.: They believe in the imminent return of Christ, don't they? Within their lifetime. Is that one of your beliefs?

Serious: We believe it's a possibility.

S.A.: In physical form?

Serious: Yes. We expect Jesus Christ to come in the clouds, and we'll see him that way, but we're not *waiting* for that. In a way we are, and in a way we're not. There's a doubt in everybody's mind, but our belief in Jesus Christ means we are waiting for that.

S.A.: I believe the Mormons, too, have that same belief in the imminent return of Christ, in physical form, to the earth.

Now you mentioned yesterday the matter of having certain insights which come by the aid of one chemical agent or another. In connection with having already seen Christ in the physical sense, just as you see me sitting here in this chair, is there any relationship between that belief or experience and drugs or chemicals?

Serious: The drugs are all the same. I know I prayed for that for a long time. I've seen *something* about Jesus Christ, but I can't say I've actually seen Him in reality. I recognized Him. He said we would see Him, but I *recognized* Him, for sure, as Jesus Christ.

S.A.: Was it a matter of physical presentation only, or was there any communication involved?

Serious: He didn't say He was Jesus Christ. It was a matter of *Love* somehow being changed into the figure of Christ. I suppose it's hard to explain; just all of a sudden *the person in front of me was Jesus Christ*. It lasted only a few seconds.

S.A.: Was it similar to your experience, Brian? Was it the same moment? Was it a shared experience? In other words, was it the same factor as *Love* Israel somehow seeming to be Christ or turning into Christ for a few seconds, as distinguished from, say, seeing Christ walking toward you down the street?

Brian: I've never seen Christ materializing into the room, but He's been seen by many people. . . .

(In 1981 Brian enlarged on his description of this experience in the following profoundly moving report:

An experience that *Love* Israel and I had (before the forming of the Family and before we had the names *Love* and *Logic*) is in many ways at the root of our community gathering together.

Once, while meditating, and on looking into each other's eyes [a common device of the human potential movement of the 1960s] I became aware of a tug-o'-war of feelings within me. On the one hand was a simple good feeling of looking lovingly into someone's eyes; on the other hand there was a fearful feeling of being on-the-spot or exposed. It's important to note that at this time both of us were into Eastern, Zen-type thought and meditation as a way to higher consciousness.

As we continued to stare, the feelings increased; a battle between love and fear began to rage within me. I kept loving as best I could. Each time I could concentrate on loving, the feelings of fear would leave; but as my concentration slipped, my mind would wander back into fears, worries and guilts. I felt as if the thoughts and feelings were all easy to read on my face, and after a while I felt as if my mind were easy to read. I felt embarrassed and ashamed. Yet, I was always able to stop thinking and get back to loving, and each time I did, the feeling was better.

Then, as I looked I saw *myself,* like a reflection. It was a shock; I felt totally exposed. Then I saw the face of Jesus Christ. At first it was beautiful, and then it was terrible because I was overwhelmed with guilt. I knew that I had never really thought of Jesus Christ as *this* real, and my whole life seemed off-balance because of it. I looked back on my life and realized that I hadn't treated everyone as well as I should have. I felt as if I were being judged by exactly how I had treated all other people.

I felt at one with all mankind. It was judgment day and I was coming up guilty. Then I realized that *Love*'s eyes were filled with love and compassion and forgiveness. I felt a terrific surge of relief, love and ecstasy. I felt deep compassion for everyone else who, like me, was asleep to the fact that Jesus Christ is real and is in us all.

As all of the good feelings began to rush through me we began to melt together. We became One. We went to a place above You and Me, to the I AM of us all, pure light. Then down again to looking at each other, seeing Jesus Christ, seeing myself, seeing my friend. Then, back up again, to I AM, then down again to two of us.

We did this several times, until it was totally clear that God is love, that we *are* One, that Jesus Christ *is* real, that the real part of me and you is loving, forgiving—which is to say Jesus Christ, that love *is* the answer to all problems, and that in this present moment is the only place we will ever find God. I knew then that the way to love God was to love each other. And I knew that it was fear that was keeping us all apart.

The experience was the same for *Love.* To this day, when asked what woke him up, he tells the story of seeing Jesus Christ in me.

After this experience I understood Christ's last prayer before his trial and crucifixion (John 17):

Neither pray I for these alone, but for them also which shall believe on me through their word; that they all may be one; as thou, Father, art in me, and I in thee, that they also may be one in us: that the world may believe that thou hast sent me. And the glory which thou gavest me I have given them; that they may be one, even as we are one; I in them, and thou in me, that they may be made perfect in one; and that the world may know that thou hast sent me, and hast loved them, as thou hast loved me.

Father, I will that they also, whom thou hast given me, be with me where I am; that they may behold my glory, which thou has given me: for thou lovedst me before the foundation of the world. O righteous Father, the world hath not known thee: but I have known thee, and these have known that thou hast sent me. And I have declared unto them thy name, and will declare it: that the love wherewith thou hast loved me may be in them, and I in them.)

S.A.: Do you do what the Apostles who were physically present with Christ did, which is make written records of your impressions?

Serious: We haven't done very much of that, but it would seem to be a good idea. Some of the dreams meant something only to the person having that dream. . . .

S.A.: In any of these appearances . . . have there been specific messages that represented anything not already received from Christ, such as that we should all love each other or that sort of thing?

Serious: Yeah, there have. The first sort of vision . . . was that I was born in everyone. I wouldn't tell my family, even though I heard it.

S.A.: I meant—have there been any instances when Jesus Christ appeared to one or another of you and delivered a particular message? Such as "The world will end in 1976" or something that specific?

Serious: I can't think offhand. There have been visions of angels giving some instructions. There were a couple of groups gathering.

S.A.: On another subject: *Logic* was telling me about the happy ending of your difficulties in trying to get driver's licenses under your new names. Was it a matter of the police adopting one attitude and the authorities eventually being more fair?

Serious: Yeah. We were cutting ourselves off from our past. In time we took the stand that we'd rather die than give our old name. For one thing, we were trying to build a sense that we were now *real* people, and our past was just a *lie*. That position was a pretty rough one for the authorities to accept, and where we ran into most of our problems—for something like jaywalking or hitchhiking—we would just give them our real names, and they wouldn't accept them. They would say, "If you don't give me your name you were born with, we will throw you in jail." So we ended up in jail almost invariably, no matter how minor the charge was, until the judges finally saw we meant it and they couldn't hold us, as there was nothing illegal about what we were doing, and they let us go.

So what we did with the officials was, first of all, we went as high as we could and went to the Department of Motor Vehicles to see if they would recognize us, and they would not. They said it would take an act of the legislature to overrule their basic rule that they have to know what your old record is. We finally did concede in giving them our old names but on a confidential basis. So they agreed to this.

S.A.: How many parents have paid you visits?

Serious: Very few. There's only a few who are really offended. . . . Most of them judge us because we don't work or make money—"One of these days they will wake up and get a job and support themselves." That kind of opposition is what we get, as that is what most people have done all their lives.

Or there is a lot of opposition as regards our cutting off all old relationships. They know they're welcome here, but they're unable to communicate with their children. That's one of the biggest things we have to deal with. . . .

We tried it all different ways. We tried to write letters, and it just hasn't worked. We found the best thing for all of us is to just go right ahead and hope what we're doing will be understood by others. If the people still doubt us, we will never get this thing built. We believe God can take care of it.

S.A.: Your theories of child rearing are very interesting. I didn't quite get it clear. As regards the role of the *real,* physical parent—the mother or father—to what extent is that similar to the mother and father role in taking care of a baby in the outside world?

Serious: Very similar. For one thing, we see people come here who have very negative patterns built up when they come in with children. *I* came here with a child, and the first thing this Family did for me was to release me from the responsibilities of that relationship so I could build new relationships, different from those in the outside world.

S.A.: Was that release made possible simply by the fact that previously you had been spending five hours of your day taking care of the baby whereas now you had maybe twenty people sharing that obligation, so you had to do that only *one* hour?

Serious: Yes. For a period of time I didn't live in the same house with my child. His natural mother doesn't live in the house. They've had a lot of negative patterns, the boy and his natural mother. So they have never lived together and won't until they're ready. The natural mother and father are free to spend time with any member of the family. There's a lot of sharing of responsibility, but in keeping with Jesus, it's mainly the responsibility of disciplining, structuring of the child.

S.A.: Do the children receive physical love and affection and certain kinds of protective care from all of the adults?

Serious: Yes. They get a lot of attention.

S.A.: How old is the oldest child?

Serious: Over three.

S.A.: They seem like very happy children.

Serious: Rather than follow in the mistakes of *my* parents—they thought, "I believe my son knows better than I what's best for him." Now I see that that's nonsense. I see we must provide instruction. If you don't show him the line—what's wrong—then he'll never know what's right. The main thing we're showing him is what's right and what's wrong for this Family, what's best for us. He needs to learn to be considerate and need not to be the star of the show.

S.A.: That's an important lesson for all humans to learn, because we are born selfish creatures. It's necessary at first for self-preservation.

We have to *want* the milk, have to *want* the food, have to *want* a Mama and a Daddy and want to be changed. Babies want things because they can't do anything for themselves. The only alternative open is to want and demand.

Serious: Yes. We can start with babies and really help them grow up, and they won't have to go through what we're going through, and maybe by the time they're five or six they'll have learned it, that they're really going to get all the food and attention and things they need if they trust God.

S.A.: Are the roles of the different members of the church—of the work they do in this environment—assigned or just naturally assumed? Does each person decide what he can do? For example, the women do work in the kitchen and the work of serving food, although one of the men was helping serve last night, too. How is that determined?

Serious: It's a matter of wherever you feel you *want* to serve. The idea is that if people do what they really want to do, the whole body will work together more in harmony; so just take on the point of view: OK, now, I'm giving my life, that means my *time,* to this Family, and I'm willing to work wherever I'm needed and will set up opportunities to serve.

S.A.: There's an old saying, "Cleanliness is next to godliness." It's very impressive to see how spotlessly clean all the houses here are and, even more than that, how simply they are furnished. Is that a result of a philosophical or religious point of view? Or did it just gradually come about that way?

Serious: This is the way we feel best. We recognize that this home is our gift, and it's ours forever, as we know it, so we might as well clean it up.

Our main gift to each other *is* each other, and then God gives us the gift of time, to experience each other, and gives us the urge to carry on. We're just beginning to get our environment cleaned up, just starting.

S.A.: The role of women in your church seems somehow different than in other churches or in the world. That is that women do the housework, the cooking, washing of dishes, and making of beds.

Serious: We share a lot of those jobs. The women do most of the cooking, but not all.

S.A.: Is there any sense in which the woman's role is inferior to that of the man? As regards positions of authority?

Serious: The Bible talks about the parallel between man-and-woman and Christ-and-the-church. Christ is the head of the church, and man is the head of the woman, but they're both one. Together they make up one, so when we talk about man or Christ, that includes woman. They work together as one, and the best *way* they can work together is for one to represent the direction. That's man; he's the direction, he's the head, and the woman is the supporting element, the heart, the loving heart to the man's direction.

S.A.: This has practically never been challenged, historically, until just recently by the Women's Liberation Movement, which emphasizes the ideal of equality. They say if equality means anything, it means women should be equal to men.

Serious: For us equality is the fact that all are equally forgiven. We were sinners. We were living lives that weren't with God, and we were equally given the opportunity to change. God can give us a variety of gifts, or He can put us in any place He wants, as you were designed to do one thing and I was designed for another. The hand isn't inferior to the foot. They just have different functions. If the woman is inferior to the man, she has a different function. She's not performing that function if she is doing what a man is doing.

S.A.: Some of the women's liberation people seem angry women, for the most part, and—

Serious: They get hurt, I guess. Probably a lot of them have had bad experiences with men. So, in a way, it's men's fault they are like that. The first thing we have to do is we have to get them to our way of thinking, which is Jesus Christ's, and when they get in line with our head, the women fall in with us. It's the natural order; the Bible describes that.

S.A.: Within your own context here, there would be no problem with that anyway in that they are *willing* to accept the arrangement, so there can be no conflict in their minds. Right?

Serious: Well, they don't always agree. But then they go out and see what the world has to offer and then come back, as they have it better here.

S.A.: In the average year, what percentage of those who are drawn to your church and come here to reside for a while ultimately make the decision to stay with you, or not to?

Serious: We feel like anybody who comes through here will eventually be back. I couldn't estimate. The stronger we get, the more obvious our life is here, the clearer it becomes to people who visit us. Lately people do come and stay and do not *have* to go out and doubt for a while longer before they make up their minds. I've noticed it more and more that way.

S.A.: There are about sixty of you here now?

Serious: Something like that.

S.A.: Your son seems like a very fearless child. I suppose two is a fearless age. Children have great confidence in their own safety at this age.

Serious: He has a very hard head.

S.A.: I guess fear is something we gradually learn. A degree of it is necessary for physical self-preservation, but with most of us we go far beyond that reasonable minimum and become victimized by irrational fears.

Serious: We discipline the child ourselves and teach him everything he knows.

S.A.: In other words, you don't plan—when he reaches school age—to send him to public school?

Serious: We will have our own school by then, our own teachers. The public schools teach too many lies. They don't believe in the Bible, and that's what we're based on, so it would be crazy for us to send them to public schools.

Older schoolchildren have gotten the basics enough to see that we can do a much better job teaching them on a one-to-one basis than the schools. We have a seven-year-old boy here. *Logic* taught him. He knows algebra, geometry, astronomy. He knows far beyond what the regular schools could do for him.

The idea is to give them the tools they need, to go ahead and explore and read the Bible on their own. Learn how to do things, work with people, learning to pay attention to God. The home and the school would be one and the same. Children would go to school twenty-four hours a day, that is.

S.A.: There isn't much agreement between astronomers on the one hand and astrologers on the other. Astronomers are scientists; and, though they may be personally cordial in their relationships, astronomers have intellectual contempt for astrologers. Is there any element in your religious philosophy that relates to that historic debate?

Serious: We studied astrology before we got here, but we've pretty much dropped that for now. I don't really know about astrology, if it's of any use to us or not. It doesn't seem to have anything much to do with the Bible. It holds people to conceptions of how they are. Because you're a Gemini, I can expect you to have certain limitations. We want to *free* people from that. But that should be a full manifestation from Jesus Christ. We're not doing anything in that area right now. We don't have any particular stand. It's not useful to us now.

Astronomy is interesting and useful for navigation. We'd like to get into sailing, like to build some big sailing crafts. Perhaps sail around the world and be able to chart our course by the stars.

S.A.: Have any of you had any previous experience with sailing?

Serious: A few men have had some experience.

S.A.: Roughly how many of the Family members were Seattle-area people to begin with?

Serious: Very few. Less than half a dozen.

S.A.: How did *Love* happen to select this area? Just by chance?

Serious: Just . . . God. He had in his own mind the idea of going to Mexico—getting back into the ruins and jungles of Yucatan, finding old pyramids and rebuilding them and gathering people there. But it didn't work out. Obviously God wanted to take care of us in *this* area. This is where people can find us easily. There is a huge flow of people toward the Pacific Northwest, people coming out and escaping other states. . . . California was one of them.

I was looking for just a hope that there was a land somewhere that wasn't messed up to the point of no return. Coming out to Los Angeles and seeing what a beautiful place that once must have been and seeing how man had totally ruined it, I thought I was going to have to go back into the woods again to have a chance to start over there. And then I met this Family and saw if we just got people together we could do it anywhere.

Now I keep looking for another virgin land, because this was a virgin land, but the people messed it up, so let's do first things first. It's an ideal location. Things are so clean up here; water is still pretty clean.

S.A.: I noticed something in the charter book [the Love Family's statement of their beliefs], but didn't get to finish it, about husband-and-wife relationships, or man-and-woman relationships within the context of love between them. In what detailed degree are those things worked out in your philosophy?

Serious: They're just beginning to get worked out. The first couple of years around here we stayed away from *any* man-and-wife relationship and sexual relationships.

S.A.: Even on the part of those married people who came in?

Serious: Yes. It broke up their relationships. There were too many other areas to work on, and that man-and-woman thing was so full of problems we just thought it was the easiest thing to do to give it up for now.

Lately I think we've evolved to the point where we can begin to work out that other relationship, that husband-and-wife working closely together as a team. And so there are a few couples now in the church that have been sanctioned by the church to live together as man and wife.

It has to be a thing where it's for the good of everybody, not just for me and my woman. That's what we saw out in the world, "my woman" and "your woman." Here it's got to work in harmony with the whole Family. That has to come first.

Logic has one of those relationships—with *Simplicity*—and I had one for a while. I have to say I abused it, because it was not good for everybody. I see that the most mature people in our Family are the ones who are taking the responsibility of working out that kind of relationship. The rest of us are still working out the relationship of brothers and sisters.

S.A.: In what way does your interpretation of the commandment "Thou shall not commit adultery" differ from what would be the Methodist or the Catholic interpretation?

Serious: It differs greatly because we're the first people I ever met who really recognize that we're all one-in-Christ. We really *live* that, so we see there *can* be no adultery in our Family. The only adultery we can have is to go outside of our Family. For me to have a relationship with a *non*-believing woman would be adultery, because it would be like linking myself up not to Christ but to the world. It would be like going with a whore. But within our families we're all married to each other. We're all one, one man and one woman.

S.A.: It is then, by your definition, impossible to commit the sin of adultery within the Family?

Serious: Yes. Oh, we have certain customs that are beginning to be established, like there's not any kind of permissive sexual thing happening between us. It's all couples that are sanctioned by the church. We like to know, if children are born, who the father is.

But keeping a relationship between one man and one woman at a time is like a bond between them, until they decide they don't want to be together anymore. That way if a child is born we'll know who the parents are.

S.A.: That factor is reasonable enough, although I'm confused trying to see where that meshes gears with what you said a couple of minutes ago about adultery. Suppose any young man and young woman in the community, to use the common expression, *fall in love,* which is something more than the love between two men or the love between brother and sister. In other words, a love which has the *sexual* component and the *romantic* component, in which the beloved's face seems more beautiful to you than it does to anybody else. In that kind of a situation you just suggested that you would recommend each being exclusively the property of the other, so that if another man were to find himself attracted to the same young woman and if he would announce his intention to you to make physical overtures to the young lady, then I assume you would say no—isn't that right?

Serious: It's up to us how we do that. This is the way we're doing it right now. It may not always be this way. The Bible itself is not clear about this. One of the things it says is that in the Resurrection we'll live as the angels.

S.A.: Angels do not have bodies.

Serious: Maybe that's not true. Maybe *we* are the children of the Resurrection and this is our new life. We may go through changes.

S.A.: You've mentioned that it *would* be possible to commit the sin of having sex with a man or woman who is *not* of the church. Is that the only possible sexual sin which can be committed?

Serious: No. It would be disobedience for a man or woman to have sexual relationships without the sanction of the church. That has happened a few times, and some disciplinary action is taken. A young man in the church here had a sexual relationship with a female guest, and when it came to light we sent him out for a period of time.

S.A.: Both the Old and New Testaments, as well as the last two thousand years of Christian tradition, have been very clear in condemnation of homosexual behavior. To what extent does the viewpoint of your church differ from or resemble the traditional belief?

Serious: Well, we have seen that in a sense we were all homosexuals, that we all had that in part of our minds.

S.A.: You mean every human mind?

Serious: Yes. Every man or every woman had that as part of his mind. We share the same mind. Maybe some people act it out more than others, but it was all in there, and it was all possible, so we had all done it in our imaginations, perhaps physically at one time or another. So we were all equally guilty, if there was any guilt.

S.A.: There's a sense in which we all have in our minds, in terms of our *potential,* the ability to do many forms of evil, to take someone else's money, to do all the classic human acts regarded as sins or mistakes. There is a real sense in which every man is a sinner, so what you say would apply presumably to the homosexual factor as well as to all other problems. Nevertheless, this specific human failing has been condemned in the Old Testament and the New as well as during the two thousand years since.

Serious: We don't condemn it; we just see that it's not a natural use of man. We're not *condemned* if we do it. God made man and *woman* to live together naturally.

S.A.: Suppose a young man with an honest interest in religion were to come to you and say, "I've heard about your church and it seems to me reasonable. I'd like to know more about it. I find myself drawn sympathetically to it, but I think you should know I'm a homosexual." What could you say to him?

Serious: We have people now living here who were involved actively in those actions.

S.A.: Would your approach be to try to change them?

Serious: Sure. We'd like to see that they are happy. That's something they have within themselves; it's a false image; it's a misunderstanding. It's an imbalance, so as their friend I would help them to see that homosexuality is what the world drove them to. Now in this world they have a chance to get themselves back into their right place. When we do what is most natural, what God created for us, then the homosexual part of us just disappears.

(In 1981, Brian commented, "In reading over this interview of 1972, I see the youth in it. Our basic beliefs haven't changed, but our expression has matured. It's like looking back at yourself as a child. It's undeniably you, but the younger self doesn't express itself very well. As time went on the bare bones of our belief gained much more heart.")

My visit was too short, but important. Brian and I had seen each other again, broken the ice of our separation. It was a significant step forward.

CHAPTER 10

The Case of Kathy Crampton

Parents of Love Family members have had sharply different reactions to their children's participation in the group. Among the most bitterly critical is Mrs. J. C. Crampton, mother of Kathy Crampton. In July of 1973 she wrote to tell me that the Cramptons had removed Kathy for "deprogramming," and went on to say that she had begun a letter-writing campaign: "*Love* Israel is going to regret the day he 'set eyes' on our daughter because we are dedicated to exposing him. I hope other parents feel the same. All the evidence we have against him and others like him needs to be brought out into the open."

The Cramptons also permitted CBS News to film the "kidnapping" of Kathy. Explained Mrs. Crampton:

> We had hoped that by allowing her case to be seen on TV the nation would wake up to the menace these cults are to our young people and our country. Kids don't know enough about it to protect themselves. They are innocent and believe that in religious communes they just grow vegetables and pray. We are concerned for the thousands caught in this horror.

Thus TV viewers who were tuned to the CBS Evening News on August 13, 1973, heard Roger Mudd introduce the story of Kathy Crampton. "Groups like the Children of God have become a phenomenon in this country," he began.

Mudd: They exist in dozens of varieties and have thousands of followers. Often they are Fundamentalist in their religious point of view. Frequently, they completely control the lives of their members. Some appear to be churches; others, more like communes. Tonight we begin a special report on a new phenome-

87

non. It's called "deprogramming," an attempt to force those religious cultists to renounce their beliefs. It involves parents, the police, and a man named Ted Patrick. Stephen Young reports from the West Coast.

Stephen Young: Five-thirty A.M., Wednesday, June 27th of this year. Kathy Crampton is being abducted. Kathy is nineteen, legally an adult in Washington State. . . .

The abductors are her mother, Mrs. Henrietta Crampton, a housewife from Redondo Beach, California; twenty-four-year-old Gregg Temple from Eugene, Oregon, who plans to marry Kathy's older sister; forty-two-year-old Ted Patrick, known as Black Lightning. They have turned to him as a last resort. For Kathy, since February, has belonged to a Fundamentalist church and commune they consider sinister. They want to free her of its control. None of these people has been involved in anything like this before, except Ted Patrick. He calls it a rescue and says it will lead to the 135th deprogramming he has personally conducted.

When she joined the Church of Armageddon, Kathy became a member of the Love Family and took the last name Israel. They all do that here. [Music in background] Kathy chose a first name from the Bible, *Corinth*. About eighty members share seven houses. Their leader, *Love* Israel, lives here. Their beliefs may seem peculiar. They add sixty-six years to their actual age. *Love* says he is ninety-eight. He is a thirty-two-year-old former salesman. They say their spiritual parents are God and the Universe. Music is a central part of their lives. . . .

They keep these homes and make a point of cleaning up the neighborhood. Last year, in a so-called religious rite, two of their members died after sniffing an industrial solvent. *Love* says the only drug now used on occasion is marijuana. He allows no newspapers, radio or TV, and screens incoming mail. The only book allowed here is the Bible. Kathy Crampton's parents and Ted Patrick believe *Love* Israel uses the Bible to brainwash.

Love Israel (A.K.A. Paul Erdman): We don't really have any big brainwashing program other than loving each other and living a regular life, and our book's the Bible, and that's the one we read, and, as far as cleaning up your mind, you know, I think we're all cleaning up our minds. If that's called brainwashing, I don't know. I just think that we all need it, real well. I think we could all use a lot of it.

Young: Mrs. Crampton stayed at the church with Kathy the past two nights and jogged with her both mornings past a cemetery. The invitation to an abduction has worked today. Kathy is forced into the back seat. Patrick prefers two-door cars. It's harder to escape. They move out of Seattle on a two-car convoy on the main highway heading south. Patrick has allowed CBS News to be present. He says he wants to document the national brainwashing menace posed by sixty-seven different groups. CBS News has informed the Seattle police in advance, but they did not intervene.

The first crisis comes some two hours out of Seattle during a refueling stop. Kathy cries to the gas station owner that she's being kidnapped. [Sound of highway traffic] For the second time this morning she is dragged away against her will and forced into the back seat of Patrick's rented car. He stays behind, after ordering the others to speed away and wait for him at the side of the road up ahead.

A curious Washington state trooper who happens to pass by pulls over. Gregg explains what's going on.

Gregg Temple: A Mr. Ted Patrick [Sound of highway traffic] is the man who takes religious people out of love families, so to speak. He has just taken the mother's daughter out of the Love Family in Seattle, and we're on our way down to San Diego for a reprogramming.

D. O. Mahoney (state trooper): My God, it's—[Pause] I feel awful uncomfortable.

Young: Uncertain what to do, he radios for assistance, and a state police sergeant responds to the call.

L. E. Walter (trooper sergeant): Hi, how are you?

Kathy Crampton: I'm fine. [Indistinct: much highway noise throughout this sequence]

Walter: What is your name?

Kathy: *Corinth* Israel.

Walter: *Corinth* what?

Kathy: *Corinth Love* Israel.

Walter: *Corinth Love* Israel. How old are you?

Kathy: I'm eighty-five.

Walter: Eighty-five years old? I see.

Young: The sheriff's department is next to arrive. A gas station owner has reported a possible kidnapping, he says. Ted Patrick has been placed under arrest.

Walter: The mother and he and the fiancé of one of her other daughters went up to get this girl. They took her from this environment. The girl is so out of her mind and drugged. I asked her a minute ago, for instance, if this was her mother, and of course she gave me something like, No, my mother is somebody, the mother of the universe. So she's all ripped up inside.

Det. R. Covington (sheriff's office): Rattled. Right.

Trooper: In the physical life, who is she?

Kathy: She claims to represent my mother.

Trooper: Is she—in the physical life?

Kathy: No, my mother is the spiritual—is the spiritual vision of peace.

Trooper: But in the physical life, is this your real mother?

Kathy: I don't see that this is the question. The question is that I've been taken against my will. I would prefer to go with you, sir, to the police station, than to go with these people.

Trooper: Well, we have to identify you and establish who you are.

Kathy: I'm *Corinth* Israel.

Trooper: You're *Corinth* Israel. Is that your legal name?

Kathy: Yes, it is, as far as I know.

Trooper: Do you have any legal documents to show who you are?

Kathy: These people kidnapped me, and I didn't have my papers with me. We were jog—we were running; this woman and I were running; and I didn't carry my papers with me just to run around the block.

Trooper: Well, I'll let the deputy sheriff talk to you, okay?

Covington: How old did you say you were?

Kathy: I'm eighty-five.

Covington: You're eighty-five.

Young: At the Cowlitz County Courthouse in Kelso, Washington, the question: what to do? They checked the statutes and doubt this is a kidnapping. Kathy's mother was present. There was no try for ransom, and the Seattle police confirmed that they knew in advance. Legally, Kathy is an adult, but Patrick insists he and the others are acting within their rights.

Ted Patrick: Well, I'll say the parents got a right to rescue their child, if they feel they are under some type of spell or influence of drug or alcohol, or in trouble, period. They have a right to go and give as much help as possible. That's a human right and constitutional right.

Young: Asked if she is a menace to herself or the community, a psychiatrist says no. Charges against Patrick are dropped, and Kathy is released. Her freedom is short-lived.

Kathy: Okay, now. I don't want to go—[Indistinct] I'm gonna—you're gonna physically take me—I'm going to walk this direction. [Indistinct] I'm free—[Indistinct]

Mrs. Crampton: Gregg! [Sound of running footsteps]

Kathy: Let me go. Let me go!

Young: For the third time today, Kathy is forced against her will to go with her mother and Ted Patrick.

Steve Young continued the next evening, reporting that Kathy's third capture had occurred in broad daylight as passers-by watched. Her abductors headed toward Chula Vista, California, a suburb of San Diego, where Patrick and "members of his best deprogramming team" live. Arriving after an all-night drive, the group settled in at a motel Ted Patrick had used before. "It will be part home, part prison, for the next six days. . . . In Seattle, *Love* Israel controlled Kathy Crampton's life. Ted Patrick rules it here. They choose a small corner suite, a bedroom inside, a combination sitting room–kitchen closest to the pool. Patrick's constant companion is his tape recorder, always near at hand, always switched on."

Ted Patrick (Deprogramming, first hour): Only God that you know is *Love* Israel. That's your God. You know nuthin' about God. You hate your parents. You hate everybody other than the Family, Love Israel. Kathy, stop meditatin' now, 'cause you don't want to reprogram yourself.

Young: Kathy's parents will remain present for most of the deprogramming. Mrs. Crampton is the first to take an active role this Thursday afternoon.

Mrs. Crampton: It's ruined everything else you believed in—all this evil that makes you happy? Huh? Oh, honey, come—come on—please, come—speak up, honey. [Sobs throughout foregoing]

Patrick: You still say she's not your mother?

Mrs. Crampton: [Sobs uncontrollably] This whole thing is a horrible nightmare.

In the fourth hour of deprogramming, Patrick's team members, Mrs. Ila Meese and her daughter, Barbara, arrived to help. Barbara herself had been rescued from a mind-controlling group, the Children of God, she said. Patrick "prefers a harsh technique, but this time he'll let the Meeses try their soft approach first," said Young.

Patrick: Every person always hate my guts from the very beginnin', which is good, because in that situation, I can upset 'em and then force 'em to think. And, in order to be angry with a person, or dislike a person, you got to think about 'em, what they said or did. And this is the reason I've been successful in all the deprogramming, because we use the big outpush first and then afterwards we open up their minds. Okay, the good guy come in and put that soft touch and bring 'em right out of it, see?

In the eighth hour, Young reported,

A significant moment, they say. Kathy has agreed to eat. Someone resisting programming usually refuses to break his fast. Most of those surrounding her call themselves born-again Christians. They attend church twice on Sundays, study the Bible and pray an hour or more each day. [Some laughter is heard here] It appears that Kathy may be willing to question the teachings of the Love Family in Seattle, which she joined last February. She stays at the Meese house that night. Patrick will later call it a mistake. While they sleep, Kathy climbs the back fence and slips away. She is recaptured by Ted Patrick and her parents through a series of accidental circumstances. She tells the Chula Vista police of her wish to escape, but they allow her parents and Ted Patrick to take her away.

Kathy: I just want to be free. I just want to be out of bondage.

Young: This violates her civil rights, says American Civil Liberties Union lawyer Mike Pancer. He also considers it a crime.

Mike Pancer (ACLU lawyer): Most young people, while they might be very happy to prosecute Mr. Patrick for kidnapping, or complain against him, don't want to see their parents get into any trouble, even though their parents have wronged them. Another reason is that law enforcement officials tend to take the side of the more established group involved in this whole operation, and the more established side tends to be the parents and Mr. Patrick. There's a real bias against the young people. There's a real bias against the Jesus Freak movement on the part of the law enforcement people.

Young: From now on, until the end of the deprogramming, Kathy will spend her nights in the motel, and her mother or father will sleep on a cot blocking the door, so she can no longer get away.

The next evening, Young began,

It is Friday night in the living room of Ted Patrick's house in Chula Vista, California. Kathy Crampton's parents and Patrick's deprogramming team pray that Kathy will denounce *Love* Israel. His followers in Seattle are praying that they will fail.

Mrs. Henrietta Crampton: We're all here together praying for her. Just—just please help her.

Kathy Crampton: [Indistinct] [Pause] I know that *Love* Israel rebukes you also. I believe in the Lord Jesus Christ, and I'm not of Satan.

Woman: Right. Right.

Kathy: And I know that *Love* Israel feels the same way that I feel, and *Love* Israel is not of Satan.

Woman: Honey—

Ted Patrick: You've been served with Satan. This is what we try to tell you.

Kathy: I know that, Mrs. Meese.

Mrs. Ila Meese: Honey, you've been deceived. You've been deceived.

Patrick: And you've been served with Satan.

Young: This is the first time Patrick has ever done a deprogramming at home. Much of the time his family looks on in a detached sort of way. The Patricks have five children. He says his anti-cult crusade began after his eldest son was approached by the Children of God. He is a former community relations consultant to Governor Ronald Reagan. Patrick's wife, a schoolteacher, is the only apparent source of steady income.

The deprogramming [48th hour coming up] is almost nonstop. Usually it is in the form of doctrinal questions. Sometimes it reverts to emotional attacks.

Patrick: The worst death a person can die is at the hands of their own child that they birthed in the world. Piece by piece you cut your parents to death. Now, you've been told to kill your parents.

Mrs. Crampton: Something has happened to your brain that's changed your whole attitude about people, relationships, family. It's changed your—your—your whole intelligence. [Sniffs] It's changed your intelligence so that you don't think that one thing—you can say anything you want; it doesn't mean anything to you.

Patrick: Answer—[Indistinct]

Mrs. Crampton: Will you answer?

Patrick: Can you answer without deceit?

Mrs. Crampton: Can you answer without deceit? Can you say, My God in heaven, I can answer a word that means something?

Kathy: My words don't mean the same as yours.

Mrs. Crampton: They damn well better!

Mike Pancer: I have a lot of sympathy for parents involved in—in these cases, not for the parents who go around kidnapping their children, but for the parents who have lost the ability to communicate with their children.

Young: American Civil Liberties lawyer Mike Pancer has dealt before with parents who feel that their children, legally of adult age, are unduly influenced by religious cults.

Pancer: It's a sad situation, and I'm not sure that I know the answer. However, their only legal alternative is to try to contact their children, and to speak with them, and to reason with their children, to get their children to do the thing that they want them to do. That's their only hope, to try to reestablish communication with their children, if they can. It's probably as much their fault as anybody's. [Singing]

Young: Kathy is taken to a spirited Saturday night gathering of religious young people. In low key now, the deprogramming continues. [58th hour] She is moved to the point of tears. Kathy will spend Sunday with some of these people at a church picnic. [Singing]

Monday, she still has not broken. Patrick plans to sharply increase the pressure, but he is ninety minutes late for the start of the deprogramming. Previously, Patrick has said we could talk with Kathy during the process. She suggests this might be a good time. Her parents agree and leave the room. They are troubled by possible promiscuity at the Church of Armageddon.

Kathy: To my knowledge, when I—when I left, there were only five or six bonded couples. That means these are people who have sexual intercourse with each other. Then these are—a bonded couple is someone who's been approved by the Family, that their relationship is not a relationship that would exclude love for any other member of the Family, and then they're bonded, and I haven't been bonded, so I haven't had any sexual intercourse with any member of the Family.

Young: How much power does *Love* Israel have over the lives of the people in the Church of Armageddon?

Kathy: As much power as the individual gives him.

Young: How much do they give him?

Kathy: It varies with the individual. I've given him my life.

Young: Patrick returns and demands that the interview stop. He wants no more filming until the deprogramming succeeds. He thinks the presence of CBS News personnel may have slowed down the process.

There followed a scene in which Patrick, faced with Kathy demanding her civil liberties, became angrier and angrier at the CBS News team. When he threatened to smash the camera—and crew—with a hammer, they agreed to leave. Young reported,

Patrick calms down but sticks to his condition: no more filming until Kathy breaks. We go. And Kathy's parents are asked to leave. The Patrick family also is locked out, or told not to come downstairs. Some sort of ceremony is going on in the living room, it is said.

Five hours pass, and then it is over. [102nd hour] Mrs. Ila Meese and her daughter, Barbara, say Kathy has been delivered. At least fourteen demons have been removed.

Mrs. Meese: It's just really a miracle of God. She had all these spirits ministering to her, and—

Young: Fourteen, you said.

Mrs. Meese: No—we didn't count 'em, but I mean at least that many.

Young: Kathy is on a bed upstairs, exhausted.

Mrs. Crampton: You look so free, Kathy, even though you're dead tired. You look—your eyes—you look like Kathy again.

Mrs. Meese: Yeah. Her eyes look so clear.

Mrs. Crampton: Yes, she looks—doesn't she look different?

Young: She is unable to rest longer than a few minutes. Confident of their success, the Patricks, the Cramptons and the deprogramming team all leave with Kathy for dinner. It has been six days since her abduction. The Seattle police had prior knowledge. They did not act. State and local authorities in Washington and California learned what was happening and did not intervene. Patrick says the authorities usually respond this way. Lawyer Mike Pancer believes the police thereby commit a crime. The significance, he says, goes beyond deprogramming and cult religions.

Pancer: Each individual in our society is given the right to live according to his own decisions, so long as he doesn't interfere in the life of anybody else in any illegal way. That principle is being violated by Ted Patrick and his cohorts, and it's also being violated by the law enforcement officials, who either refuse to take action, or, as in Kathy's case, actively assist Mr. Patrick in his work.

Young: Somewhat rested, Kathy reflects the next day. She forgives her parents and Ted Patrick and the others for doing what they thought was best. Her faith in Christ has been strengthened, she says. What faith she once had in law and order is now shaken.

Kathy: I do care. I don't—I don't know that I would go right out and—and really make a big deal and take it all to court and everything. I don't know if I feel that strongly about it.

Young: Did you, in fact, just tell them what they wanted to hear?

Kathy: No, I—I sincerely gave *Love* Israel up. I sincerely did, with all my heart. I really believe that.

Young: Do you feel you're free now? I mean, free physically? Can you do what you want, go as you want, go where you want?

Kathy: I—I don't feel I'm really free yet, no, physically. If I said I wanted to go back to *Love* Israel, I think the whole thing would start again. I have no idea what the future holds. I only know that I'm here now.

Young: But you might go back to the Church of Armageddon?

Kathy: Yes. I might.

Young: The next day, July 4th, Independence Day, at a beach, Kathy Crampton got into a passing car and escaped. [Singing]

Young: Five days later, she returned to Seattle and the Church of Armageddon. For her perseverance in resisting the deprogramming, *Love* Israel has renamed her *Dedication* Israel. The Love Family has decided not to press charges against Ted Patrick. They say that would be to live in the past.

Eight years later, in May of 1981, Kathy Crampton left the Love Family again. One of the reasons for her departure—according to her mother—was that when her latest child was born Kathy received no medical attention, even though the baby was a month overdue; Kathy had a fever of 102 when the baby was born; the placenta did not emerge for two days after the birth; the child, ten pounds at birth, was anemic. Kathy apparently objected to the fact that the baby was born without the supervision or advice of a medical authority.

Kathy was understandably having difficulty readjusting to the outside world after so long a time with the Family. According to her mother, she did not even have enough identification to get new legal identification.

The baby's Family name was *Glad,* which Kathy has changed. The baby's father, as of June 1981, was still with the Family.

Before this book went to press, I asked Brian what had become of Kathy. He felt that some of what Kathy's mother had said didn't describe Kathy's present situation accurately. "Her leaving the Family had been more a matter of separating from the man *Helpful* whom she'd been with in the Family. She went down and lived with her parents for a short while and, I guess, felt uncomfortable there. Consequently she's now moved back into our neighborhood. . . . We see her every now and then and she visits us."

(On December 21, 1981—after this manuscript had already been set in type—Kathy Crampton phoned me to say that she had heard I was planning to go to Seattle in late January 1982 to participate in a program sponsored by the Church Council of Greater Seattle, and that inasmuch as the Love Family was to take part in the entertainment (though the

Love Family is not affiliated with the Church Council), her family felt that some people might interpret this as my public stamp of approval on the Love Family.

I explained to her that I had no intention of putting my stamp of approval on any specific religion. More importantly, I was interested to learn that she had, once and for all, put the Love Family experience behind her. She was now living in Redondo Beach, California, her parents' home town, and took a generally dim view of *Love* Israel and his group: "There are some very good people up there," she said, "and some good things are done." But she had criticisms.

I have heard—not only from Ms. Crampton—that some members of the Family have objected to expenditures made by *Love* Israel for himself at times when there was not enough milk available for the children of the commune. It also became clear in our conversation that, like other women who have left the Family, Kathy felt that the commune's social structure was generally unfair to women.

The search for truth is never-ending.)

CHAPTER 11

The Case of
Vicky Sinunu

The story of Vicky Sinunu was different.

It came to my attention quite by chance. In 1973, without advance warning, two members of the Love Family, *Cooperation* and *Courage,* appeared on our doorstep. They were in the neighborhood, we gathered, because of a young woman whose family lived nearby. She had been "kidnapped" from the Love Family and deprogrammed, and *Cooperation* and *Courage* were attempting—I know not how—to get in touch with her, to see if she needed or wanted their help. To us, the two represented an opportunity to learn more about the Love Family, about Brian and about his adjustment to the life there, so we invited them to stay with us for a few days.

In my life there are often comic elements to otherwise serious proceedings. At the time I was preparing "Meeting of Minds," a television project later shown on the PBS network. The program is a talk show with a twist; all the guests are important personages from history. On the show we were then rehearsing, for example, the guests were Cleopatra of ancient Egypt, President Theodore Roosevelt, Catholic theologian-philosopher Saint Thomas Aquinas, and American revolutionary firebrand Thomas Paine. Rehearsals for the show were held at our home. Because taping day was fast approaching, the actors were rehearsing in costume. So for three days we had walking around the house a woman in the raiment of ancient Egypt, a President in turn-of-the-century dress, an Italian churchman of the medieval period, and a New Englander in the britches of the Revolution—these four, along with two others, *Cooperation* and *Courage,* who, with their Biblical robes and long hair, looked like John the Baptist and Saint Paul.

At the same time our kitchen was being rebuilt by a couple of Archie Bunker types. Exactly what they thought of the household's colorful inhabitants we never learned, but we did observe a certain amount of eye-rolling between them. *Cooperation* and *Courage* made a few good-natured attempts to bestow the message of Christ on these hard-hat construction men, but I'm afraid the Word fell on stony soil.

Vicky Sinunu's case differs from that of Kathy Crampton primarily because Vicky did not return to the Church of Armageddon after deprogramming. Like Brian, Vicky joined the Love Family in 1971, sending her parents the same sort of letter we had received. During the next year, her mother visited her a couple of times, sadly observing that Vicky was too indoctrinated to leave the group. She did abandon it for a month to be with Steve Fisher, a medical student she had been living with, but returned to Seattle—pregnant. When her little boy was born in July, *Love* Israel named him *Light* Israel.

Early in 1973 Vicky's aunt sent the Sinunus a news item about the deprogramming done by Ted Patrick and Mrs. Meese. After talking with families who had been through it and recommended it, the Sinunus decided they would try to liberate Vicky. Mrs. Sinunu and a close friend met Ted Patrick in Seattle on February 4. Mrs. Sinunu took Vicky—and, as it happened, *Logic,* who was with her—out to lunch; unfortunately the baby was not allowed to leave the church's quarters. After lunch the car stopped on a freeway to pick up Ted Patrick, posing as a hitchhiker. *Logic* was forced out of the car; Patrick gave him money to get home with, and they drove off. Vicky did not fight. When her mother explained, "We are taking you home because we love you," she replied, "It must be God's will or you wouldn't have done it." They proceeded in stages to Chula Vista, where the deprogramming began. Although Vicky defended the Love Family, she did listen to Barbara Meese and Mrs. Meese as they talked to her. The next day, Wednesday, she cried for the first time, saying she wanted her baby, and talked at length with her mother. As Mrs. Sinunu put it,

> She told me that one reason she had doubts about the Family was because I have never liked them. She also said that she had always thought it wrong that they did not communicate with their families. This was the first time she had shown any sign of relenting her stoic expression and now she started releasing her pent-up emotions in tears. I told her how sad it had been for us—and she put her arms around me and we both shed lots of tears.

On Thursday, when Mrs. Sinunu returned to the Meese house from an errand,

> Ted was in the kitchen talking to Vicky with Barbara. He was talking softly and listening carefully to Vicky. In a few minutes he called me

to come in. Vicky prayed the most beautiful prayer I ever heard, confessing that she had been deceived, asking God to forgive her for worshipping a man, etc. Then Ted started to pray and cried like a baby. It was the most miraculous thing I've ever witnessed. We knew that God had truly answered our prayers.

The focus then shifted to the baby. Mrs. Sinunu and Ted returned to Seattle that night, armed with Vicky's notarized petition asking for her child. On Friday they got a court order and, with police support, went to the Church of Armageddon, where Mrs. Sinunu asked *Serious* for *Light* and was refused. Love Family members said they would give the baby only to its mother. Since Monday was Lincoln's birthday, nothing could happen until Tuesday. Ted returned to San Diego, and Mr. Sinunu arrived in Seattle to wait out the long weekend with his wife. At a court hearing on Tuesday *Charity, Logic* and *Strength* refused to believe that Vicky had not been kidnapped and held captive. The judge asked the Sinunus to have Vicky in court on Wednesday; the Love Family members were asked to have the baby there then.

Vicky returned to Seattle with Steve Fisher, *Light*'s father, and with Ted. Under oath on Wednesday she and Steve declared they were the true parents of the child. The judge ordered that the three Love Family members be held in jail until the baby was produced. But by nine that night, the baby had not been brought.

Finally, the next morning, *Serious* came down from Queen Anne Hill with him, and Mr. Sinunu met his first grandson, renamed Seth Steven Fisher, for the first time. Reunited, the happy family left Seattle.

But the story does not end there. That evening, wrote Mrs. Sinunu,

Steve and Vicky announced that they had loved each other for three years and would like to get married. It was another long weekend—and God kept adding to my failing strength. So Friday they had a conference with Bill Craig (our wonderful pastor), got blood tests, marriage license, took Seth Steven Fisher to the pediatrician for his very first check-up, and this left all day Saturday to buy wedding rings, clothes for Steve, a wedding dress for Vicky and plan and prepare food for the guests. It worked! The wedding was beautiful! The food delicious. The day was perfect—temperature 73° in February. "GOD BLESS US EVERY ONE."

Shortly thereafter, *Courage* and *Cooperation* returned to Seattle.

Twenty-five-year-old Vicky Sinunu Fisher was generous enough to visit our home and answer my questions about the Love Family, giving me both straight information and her thoughts and opinions. Our discussion enabled me to clarify impressions from my 1972 visit. For instance, I had been struck by the fact that one young man did not talk; he even seemed almost catatonic. From Vicky I learned that while this particular fellow had had emotional problems, the younger members were indeed urged not to talk, especially not to guests. The elders did the talking. "All the energy goes to the elders. That's just the way it is. The elders say we're all one mind. I can speak for you or you can speak for me. The man can speak for the woman. And the elders can speak for the younger ones." *Logic* had become one of the elders, she told me, the head of one of the two guest houses. That struck me as an appropriate post for someone of Brian's ready, easy charm. Vicky also corrected my false impression that only women served men. Whether you are male or female, if you are a new member, you serve the more senior people—at meals, for example.

I learned about members' names. A member first gets an Old Testament name, which he or she chooses, upon baptism into the Family. "Eventually," Vicky said, "you get a name which comes down from God." (Hers had been *Godliness*.) Actually, the Family creates something like its own language, even naming the days of the week after the names of the churches mentioned in the New Testament. Saturday is Laodicea, Sunday Ephesus; Monday is Smyrna, Tuesday Pergamos, Wednesday Thyatira, Thursday Sardis, Friday Philadelphia (which, I could not resist saying, might be a little confusing if you ever had to go to Philadelphia on a Friday).

In 1973, Vicky told me, there were close to ninety members, sixty-five or seventy of them men. I could not remember what the sleeping arrangements had been when I had visited. "In most of the houses," Vicky explained, "there's a women's room and a men's room—for the elder women and the elder men. Then usually there's a basement with a large area for bunks, which is mostly used by men because there are generally more men than women. But if there are extra women who can't fit into the women's room, then they sleep in the basement, too." That reminded me that Brian had mentioned something about a crew going around twice a night to wake everybody. "It was supposed to be just to keep you sleeping lightly," said Vicky, "so you could always be aware. So you won't go into a never-never land. So you can always be conscious." To me that made no sense. Being awakened so frequently could produce irritability.

Vicky's view of *Love* Israel—who was thirty-two, she said—was that he was not a religious fanatic, as most parents assumed, but the kind of person "who likes to be powerful. To control people." She did not talk about his past, and explained that members "were urged instead to talk about now. Not the future either. Right here and now."

We covered other areas, briefly. I learned that the Family had recently had a policy of not using money. They used a school bus for transportation and bartered for gasoline. They were trying to work out something with the power company to pay for electricity; the alternative was to trade with a third party, who would give the money to the power company.

I asked, of course, about drugs. Was *Love* or the group critical of any particular drug? Would he say, "Heroin is wrong but marijuana is okay"? Vicky's answer perplexed me. "Mostly they say everything is a gift from God."

"*Everything* is okay?"

"Yes."

"If that makes sense, then heroin is okay. Which I think is stupid."

I took Vicky's reply to that, however, to be an indirect, tacit rejection of something like heroin: "You don't want to get addicted to anything," she said. "You don't want to get addicted to food even." Apparently it was so important to the Family to consider themselves spiritual beings that they claimed they could go on forever without food. This reminded me of their strange claim, a year earlier, that the dead would revive; they seemed at times to dismiss the body entirely.

Of this assertion *Logic* later said, "This is not true. We do feel that people need to be masters of themselves and not be led by habits and desires. As you know, controlling food intake is as difficult for some people as controlling a drug habit is for others."

At the time, though, I was concerned that their depreciation of the body might extend to medical matters. Vicky had given birth to her baby in her house and said that for childbirth some of the members were competent midwives, but she observed that "For a people who didn't believe in doctors, they put a lot of reliance on" the one woman who was trained as a nurse. That woman didn't prescribe medicines, but helped out. But the Love Family were not like Christian Scientists, she agreed; if someone was seriously ill—"something really big that faith couldn't heal—they'd try regular medicine." She had seen a little boy in real pain, badly burned when hot tea spilled on him; faith had stopped his pain. "When someone came in and put their hands on him," he had stopped crying. There was no question, I concurred, that that works when you believe in the power of the person who is helping you.

I raised the question of violence. Ted Patrick was worried about it, perhaps because the Family had bows and arrows. They were just for hunting, Vicky said. But she wasn't sure when I asked if that meant that the Family condoned the killing of animals. They were not pacifists, though fighting was discouraged; they would fight in self-defense or to defend Family members.

I was curious to know what policies governed family and sexual relationships. Vicky knew of only one woman who ever had relationships with more than one man, but she added, "*Love* himself had two wives," and acknowledged that jealousy between the two women had been a problem. As for child-raising, she said that they espoused the same kind of theory that underlies the Israeli practice on the kibbutz: since children get their hangups from whatever is wrong with their parents, if the children can be gotten out from under their parents and into living with their peers under adult supervision—including that of the parents—they will be healthier.

And there are rules governing love and sexual relationships. A relationship must be between an older man and a younger woman. Couples have to be sanctioned by law, which means that *Love* gives his permission. "But," said Vicky, "it happens very seldom. Most people in the Family of Love are celibate." She knew of only one homosexual and he too—she said—was celibate. I was surprised that young people should be so ascetic. She explained that when she had first joined, "people had given up sex altogether until the Marriage Supper of the Lamb, whenever that would be. And for all we knew it would be in the future sometime. . . . And then things changed. Some people had been celibate for two years or more . . . the idea was to cut out wants and needs. . . . " Everything was to be "a gift." "You're just not supposed to want." The ascetic life meant giving up wine and cigarettes and drugs, too. Vicky said you had to go to *Love* and ask permission, to turn on, for instance. *Love* would say, "Would you like to?" "He usually gives it to them, but he doesn't *like* to. He gives them a talk about asking," Vicky said.

I questioned her about my impression that the FREECOG (Free Children of God, an anti-cult group) felt that the Children of God and the Love Family were practically identical. "No, they're not," she said. "The COG are a lot more heavy-handed," and while the Love Family occasionally preach on the street, "the COG do a lot of that, trying to convert others on the spot."

But even more interesting than the basic information Vicky gave me was her evaluation of the Love Family and her own experience in it. When I observed that many parents fear that in communes young people are victimized or hypnotized, Vicky flatly rejected the idea. "People join just because they think it's a right," she said. "In my case I was just looking for a Christian house. I asked around the University up in Seattle and somebody told me about the Love Family, so I just walked in, without being enticed or hypnotized in any way."

Instead, another motivation for joining began to emerge in our discussion. I noted that some of the men in the Family—more so than the women—looked like people who weren't making it in the world. "*Everybody* there wasn't making it in the world!" Vicky exclaimed. According to the standard American picture of things, we agreed, a man is supposed to make something of himself—he should become a doctor or lawyer or businessman. Vicky—whose father is a businessman, whose mother had been a schoolteacher and whose brother was in law school—said that she felt that she and most of the women in the Love Family had also felt that they, as women, should *be* something. But when I asked what she would have liked to be, she said, "It wasn't what I'd like to be; it was what I had been urged to be. I didn't know what I *wanted* to be." She hadn't been urged to be anything specific, just "something great." To be nothing specific, but "great," must be an awful burden. I thought we were getting somewhere.

Most of us, I suggested, even knowledgeable people, are tentative about even our most important beliefs and feelings. We will take a position, but we know we might not be totally right. But leaders of groups like the Love Family are *sure* they're right, and that has great appeal to others living in an uncertain world. Vicky agreed. "Usually when you come into something like the Love Family, you're sort of searching and not too sure of yourself. Then you find these people who are absolutely sure they are right, and so you begin to think maybe they are. Maybe they *do* know something you don't."

This conversation suggested to me that the Love Family may have offered both Brian and Vicky and people like them their first chance to feel important in an organized social framework. " . . . That was another reason that I joined," Vicky said. "I wanted to feel like I was better than anybody else. That's one thing that the Family has to offer: 'We *know* we're better than the rest of the world.'"

I pointed out that the trap of pride had troubled all religions. On the one hand Christians quote the humble, meek Jesus. But then they feel, "We're the best; others are beneath us."

"Within the Family," Vicky replied, "you were humble. But you do think the Family is all there is. And all those other people—when they join the Family, they'll change. But now they're not as good as we are because they don't have this kind of life-style."

She characterized the life-style as "elegant." "Mostly what the Family has to offer is its style. It's really a classy style of living."

"Whereas," I interjected, "for many young people their previous life was disorganized."

"Right," said Vicky. "That's it."

Yet she complained that both children and adults were constantly criticized, until "you start thinking 'I can't ever do anything right.'" This applied to tasks like bedmaking and cooking, for example. "And I kept feeling . . . I should be able to do everything perfect. But everytime I'd be getting better I would always be told I wasn't doing something right. I just always felt a little bit guilty." She paused, then went on, "And the little kids do that much heavier than the adults do, 'cause they're just expected to change. They do something or act a certain way, and they're spanked until they change. And they're just told over and over again that they do wrong, so they just can't live up to the standards that are set for them."

The women got into trouble, for instance, for being late when the whole Family was meeting to go for a walk. To get ready, "the women first had to take care of the children and get them all dressed, getting stuff ironed to put on, etc. And the men would be out there saying, 'What if we had a real emergency and we all were going to leave; what would happen?' It seemed that all the women were always late. So we were criticized." *Strength* and *Love* were both critical, but it was also the attitude of the group. "Anybody who is not perfect is in trouble," said Vicky. Occasionally, she said, someone criticized the elders, but only if asked.

"Did you ever think about leaving the Family when you were up there?" I asked.

"Part of my mind wanted to be out of the place, but I felt guilty about those thoughts. . . . We talked about it and thought about it," she said, "but we always felt it was wrong." She would never have left on her own, she added, and she was glad now that she had been taken out, though she had found the abrupt move a psychological shock and had felt lost at first. When I said that in deciding to remove a young person from a commune one had to consider the alternative life he or she faced, Vicky agreed. For a young person on the streets, living a freaked-out life, the Love Family was a step up, and Vicky observed that some Family members had been in "serious trouble" before joining.

About a third of those who arrive in a given year drift away by themselves, she said; occasionally people are asked to leave, but if they change they can come back. Some have left apparently because of the food. The Family obeys the Old Testament rules, eating "no pork, no rabbit, no shellfish." (This may have changed by 1981, when I was served shrimp while visiting Brian.) They grow vegetables and have chickens and make good wine, though it is served only on special occasions chosen by *Love*. They did not eat just health foods, Vicky stated, but "whatever came in." More importantly, she observed, "There were interesting attitudes about food. There were no formal religious services—like the

Catholic mass or anything like that—but every meal was made to seem important. The act of eating was important. We concentrated on eating and the serving of meals because that was our equivalent of communion. *Love* said that everything we ate is the body and blood of Jesus Christ."

Vicky did not see the Love Family as the evil plotters described by her own family or Ted Patrick and his associates. In her words, "They are really good people, but they're just wrong." Since that was the way they looked to me, too—at least in regard to certain beliefs—I asked her how they were wrong.

"Well, as I see it," she said, "everybody's serving *Love,* but he's serving himself. He's supposed to be serving us. . . . I don't know just *where* he stands. The whole thing is supposed to be serving Jesus Christ. That's what the whole Family's *supposed* to be doing."

"Do you think they're deluding themselves?"

"Well, they just—I don't know—it seems real because it's so peaceful and harmonious. . . . And yet that's not real. Something is lacking. People are talking about serving Jesus Christ, but all they're doing is playing a game. But I did like the elegant life-style. Yet, it was wrong because they think they're better than everybody else."

Finally I asked, "Now that it's all over, how do you feel about it?"

"I feel like I don't have anything to hide about the Family," Vicky said. "It was a hassle, but now it's closed. Now in my mind it's okay to be just like everybody else. I don't have to see myself as a big deal anymore."

The letter we received from *Courage* after he and *Cooperation* returned to Seattle adds the Family's perspective on Vicky's case to hers and her parents'.

Dear Steve and family,

Cooperation and I made it to Seattle at about Saturday mid-afternoon. It sure was nice to get home. Everybody was here and happy. Music was playing by the Family band in the front yard, and the sun was shining.

All my worries had been to no avail. We gave the child up to the girl and her parents, so everything had smoothed out for the Family.

I am so sorry we took off when we did without seeing you first. I hope you understand what was going on in my mind, waiting for a phone call from *Logic.* And it was just as well, because they had decided not to use the phone anymore, and also *Strength* and *Logic* and *Charity* spent a day in jail for not bringing the child to court on Thursday. According to *Strength,* it was all set up in order to get the child from us. All charges on us were dropped upon giving up the baby.

As far as the girl is concerned, we hope this experience makes her stronger. I am not sure what she will do or anything, but I hope she finds her happiness in whatever it may be. Maybe this whole thing is just to show her what her parents are about. Whatever, I see it all good, and we love her a lot. God will not allow his children to be harmed; he only lets them learn lessons through experiences, so we'll finally learn to do what is right. . . .

CHAPTER 12

Yod and the Brotherhood of the Source

December of 1973 brought a letter from Brian that began:

Dear Family,

This time of year brings many thoughts of you all to my mind. They are mostly good, but sometimes I can look back and regret that I wasn't a more loving person and a better friend to each of you. . . .

Last night (after having had some of our parents stay in my house for a few days) I was sitting quietly and sort of meditating on stopping my thoughts for a while and just sending out love to everyone. After a while of letting the thoughts go it seemed so clear to me that, since there is no way to go back in time in order to more fully appreciate the people around me then, all I can do to help is to love the people I see around me now as my true relatives. In other words, with the experiences God has given me (both in what to do and what not to do) I want to love and appreciate the people around me, as parents, brothers, sisters and children, more than ever.

I see that in this love for everyone lies my happiness—and yours. . . .

May of 1974 brought Brian himself. He came down to Los Angeles for his first visit since 1971 and spent a few days with us. The purpose of his visit, he explained, was to see us and also to make official contact with Yod, the leader of a local religious commune called the Brotherhood of the Source. Apparently the Love Family and the Brotherhood were considering a merger. Yod's group had been founded in 1969 with only three followers. Like most adherents of 1970s religious communes—and many born-again conservative Fundamentalists—the group's members believed that the end of the Establishment was imminent, although no one claimed to know how or when the final collapse would take place.

108

They considered, Brian said, that the present inflationary and depressive economic patterns were indicative of the ultimate collapse of our economic system. If money fell apart, they argued, the police, the Army and other protectors of order would not be able to function. Consequently general chaos would result.

They believed, therefore, that the only salvation for mankind was to form a bond that, in time of disaster, would be stronger than nationalism, stronger than a desire for money, stronger than business connections. That bond, they believed, was universal love growing out of a recognition of God's place in the universe.

As it happened, I had known the group's leader—as Jim Baker. But I did not recognize him at first when we met a few days later.

The fact that he was a con man, thief and killer is a matter of record. Unfortunately for clarity of analysis, however, the act of religious conversion, whether actual or alleged, greatly confuses the task of those who would judge the man, since if his spiritual conversion was authentic, none of his past crimes could be held against him. Charles Colson, of Nixon's White House staff, was a moral monster during the period that the Watergate crime and cover-ups were being committed. He had a reputation, even among his associates, as an utterly ruthless individual. But the shock of his public disgrace apparently led to a sincere spiritual reassessment. Eldridge Cleaver, too, was a criminal, and a dangerous one, but I have not seen the legitimacy of his religious conversion subsequently brought into dispute.

Baker was born in Cincinnati in 1922 of parents who were divorced not long after his birth. He was supported during the Depression by his hard-working mother, who acquired experience as a chef, a talent that was in time passed along to her son. After a teenage marriage at nineteen, Baker signed up for a tour of duty with the Marines and saw action in the South Pacific during World War II. His specialty was hand-to-hand combat, a martial art at which he became expert enough to achieve a Marine Corps championship. Later he was sent to Idaho to train other Marine judo instructors.

After the war, having heard that Hollywood was looking for a new actor to play the role of Tarzan, Baker—believing that his physical skill and good looks equipped him for the role—went West. That ambition was not to be realized, but in Los Angeles he met a woman named Elaine who five weeks later became his second wife. Baker, it gradually emerged, never had any interest in conventional work but was always able to support himself by original and creative means. At first he made and sold sandals and belts.

A year later he became involved in a fight with another resident of

Topanga Canyon who, Baker claimed, had attacked him with a knife. The judo champion naturally had no trouble disarming the man, but, not content with that, he broke his alleged assailant's neck with a fatal judo chop. Having been able to convince the police that he acted in self-defense, he was shortly released.

In 1958 Baker and Elaine opened the Aware Inn, thus getting in on the ground floor of the health food, natural-ingredients fad. The restaurant, in the Sunset Strip section of Los Angeles, was an immediate success. A second branch was opened on Ventura Boulevard in the San Fernando Valley. By this time Baker was involved with a third woman, Jean Ingram, a young TV actress. Her jealous husband, however, threatened to kill Baker, something that—according to Baker—he attempted to do the morning of January 29, 1963. Since Baker killed the man instead, the police had only his version of the incident to go on. As in the case of the first killing, the method employed was a judo blow to the neck. This was Baker's second offense, so the district attorney brought him to trial. He was convicted of manslaughter and sentenced to serve 1 to 10 years in prison. After spending several months behind bars, however, he was granted a new trial, at which the charges against him were dismissed.

Later Baker and book publisher Lyle Stuart opened a restaurant and ice cream parlor called "The Old World" across Sunset Boulevard from Tower Records. Several months thereafter, Baker sent a letter to Stuart, who was vacationing in Jamaica, saying, "Congratulate me; we now own a Rolls Royce."

Baker had bought a purple Rolls for himself and a Mercedes for his wife, charging both to the ice cream business. Like his earlier restaurants, the shop was an enormous success. Musician Herb Alpert, film actor Joel McCrea and other celebrities frequented the place.

Baker was heavily into narcotics at the time. He was also stealing large amounts of money from the business. Waiters who wanted to tell Stuart the truth were literally afraid that Baker—already a double killer—would murder them if they informed on him. Stuart insisted on an investigation. His attorney was Norman Olmstead, a former FBI man.

Stuart has told me he reported to the arbitration meeting with a tape recorder in evidence. Almost immediately Baker's attorney asked to talk to Stuart out in the hall and said, "What do you want to agree not to put Baker in jail?"

"The whole business," Stuart said.

Baker agreed to these terms on the spot, but not long thereafter came close to physically assaulting Stuart in the restaurant. Stuart was saved by a tough lesbian who called herself Gus. According to Stuart, Baker had been stealing $300 to $600 a day for a year and a half.

The Love Family's views were generally similar to those of Yod's Brotherhood as regards the Last Days of the World. Presumably this was what had led to the consideration of a blending of the groups. Personally I find it difficult to envision either Baker or Erdman willingly conceding the supreme authority of the other.

When I expressed an interest in Yod's group and Brian's intention to spend time with them, he asked if I'd like to join him there. I at once agreed to visit the Brotherhood's headquarters two days later.

"What time shall I meet you there?" I said.

"About 3:45 in the morning," Brian said. "Their day starts at four."

On the night before my appointment I set the alarm for 2:30 A.M., to give myself plenty of time to breakfast, shower, dress and drive to Yod's house, somewhere in the hills above the Sunset Strip.

When I arrived I could see that the place was already awake and bustling. Brian met me in the dark parking area and ushered me into the large, comfortable house. Everyone present was dressed in a white robe. Mattresses were scattered about. A few people, with sleepy children, seemed to have just awakened. The mood was subdued, but there was the low hum of conversation. I was introduced to several members and, after a few minutes, seated myself against a wall and took out a tape recorder, prepared to record both my own observations and whatever ritual or preaching might take place.

At the opposite end of the large living room a wide window provided a still-dark view of the twinkling lights of the city below. The moon was visible. Cool morning air blew in from the open front door. More candles were lighted. I smelled incense.

After a few minutes, amid a rustle of murmurs, Yod descended the staircase to my left. Although I had known him before, I could not possibly have recognized him, since his appearance had changed completely. The James Baker I had casually known had looked like what he was, a well-to-do Beverly Hills restaurant owner, modishly dressed, with a sort of hip, cool attitude. The figure that now appeared looked like Michelangelo's version of God the Father. Long flowing gray-white hair, a full beard, piercing eyes. I rose. Someone introduced me.

"Oh, Steve and I already know each other," Yod said warmly. "I used to be Jim Baker."

"Oh, how are you, man?" I said. "Good to see you again." He still spoke in the manner of a musician rather than a mystic or prophet. He smiled, almost winked, as if to say, "How about *this* scene?"

He then proceeded through what must be described as a throng of fervent admirers. The young women, particularly, almost swooned as he smiled and touched their hands or shoulders. In a moment he was at the far end of the room, where he seated himself against the majestic panorama of the still-dark sky and the sleeping city below.

The leader then began to speak and continued, to the best of my recollection, for at least an hour. He began slowly, quietly, rather in the manner of Oriental gurus and swamis, one of whom, in fact—a Sikh leader named Yogi Bhajan—had converted him to a sort of vaguely Hindu mysticism. Bhajan is an Indian word meaning "listening to the heavenly music within."

Gradually Baker warmed to his task. His volume increased. His eyes flashed. He was, in various breaths, solemn, wise, amusing, hip, reasonable and—one must report—nutty as a fruitcake, though the man himself was perfectly sane.

Many of his observations, both those which reflected true wisdom and those which would strike the average person as sheer nonsense, were greeted with appreciative "Oh, wows," "Right-ons," murmurs, and strange, soft giggles by the young women kneeling at his feet. The men seemed no less in agreement but not so prone to comment aloud.

That Yod-Baker was a father figure to his young followers was obvious.

There were several cultural streams which flowed into the river in which Yod's followers seemed pleased to immerse themselves:

One source was the Hebrew Scriptures, the Old Testament. A second source was the Christian Scripture, the New Testament. A third was the Hip Culture, which originally grew out of urban middle-class black language and customs of the 1930s, specifically that branch of it connected with the performance of jazz music. A fourth influence was astrology. A fifth was the Oriental-Hindu-Yoga philosophy. A sixth was an amalgam, confusing to the initiate, of ancient Egyptian, Persian and Middle-Eastern pagan belief and mythology.

One of the symbols on the hat Yod wore was the ancient Egyptian *crux ansata,* or key of life, with which the gods could bring the dead to new life.

The seventh stream of Yod's discourse would be what the average American thinks of as the philosophy of Christian Science, Science of Mind, or the Power of Positive Thinking: Very little is impossible. Man can do whatever he sets his mind to. If you think positively and constructively, your actions, health, and personal relations will all be the better for it. An eighth influence was the pseudo-science of numerology.

Those inclined to a reasonable frame of mind tend to react to this sort of material with an almost automatic mixture of contempt and rejection. The irrationality of it is so evident that one is inclined to dismiss it out of hand as almost totally nonsensical.

Fundamentalist Bible-Christians, however, are at something of a disadvantage in arguing against such combinations of symbolism, poetic imagery, prophecy and fantasy because the same factors are found in some Scriptural passages.

Consider, in this context, the following passage:

I turned to see whose voice it was that spoke to me, and when I turned I saw seven standing Lamps of Gold, and among the lamps was one like the Son of Man, robed down to his feet, with a golden girdle round his breast. The hair of his head was white as snow-white wool, and his eyes flamed like fire. His face gleamed like burnished glass refined in a furnace, and his voice was like the sound of rushing waters.

In his right hand he held Seven Stars and out of his mouth came a sharp two-edged Sword; and his face shone like the sun in full strength. . . .

After this I looked, and there before my eyes a door opened in heaven; and the voice that I had first heard speaking to me like a trumpet said, "Come up here, and I will show you what must happen hereafter." At once I was caught up by the Spirit. There in heaven shone a throne, and on the throne sat one whose appearance was like the gleam of jasper and cornelian; and round the throne was a rainbow, bright as an emerald.

This sounds remarkably like Yod's stream-of-consciousness sermons. Its raw material is classically fantastic, the stuff of myth, dreams, even insanity. And yet, as those familiar with the Christian Scriptures will be aware, this portion of the Book of Revelation is accepted as the literal, sacred word of the Almighty God by millions of Baptists, Presbyterians, Methodists, Jehovah's Witnesses, Seventh-Day Adventists and other members of faiths not commonly thought of as fanatical and extreme.

Atheists and agnostics are at least consistent in rejecting all such religious literature. But Christians who accord Revelation the same respect they show the Sermon on the Mount do have a problem in criticizing such material when it emanates from Yod, the Mormon's Joseph Smith, or other founders of modern religions. Again the difficult question: how does one differentiate among various aspects of the nonrational?

At 8:15 in the morning, after the serving of breakfast, casual conversation, the playing of some jazz music and a tour of the premises, I explained that I had to leave.

Yod thanked me for having joined the group.

"Thank *you*," I said. "It was most illuminating."

"Leave it to you," he said, smiling, "to choose the right word."

That Yod was sincere seems beyond question. It is difficult to imagine that if he were still an out-and-out con man ruthlessly victimizing impressionable young followers for financial or material gain, he would go to that much trouble for so slight a personal reward.

The television drama "Can Ellen Be Saved?," a thinly disguised indictment of the Children of God, portrayed two leaders of the sect as consciously evil, not even believing in their own teachings but advancing them hypocritically merely for the purpose of acquiring material holdings.

That such churches or communes do, in fact, acquire property is clear enough. But there would seem to be little attempt on the part of the leaders to appropriate the money, real estate, jewelry, cars or cash as their own. Most do not go to South America with the money. They remain with their followers. To those determined to view clergy of all kinds as conscious hypocrites interested only in material gain, the activities of the leaders of the Love Family, the Children of God and the Jesus Movement generally may seem consistent with the most critical hypothesis. For that matter, such skeptics see all Popes, bishops, priests, ministers and rabbis as hustlers motivated solely or primarily by selfish considerations. But I do not believe this hypothesis is productive in trying to understand either religion generally or the contemporary communal movement. As an historic phenomenon, religion has been characterized by sincerity, the *sine qua non* of both fanaticism and more rational belief. That there have been charlatans within the fold is evident, but such cases are the exception, not the rule.

All of us who loved Brian thought that if the Love Family merged with the Source group he might move to Los Angeles, but not long after he returned to Seattle, Brian wrote to us.

Dear Family,

I am now happily back in Seattle with my Family! As time went on with my stay at the House of Father Yod the chances of our two families overlooking their differences and joining forces became less and less likely.

By the time *Love* and some of our Family arrived down in Los Angeles to meet Father Yod, my mind had a lot of confusion in it. In my hopes for unity I had to accept too many things contrary to our basic understandings.

The contrast of *Love* Israel and Father Yod was much the same as when you met him, and *Love* was a humble yet sure witness of JESUS CHRIST.

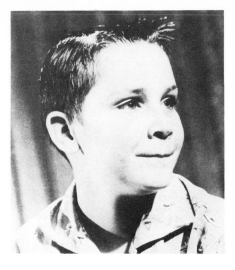

Brian at about age six with
his typical cat's smile.

Steve, Jr. and Brian with me
on the "Tonight Show," 1954.

Brian on my back and David
at our house in Amityville,
Long Island in 1954.

Jayne and Brian in Rome,
1958.

Steve, Jr., Brian, Jayne and I
on a boat trip.

Logic Israel, a member of the Love Family, 1975.

acing page): Brian at twenty-two with me at a
nference at the Center for the Study of
emocratic Institutions in Santa Barbara in 1969.

Logic, Honesty, Love Israel and I at the Seattle Center dinner, May 1981.

Safety Training and Research Association of Washington

Liberty, Logic, Purity, and Brian's wife, *Simplicity,* September 1981.

For me the whole experience was a good and strengthening one. It was the first time I have ventured out and away from the mind of the Love Family. The result was that I saw just how totally precious my relationships to the members of this Family are, especially to *Love* Israel.

I felt the pains of separation from the people I love. It gave me more understanding of the position of our parents. I am glad to have gotten the chance to see you and Jayne and Bill and David and Robin, and most of all Mom.

Love felt all the same things while I was away and decided that *from now on, when someone wants to join the Family, they should first of all go back and see their parents to explain themselves and to express their love to them before returning to join the Family of Jesus Christ.* [Italics added.]

I am glad to be back helping to build a simple family, based on the Bible, one that includes the most people.

I see the most that I can do for unity is to be one more of God's gathered sheep. I am grateful for the gift of representing *Logic* to these people. This experience reminded me of the importance of giving real meaning to the name of JESUS CHRIST.

I love you all. Please come see us whenever you can.

—Your *Logic*

The italicized portion of the letter was important to all of us, since it related to a significant change in the Love Family's rules and regulations. I have the feeling that if the various Family members who have been kidnapped and deprogrammed—whether successfully or not—had, early in their commune experience, returned to their own families and had as rational a discussion with their loved ones as possible about their decision, rather than suddenly sending a bolt-from-the-blue letter followed by a long period of silence, relations between the Love Family group and interested parents would have been considerably more serene during the past decade.

Yod did not live much longer. Later that year—1974—after he sold the group's restaurant, The Source, on Sunset Boulevard, his entire commune moved to Hawaii because they had become convinced that the end of civilization was fast approaching and that the American mainland was going to be destroyed. Some family members took up the sport of hang-gliding. One of them—he called himself Mercury Aquarius—set a new world's record by remaining aloft for thirteen hours, after launching into the brisk sea breeze off Koolau Ridge near Waimanalo.

A few weeks later, Jim Baker—who had changed his name again, this time to Yahowha—decided to try the sport himself. The date was August 24, 1975. He chose a challenging location. No novice should have launched from so high a point. Ten minutes later the man his followers thought was God crashed into a group of campers in a nearby parking lot. His back was broken, but neither he nor his adherents believed in medical science. After nine painful hours he died.

His religion no longer exists.

CHAPTER 13

Letters from Parents

Young people who join a group like the Love Family obviously plunge their parents (and brothers, sisters, aunts, uncles, friends) into a major experience, as the Sinunus' story, the Cramptons' and mine all testify. There is evidence of this in the letters that parents exchange, offering or requesting information or just describing their feelings. One example of such a letter came from a Chicago attorney in July 1974, while Jayne and I were touring in a production of Noel Coward's *Tonight at 8:30*.

Dear Mr. Allen:

Your son and my two sons are members of the "Love Israel Family" in Seattle. My sons have been in there for a year, and for me that makes our family score 100%. I'm sure it will please you to hear that on a recent visit through Chicago with the head of the clan and 25 members of their "band" my younger son, whose name within the group is *"Resolve,"* told me that your son is his closest friend in the group and the person he most admires in the Family.

My boy is, or was, a highly intelligent kid and unusually sensitive and perceptive, and I think it's a very high compliment. I was in Seattle last month but didn't know your boy was in the group, and I don't believe I met him, but I'm sure he's all that my son says he is.

My boys also told me that you are a frequent visitor there and that you speak to the other members and, they told me, quiz them seriously and they feel you're a "great guy," which doesn't surprise me.

It's none of my business and I have no idea as to the road your son traveled before he went into the group. For all I know, from your point of view, this stop may be a step up for him. My sons are typical members of the student revolt of the 60s against Vietnam and the Establishment, and they were obviously searching for something they could believe in, and they seem to have found it, at least temporarily, in this group. They were never on hard drugs and supported themselves for most of the time.

I went out there with my wife and we expected to spend considerable time in the Northwest and make a vacation out of it, but after two 12-hour days of unceasing powerhouse attempts to "convert" us, we checked out of the hotel and came home.

You may have met or seen *"Resolve."* He's a tall, slender boy of 20, and is usually playing the piano or working on music with or for the group musicians. I know something about music, having studied it seriously and played for 62 years—although I've never achieved your skill in improvisation on popular tunes, which I much admire. *"Resolve,"* in my opinion, is the most genuinely gifted young musician I've known in my lifetime. In addition to piano, he had training from Chicago's greatest teacher of musical theory and composition, and he sounded very good to me on his last visit. The older boy is *"Solidity."* He, too, likes to think of himself as a musician and plays the bass fiddle.

The reason I am writing you is that it is difficult for me to believe that this is a permanent resting place for my sons, and yet I understand your boy has been there for some time, and I met two other very fine boys who have been in for three years each. I have to hope that mine will find their way out of it. As parents, my wife and I are naturally concerned. Outwardly, they seem "happy," but then I think most of us think of cows as happy, too, so that doesn't impress me very much.

They do no good whatever—they really do nothing except sit around vacantly or get together occasionally and "make music" as they call it, which generally consists of playing their doggerel hymns. . . . I would appreciate hearing from you as to your own opinion of the group, of their leader—who, as you may know, is a former salesman named Erdman. . . . I have met him several times and he has all the surface glibness and charm of the typical con man—a type well known to lawyers. And entertainers too, I suspect. . . . If you ever have a chance I would be very grateful if you would write me a note, and on your next visit to Seattle you might take a look at my kids and let me hear from you.

> Very truly yours,
> S. J. Sherman

In reply I wrote,

. . . I've received several letters and personal inquiries in recent years from parents of young people in the Love Family in Seattle; the letters are all much the same. They are, I suppose, the same sort I might write to anyone I thought might be able to provide me with more detailed information about the Seattle commune.

My son Brian—who has taken the name of *Logic*—has been up there now for about three years. It wouldn't be correct to say that I am a "frequent" visitor to the place since I've only been there once, about a year and a half ago. Brian came down to Los Angeles a couple of months ago and I was able to spend some time with him, chiefly at a similar commune in Los Angeles.

Brian thought for a time he might move in with that group—and we were selfishly hoping he would—but he changed his mind and went back to Seattle.

I've given the Love Family a great deal of study—and more thought—since Brian joined it. The answer you and I and the other parents involved are looking for is still elusive. I find that I sometimes think through a problem best if I do some writing about it, and when my schedule permits I may get to work on a book on this subject. It's a national phenomenon, as you know, and one that seems particularly puzzling to me. As a Christian of sorts myself, I naturally take no basic exception to my son's affiliation with a Christian group, although the Love Family's approach to religion is so very far from my own that like yourself I hope that someday my son will move through and past this particular experience.

Brian was never on drugs, although like many young people he has no doubt done some experimenting with them. You're probably familiar with the tragedy of the two Family members who died a couple of years ago after inhaling chemical fumes in some sort of religious rite.

I'll instruct my secretaries to enclose with this letter some odds-and-ends of relevant literature. But even after one has studied it all, the essential question "why" remains.

Brian, who is my second son, of four, has always had a sweet, saintly disposition. . . .

I have heard earlier reports about Erdman's past and it could certainly be more savory. It is difficult to know now, of course, whether his religious conversion is sincere or merely opportunistic. To me he seems a genuinely sincere religious fanatic, although that may be small comfort. Fanaticism, in fact, seems to me an essential ingredient of religious expression of this particular sort.

I have the same hope you do, that Brian will not spend the rest of his life with the Family, but I doubt if there is anything that either of us can do to change the situation at present.

I have to run for the plane now. I am quite aware this letter isn't an adequate answer or commentary on all of your questions but it's the best I can do at the moment. Perhaps some of the enclosures will prove helpful.

I can't honestly recall whether I've met *Resolve* and *Solidity*. I've met a great many of the young men in the group, of course, so there's a good chance that I have had the pleasure of meeting your sons. The next time I meet them, of course, the names will mean something to me and I'll be glad to ask them questions, the answers to which I will pass along to you.

Thank you for sharing your thoughts on the subject with me.

As of 1981 Sherman's sons were still members of the Love Family.

The reader will note that as of 1974 all of us were still hoping that Brian would choose some form of religious expression other than that limited to the Love Family. I responded, at the time, to occasional questions from journalists that I could think of a great many alternative possibilities for Brian that were superior to life in the Love Family but that we could also think of a perhaps even longer list of social alternatives that were far less desirable. Perhaps no other area of human activity has led to so much confusion and misunderstanding as religion, which, despite its benefits, has, through the centuries, separated individuals, families and—indeed—entire nations.

A not untypical letter came from Tennessee in May of 1975 from Nola and Tom McKnight, parents of *Helpful* Israel, whose original name was Lee McKnight. He was Kathy Crampton's husband. Note that the young man had a college education, a church background, was familiar with boating, scouting, sports—in other words, he was just the kind of young person who would seem to be a winner, a superior, likable young man. But Mrs. McKnight's letter tells its own story.

Dear Henrietta, Curt, Abe, Betty, Steve Allen and all parents of children in the Love Family:

Two and one half years ago our son Lee (*Helpful* Israel) came back from one and one-half years in Europe, India and Indonesian Island. Then he left, with his former scoutmaster, for Alaska. In Colorado he met the Love Family. Since then our lives have been changed. . . .

When our son Lee (*Helpful*) joined the Love Family and came home to tell us I really thought I was going to die, so each of us know the hell we all went through when our child or children joined this group. For two years I cried and drank and prayed. One and one-half years ago I visited my son and his group. I was in such an emotional state at the time I relied on a minister's help (this is a friend of my oldest son that lives in Washington, D.C.) who advised me to keep "my cool," to establish once again some relationship with my son that I worshipped and adored. I look back and thank God that I only blew my top at "*Love*" once. I was fortunate that I was able to get out without breaking his neck and destroying my thin line of relationship with my son.

Of course our greatest concern was that our child was being continuously drugged and if he were we wanted to try and save him. If he is being drugged now I feel it has been so long that there is no hope for his recovery.

Last October my mother was very ill and she dreamed that she had died but would not let anyone bury her until Lee, her grandson, came home. We wrote Lee and were so surprised that in two days we had a phone call from him and we sent him two tickets to Memphis, via air. We did not know who was coming with him. We were notified that he would be in the next day. Our joy was unbelievable.

Naturally we arrived at the airport early and were overjoyed when he stepped off the plane, and then our joy was doubled when Kathy Crampton (*Dedication*) was with him. They spent one week with us. Lee visited the family, old friends and 90% of the time was just like our son. Kathy was a vivacious, happy and brilliant young woman full of warmth and love. We loved being with them. Since our sons had not seen each other in two years and Lee had not seen his brother's 10-month-old son, we had them fly in from D.C. The reunion of the two was not as the two had always been. Randy, our oldest, was ready to accept Lee's way of life and to respect his life but was rather hurt and disappointed that his brother did not reciprocate this feeling. Our boys had always loved each other and it hurts to see this rift.

Since Lee and Kathy were here I have been more at peace than I have been in two years. Each person must accept his own way of life. I would love to have Lee here but he is a grown man and not a teenager. He has a college education, was raised in the church two or three times a week and with his father boating, scouting, sports, family, school and church continuously. He started writing and seeking religion in the fifth grade and after all his travels, education, scouting (serving as scoutmaster during college), sports, a $14,000-a-year job—gotten on his own—he has chosen the Love Family and I cannot change it.

I am committed to taking care of my mother and helping my sisters and brothers-in-law. I have no energy nor time anymore to fight

causes and to be a crusader. I did this for years in PTA—civic—politics—etc.; now I am tired and have too many responsibilities. I just
pray that each of you will find peace with your children and I know
the heartache and pain that each of you has felt. I pray that each of
you will be successful in your endeavor with your acute problems.

I want all of you to know that if I could get Lee out of the Love
Family and he would be a happy, whole person I would do anything
to accomplish this. But in our case I believe our son would be
destroyed completely if we took him out. We are not saying nor
believe that this is true of all the wonderful children that are there.
Each of you know your own child better than anyone and we all must
do what we think is best.

I want you all to know, as one individual, I do not agree with all the
actions and ideas and beliefs of my own church or family, just as I do
not agree with many of the beliefs and things that *Love* (I don't know
his name, but I don't believe it's "Love") does, but I do believe that I
must let my son know I love and respect him and that the front door is
always open to him. But he must choose. . . .

To Henrietta and Curt, we had a note today from Kathy and she
spoke of the love for you all. It was a sweet note. We have had two
letters from Lee, and his letters to his Grandmother since my
brother's death are so beautiful I had copies made to send to my
sisters and close friends. Kathy is such a beautiful, loving and
brilliant girl and we love her as our own daughter. No matter what
happens in the future we will always love her.

To Steve Allen: I met your son and liked him very much; however,
at the time I met him I was, as I said before, in such a state that I
cannot say that I remember much except I wondered if *Purity* was his
daughter. As you know at that time they did not let you know the
parent of any of the children.

God be with all of you and your family.

Nola and Tom McKnight

Some time later Mrs. McKnight wrote to me again. By now she was
more resigned to the reality of her son's life.

I just returned from a visit to see my son, Lee McKnight (*Helpful*
Israel). My sister and I spent a week with the Family.

One morning we visited with *Love* and his household. All the men
were working in the yard and greenhouse and there we met your son.
He was working with some of the plants from Hawaii. He looked and
sounded healthy and happy and asked that I write to you. I also saw
your beautiful grandchildren.

My son and his wife, Kathy Crampton (*Dedication*), went with us for a two-day trip to Victoria. It was really great to be with my son on a nice trip and he really enjoyed eating steaks, having a nice motel room to be with his wife. He enjoyed driving a car and just doing all the things he did at home.

There is a more relaxed attitude now than when I was there before. They (the *men* in the Family) are working on their freighter so they can go salmon fishing this fall. They were flying some of the group to Alaska in their plane. A few of them had just returned from the place they have in Hawaii.

I still do not like so many of the things they do, but that is their choice and I do not want to sever any relationship with my son due to these differences; instead I hope to make our relationship stronger by seeing him as often as possible. I do not like the poor manner in which the women are dressed, and they are subservient to the men, nor do I like everyone being able to discipline the children. It was all done in a loving manner but I don't like it. However, I feel about many of the things they do it is not my place to dictate to my son or anyone else.

When you write or see *Logic* give him my regards and I hope to see more of him on my next visit.

I visited and became friends with a Mrs. Taylor (80 years old) that lives next-door to *Helpful* and it is nice to have contact with someone there that sees and can let me know if anything happens. She is a very alert lady. I also made friends with the young couple across the street. They visit back and forth with many of the people in the Love Family. Lee (*Helpful*) had an infected eye when I was there and it was nice to be able to call Beth and Darrell Grieser and find out about his eye. They even got Lee to call me and tell me his eye was better.

I know this is a wandering letter but I just wanted you and other parents to know about their children and that I intend to do all I can to keep a good relationship with my son.

I also received letters from parents responding to stories in the press about my views of the Love Family. My public life had affected Brian when he was growing up; now it was definitely an aspect of his—and my—experience with the group. The fact that a television comedian was the father of one of the Love Family members was regularly noted by the media; I and other Allens were interviewed frequently. (Brian wrote, "I'm sorry your name gets dragged in for extra sensation.") I was aware, of course, that I got special treatment during my visits to the Love

Family—though all parents are warmly welcomed; that *Cooperation* and *Courage*'s visit with us had been a special experience for them; that the Family hoped I could be of help. Many parents, by the same token, hoped I could be of help to the parental position.

In April of 1975, for instance, I visited Brian in Seattle. He had written in late March, "Dear Dad, I am writing to ask you if you will please come for a visit. I feel like I need to talk to you." As I immediately wrote back to him, I had received his letter the day I had had a dream about him, after which I woke up with tears in my eyes. It seemed he was a small child again. Unfortunately I couldn't remember the details of the dream, but I had awakened with a combined feeling of sadness and strong love for Brian, and with the desire to see him. A month after his letter we spent a few days together.

One of the emotional high points of my visit, by the way, came with the birth of a baby in one of the nearby houses. I was invited to be present to celebrate the event. The little fellow was carried to me a moment after he entered the world and, to my surprise, placed in my arms, wrapped in a little cloth.

"We hope you'll give him your blessing," one of the Family members said.

I smiled down at the child, who seemed quite comfortable. "The implication of being asked to bless this child," I said, "is that I am morally superior to him and have some power that he does not have. But that is not the case. At this moment he is all innocence. If he could speak, it would be more fitting if he gave me his blessing. In any event I hope God will be good to us both, and to all of you."

The little visitor was then bathed in a tub of lukewarm water, still smiling. He was later named *Action*.

During that visit I was interviewed. A press story based on the interview distributed by the Associated Press distorted the truth in some respects, as short reports on complex issues invariably do. The lead paragraph was, "Comedian Steve Allen says it is fine by him that his son and grandchildren are living on a religious commune here." Later in the story, the point was to a degree clarified, but because very little of what I had actually said to the reporter was included, the quotation still represented an unsatisfactory rendering of my views. I had said that although I would prefer a different sort of religious environment for my son, if in fact the communal existence was reasonable and productive for him, then "it was fine by me." The word "fine" was unwisely chosen; I simply meant that if Brian was leading a happy and productive life I would accept his decision. "The one important question about such social experiments," I added, "concerns the ultimate fate of the children. The happiness and healthiness of the children is ultimately one of society's measuring mechanisms."

It is tragically clear that in modern society a high percentage of young people end up with psychological problems. So, as I have suggested in many interviews, it would be interesting to compare that unhappy reality with the results of an upbringing within the Love Family.

When the Associated Press reporter asked for my comments on *Love* Israel's view that women were put on earth to serve men, I said, "If they passed a law saying that every woman had to do this, it would be deplorable. On the other hand, if they passed a law saying that women could never wash another dish, that, too, would be deplorable. But since, obviously, there is no force used to keep women in this commune, they must therefore be acting on the basis of their personal decision. These people here, for better or worse, are living something twenty-four hours a day, in distinction from some other religions which usually practice their beliefs about forty-five minutes on Sundays."

Another news story, in the Washington, D.C. *Star News,* obviously a rewrite of the information given in the Associated Press account, said, "Displaying the good-humored attitude that endeared him to an older generation of television watchers, comedian Steve Allen said it doesn't bother him at all that his son and grandchildren are living in a religious commune near Seattle." It is, of course, hardly accurate to say that Brian's decision didn't bother me at all. It bothered all of us who love Brian. But since it was his choice, we had to adjust to it, and over the course of time we did gradually, continuing to love him and keeping in contact with him all the while.

The publication of the various stories led to my receiving additional letters from other parents of cult members. Some were understanding. Some, like the following, expressed the parent's own anger and sense of loss, emotions I quite understood.

Dear Mr. Allen,

Is the Israel cult paying you to voice your approval of them or are you unknowledgeable of what the group is? I cannot understand anyone approving of Love Israel or any of the other destructive mind-control cults unless he either is a member (under mind control) or they are paying him to voice his approval.

How can you say the group is productive? How can you stand by and watch your grandchild destroyed?

A person who is nationally known as you are could be most helpful in exposing and destroying the cults.

Won't you please reconsider your statements in regard to the cult?

Elizabeth M. Painter

Others, also concerned parents, were understanding.

My dear Mr. Allen:

Your son *"Logic"* of Seattle's Love Family had newspaper coverage recently, with a very good likeness of himself, in the *Post Intelligencer.* We have come to know *Logic* personally, as our daughter is also a member of this commune. The paper stated your position as regards to your son being a member of the "Family." We agree with your views, as stated.

This does not necessarily mean that we endorse many of the tenets of this group. It is that we believe that at maturity, an individual should be free to make decisions as to life-styles or whatever, and to be protected from violent seizure and forcible detention by anybody, even by or for concerned parents.

It is our feeling that after we have had a chance to shape the lives and personalities of our children, we must grant them the right to make their own decisions at some certain age, 18, or 21, or 30, or 40, or 50, or at *some* time. If they make wrong decisions, in our opinion, after maturity, we might cry a little, pray a lot, but wish them well, and assure them of our continued love and support, no matter what.

We were urged to write you in censure: "If people take Mr. Allen's view on cults, our whole cause will seem in vain." In our case, this exhortation has inspired the above response. We applaud your decision, and your point of view, sir!!!!!

> Very sincerely,
> Bodil W. Campbell
> Kenneth M. Campbell

The range of feeling extends further. In 1980, *Simplicity*'s mother, Jackie Junso, whom we consider Brian's mother-in-law, wrote to us enclosing snapshots of Brian, *Simplicity* and their children, *Liberty* and *Purity,* and said, "I live in Renton, south of Seattle, so get up to visit quite often. I enjoy each and every one of the Love Family, especially the children." In another letter she noted, "I sometimes feel like I'm on a 'one-woman crusade.' Seems like family and friends pick up on the negative reports about the Family. It's like fighting City Hall. Personally, I'll stand beside the Family on any issue that comes up."

CHAPTER 14

The Case of Larry Israel

In 1978 a young man came to my offices in Van Nuys, California. When my secretary reported that a former member of the Love Family was in the outer office I welcomed him immediately. His name was Larry Israel (his parents' name happened to be Israel). Later I invited him to visit again, in my home. He explained that he had spent four years with the Love Family, under the name *Consideration*. His story is particularly moving because he seemed by nature to be a seeker, an uncommon type in our materialistic society, and also because his extreme impressionability made him especially vulnerable to both the blandishments of the Love Family and later, the professional deprogrammers.

It became clear, as Larry told me his story, that he had suffered more than any other member of Brian's religious commune. Kathy Crampton was deprogrammed but remained loyal to the Love Family. Vicky Sinunu was deprogrammed and returned to the world. The case of Larry Israel was different. The experience of deprogramming itself was a stronger shock than his emotional and nervous system could withstand. He seemed eager to share this information with me, to have someone fair-minded about the larger issue sit in judgment on his case, as it were. He spoke quickly, somewhat nervously, his swarthy features knotted in intense concentration as he related the details of his remarkable spiritual adventures.

Larry had been Bar Mitzvahed and gone through the Jewish religious experience in a formal, social sense, but it had had no emotional meaning for him.

Larry explained that among his early religious experiences in 1970 was the sense that life must be eternal, that God wouldn't have created us just to live seventy years or so and then end our lives, as animals do. That insight led him into Far Eastern religion and had given him a new feeling of joy of living chiefly because of the conviction that life had, after all, a purpose.

He told me he was open to the message of Christ, showed me photographs taken in the Love Family, permitted me to tape-record our conversations and gave me letters he had written.

Larry: I was really searching. I was really into Eastern religion. I can't describe how *desperate* I was to find the truth. And okay, I met this girl named Fel. Have you ever met *Bliss?*

I became friends with her. She was the first girl that ever really became a girl friend with me and who really accepted me, and we were kind of on the search together. She was a nurse, and you remember how I came to say that love was the answer? I realized that, but I thought, "How do you live it in this world, where nobody knows their next-door neighbor?"

So I began to think of communal living because that was starting then in many parts of the country. I went out to New Mexico a couple of times and visited this commune called *Morning Star* and had a few religious experiences while I was there. Just going out West from the East into the open spaces was an experience in itself.

But for some reason, we weren't satisfied with it [the commune]. So we went north to Denver, Colorado, and went in a little church to stay for the night. I think it's called St. Andrews Church. I remember sitting next to a guy with long hair and a beard and didn't think much of it, but we did some dishes afterwards and . . . he began to talk about this place up North where he lived. His name was *Man.*

I don't remember if he said *Man* Israel or not. The woman's name he was with was *Woman.* Israel was already my name, but I don't think he told me his last name then. I was really attracted by him, by the peace he seemed to have. He was telling us about this place up in Seattle, and he carried around this little New Testament. He would always open it, and he was traveling on faith. No car . . . The more I talked to him, the more I was interested. So I kept talking to him. I don't remember him preaching to me, but I had come to the point of believing that all the religions seemed right, because they all talked about God and love and that's where it's at. . . . He may have said something to me about Jesus, but I went off by myself and reasoned with my own mind. I said, "Was Jesus a great man?" Now, remember, I was brought up Jewish, so I didn't really know anything about it.

S.A.: Had Christians ever treated you badly?

Larry: No, I didn't really have that. When I was a little kid the other kids used to pick on me a little bit, but I don't know if that was because I was Jewish and lived in an Italian neighborhood. . . .

Anyway, that didn't matter to me . . . It was just right to love everybody, so I said, "Was Jesus a great man?" and I answered, "Yes," and I said to myself, "Would a great man lie?" And I thought, "Well, would Abe Lincoln lie?" and I said, "No," and I said, "What was one thing Jesus said?" And I thought, "Well, He said I am the way, the truth and the life. No man comes to the Father but by Me."

So I thought, "Well, he must be telling the truth, because he wouldn't lie. So he's the Way."

At that moment I believed that He was the Way, and that God Himself had led me to these people. It all seemed to fit together and I thought, "I'm going where they're going." . . . I almost went right from there, right from Denver. . . . I went back home and worked for a couple of months, and a friend—who I had lived with in Columbus, Ohio—was also into the Moody Blues experience and a lot of stuff I was—had gone out to Seattle, as I'd told him about it.

He came back and told me how great it was. He didn't tell me why he didn't stay, but he told me how great it was, so that encouraged me even more.

My mom begged me not to go. I felt like I was going to go there for a long time, maybe forever.

I was twenty-one. I guess I kind of felt like *Bliss* or Fel would come out there eventually, but it didn't matter. I was going to have to give her up because I wanted to serve God. It wasn't like I was going there just to find a place to live. It was like I was really being led there by the Lord, although I didn't know much about the Lord, what He was or anything like that.

I got a ride all the way from Des Moines, Iowa. Right after that I opened the Bible, and it said whatever you pray for, if you believe, you're going to receive. I don't remember praying for a ride but obviously it was on my mind, and right away I got a ride.

So I got there and went up to Queen Anne Hill and there was the blue house on Armour Street and it was real peaceful.

Summertime, May, and it was like walking into another world. It didn't seem like a bunch of hippies living together. It had an organized purpose, like *class*. . . . It wasn't cluttered, like most people's houses, with a lot of furniture and stuff, but real simple.

I can't really describe to you how much it meant to me, because I had been so, so unhappy in my life. The loneliness and the despair and all that, and now the searching and waking up and having a realization that God was real. This really meant something to me. . . . They began to show me the charter, and I really felt accepted

and loved. I knew this was different than the communes I'd been in.
. . . People were trying to live together and make it and love one
another and the world, because they felt that was right. . . . I don't
know if they thought much about it, but I think the fact that my name
was Israel made them believe what they were doing was the right
thing, like a confirmation. So here's a Jewish guy with the name of
Israel and *our* name is Israel, so this is just, wow.

And then they pointed out the Scriptures from the Old
Testament and the New Testament saying how God was going to
gather His people in the last days.

This was amazing to me because I had never known anything
about the Bible. I knew about Passover and Chanukah and that type
of thing, but how what was happening on these last days on earth was
related to the Bible, I had no idea.

In Isaiah, if you've read the chapter, it talks about how God is
going to gather His people together and Jesus would say things like
there's going to be one fold and one shepherd. So I got baptized the
next day, which was unusual. They don't do that anymore; usually
they wait until a person really commits. But I *was* committed; I knew
I was going to give my life there, and I'm sure they could see that.

I came there with contact lenses and the day I was baptized, or
the day before, I broke them—on purpose—because I felt that was
like having faith in God. In other words, having the glasses was a *lack*
of faith; God would heal my eyes. I did that willingly.

As I began to live there, day by day, the acceptance and
life-style—it all seemed to be right on. I seemed to be more
convinced as time went on that this was the place.

I took the name *Man* Israel because I was just a man of Israel.
Now they have Hebrew names, as you know. That's because they
finally got to have so many *Mans* they didn't know how to distinguish
them. They were calling them *Dark Man* and *Blond Man* and *Tall
Man* and *Music Man*.

. . . Sometimes *Love* would pick a Hebrew name and
sometimes people would be given a choice. As time went on, and it
was obvious that you were solidly into it, who you were came to be
recognizable to *Love*. He would *see* who you were, that virtue of
Jesus Christ you represented, and then he would give you that name.
So I got the name *Consideration* six weeks after I was there. I
remember the day I got the name. I was working in the front yard.
We were fixing up *Love's* area, where he lives now. I remember just
thinking inside how I had really made a commitment and I was going
to be there, no matter what, and I remember coming to a firm stand;

I don't remember what led up to it. And then this guy named *Happiness* came on a bicycle and said *Love* wanted to see me. I was pretty nervous, I didn't know why. So he tells me to go in the back and he gives me a robe and I go in there. *Serious* was there, and a girl named *Unity*. I don't remember the exact sequence of events, but he said something like, "Do you know who you are?" Or he just called my name, and he anointed me with oil. I don't remember the sequence, but he called me *Consideration*. I guess I felt some disappointment, because *Courage* and *Honesty* and *Strength* had names with real meaning to them, and *Consideration* seemed not to mean much at the time.

I went into a sanctuary. It was like a really holy thing that was happening. Then he had us all sit down, and at the time we were breathing toluene. I didn't really know what it all meant. I just thought of it as a sacrament. I didn't know anything about it. I hadn't done it before, and they didn't call it toluene. They call it "tell-you-all." . . . Well, we sat down and someone brought in some plastic bags and a bottle. *Love* poured a little in each one. I guess I was a little nervous. I didn't know what was happening, but since *Love* was doing it, I thought I should do it.

. . . He might have said nothing can hurt us, you know? I know there's a scripture in the Bible that says you shall drink any deadly thing, nothing will hurt you.

So he starts taking these deep breaths. I was kind of reluctant. I would just take little sniffs, and I started getting into it a little bit. It's not like other drugs. It puts you in sort of a—totally indescribable—weird, a type of high. But taking it in the context of a religious experience—it *is* a religious experience. It's really hard to describe, Steve, because it wasn't like marijuana, nothing like LSD. All these strange things would happen while we were doing it. It was different every time. . . .

S.A.: Under opium you lie down and go to sleep. Toluene is not like that?

Larry: No. You just continue to talk.

S.A.: Marijuana sometimes makes people laugh. Does toluene do that?

Larry: No. LSD in the early stages makes you feel strong emotion or makes you laugh. Later there may be other themes you get into.

S.A.: Was there anything like that with toluene?

Larry: It's difficult to remember. I didn't consider it a drug; I considered it a sacrament. Before I knew it someone gave me some kind of a pill, and everything happens different.

S.A.: How long had you been in the place at that point?

Larry: Six weeks.

S.A.: Were the sessions always under control, organized, or would they encourage you to go out and try it alone?

Larry: No, no. An elder would always have to invite you. But at that time when I did it, *Love* was the only one who was in charge.

S.A.: Would it happen once a week, or month, or whenever the mood struck him?

Larry: It changed as time went on, but I think he was getting into it pretty often. I didn't see it as wrong. I didn't doubt anything they were doing. But just to go on with this experience, that day . . . they gave me this pill, and *Love* told me because I was Jewish I was going to be a Jewish scholar . . . and I had to learn the whole New Testament.

S.A.: What had you studied in Ohio?

Larry: The second year of college I took up accounting, only because I was good at math. I didn't like it. I was into sociology and psychology and those kinds of subjects. Always interested in philosophy. . . . Anyway, so *Love* asked me to be the Jewish scholar. I was pretty fascinated. He gave me a big Bible, and I just started reading it. He said something like, "Go find a rabbi." It wasn't like he thought it out, he just said, "Go find a rabbi." I remember going across the street and telling some people what *Love* had said. *Imagination* said, "Well, *Love* said that, and you've committed yourself, and he speaks the word of God, so you've got to be obedient to him."

That night I walked off the hill, not knowing when I was going to come back, maybe ten years, twenty years or whatever, just knowing that since I was committed, I had to obey him. And walking off the hill I felt—you know when you make a commitment about something you believe in, you feel good about yourself? So I walked off the hill and walked all night.

The next morning I went to a rabbi, and he told me he wasn't interested. I told him I believed in Jesus, and it didn't make a big hit.

I thought, well, should I go to Israel? What should I do? I remember being at the bottom of the hill. I was on Capitol Hill where I had gone to the synagogue, and I looked back up at the hill and I just felt led to go back up there. I didn't expect what would happen. I'd expected I would be gone for a long, long time. But I wound up going back to *Love's* house. He came down the stairs and looked at me, and that was one of the few times I felt the love of God was looking at me through his eyes. I felt welcomed back and happy to be back. That experience was what happened the day I got my name.

I had several unique experiences there. Like one time they sent me across the country to see Billy Graham.

S.A.: Billy Graham?

Larry: Yes. I heard he was in Africa, so we were headed over to Africa.

S.A.: You and who else?

Larry: *Ruell* and a woman named *Adiel.* In the middle of Texas Adiel would not submit to us—I don't mean sexually—so we asked her to leave. So in the middle of Texas she got out of the car by herself. It was something I began to sense in her attitude, because a woman is supposed to submit to a man. We gave her a few chances, but I came to the conclusion that the right thing to do was to ask her to leave. Not that we hated her or anything; it just seemed like we should do that because we had to be one. That's another thing *Love* used to say, "Who has seen that we're all one here?" Obviously if someone would not submit, there goes our oneness.

So we heard that Billy Graham's home was in North Carolina. We went through the North, Ohio or those states, I don't remember now.

When the Family would send you out sometimes it was because they felt you had it in you, and sometimes it would be to go and see the Family from a different point of view, so when you came back you'd be stronger.

There were a lot of people that were there who had different kinds of problems. I had certain kinds of problems dealing with—well, for myself, I was *striving* a lot. I had a lot of guilt about food, about moderation. It was really stressed there, all the time. We only had two meals a day. And we were trying so hard to do it right, so hard to please God. For me, the type of personality I was, there was something underlying in that. I had never been accepted in life before, and now here I was accepted and living for God.

But in the Family we had to do everything right. We tried to be perfect, but since we're human beings I couldn't be perfect. I was always judging myself, thinking I wasn't loving enough. A lot of people had problems with food there, because moderation was so encouraged. For four years I never went into the refrigerator except to get some iced tea. We would judge one another at the table. Like if someone thought someone took a roll too much, someone would say, "I don't think that person should have taken that roll," and they'd ask the elder, and the elder would make a comment.

Some of the women had great problems, especially the heavy ones. They had to be thin. *Love* liked the women thin.

S.A.: Did they all lose weight?

Larry: A couple didn't. They would sneak food sometimes and then be guilty. Plus most people in the Family had to fast seven days, usually in the beginning when they were first getting involved. It was kind of a sign; no one actually told people to do it, but like a sign of commitment. The first three days would be like one cup of liquid. I heard *Encouragement* did a fast for twenty-one days straight with one cup of apple juice. Usually it was juice.

I always felt like I should be fasting, and always felt I wasn't doing enough for God while I was there, and it really carried out in the food area.

How much do you think I weigh now? I weigh about 143 pounds now. When I got home from the Family I weighed 126, and I didn't know.

S.A.: Your parents must have been shocked to see you.

Larry: Yeah. I'm 5'7-½". They were shocked. They were sending me out to see Billy Graham, to make a contact with him. I didn't know about him other than that he was some famous Christian. Everyone told us there was no way, but we went on the road. We had faith that God was going to lead us there. We were headed toward Africa. First toward his home, and if he wasn't there, we were going to wherever he was. Just on faith. And we got to his house.

I remember we met a minister. We were wearing our robes and we knew we were going to see him that day. It was like a little miracle that was happening. Two of us—the woman had split. We talked to Billy Graham's wife and the minister for about twenty minutes. There was tension there because we were talking about marriage, and our marriage does not agree with the wordly marriage. Naturally we thought we had the way, the *only* way. Every other group was wrong. All of God's people would eventually come to the Family. Worldly marriage is null and void because Jesus said that the children of the Resurrection neither marry nor are given in marriage but are as the angels of God in heaven.

They interpreted that to mean they were the children of the Resurrection; thus, any worldly type marriage, if you were to come in with a husband and wife of twenty years, it would be dissolved. Then *Love*, who spoke the word of God, you know—how people get together and everything?

People gave up everything, all their wants and desires. There were stages. There was one point where they gave up sex totally, until the marriage supper of the lamb, which is a chapter described in the Revelation. And *Love* always had the power because he spoke the word of God. So when he could see that people kind of liked each other, he could put them together, or he could make them go apart. He had the final decision.

S.A.: He would say who should be together?

Larry: Yeah. I know sometimes he would ask the people and sometimes the people would go to him. So naturally, according to Billy Graham, his wife and the world, this was the wrong interpretation of that scripture.

So then Billy Graham comes in. I remember him coming in to my left and he was *glowing* like. That was the first time I'd ever seen him. He shook my hand and went over to the other side of the room and he asked me what I was doing there. I talked to him for about five minutes, real nervous, and naturally I thought we had the way and I was a messenger sent by God, and it was quite an experience. He listened for about five minutes and then he said, "Let's all stand," and he prayed for us. He asked to keep a charter and then the minister gave us some money and we went on our way. He said, "Thanks for coming by," and that was it. We were just thrilled because we had accomplished the mission and spent five minutes with him. Just recently I found out that his wife has a brother who is a pastor in Texas, and I want to call him because I now want to tell Billy Graham that I was the person who was at his house and I am out of that and tell him what has happened."

In 1975, after having been given permission to go home to Cleveland because his father was to have open-heart surgery, Larry Israel was subjected to deprogramming by Ted Patrick. In his words,

The deprogramming failed to snap me out of what they believed to be mind control and absolute dependence on *Love* Israel.

For the next three months someone slept in my room with me and they had a bed up against the door of my room so I couldn't escape. I took a trip, during those three months, with Ted Patrick, to Texas where he was deprogramming someone from the Hare Krishna group. Then I went to his home in San Diego.

People were calling me Larry and I'd been called *Consideration* for four years—not just called it—that's who I *was* in my own mind. It wasn't just being *Consideration;* it was that the name had so much meaning. Those names have so much meaning to those people. It gives them a sense of purpose. It's like who they really are in God's eyes, and—having been rejected in the world—to receive a name in the Kingdom of Heaven gives a lot of meaning to the names.

I got so depressed I committed myself to a hospital, Woodruff Hospital in Cleveland, but I don't remember much of the experience. I had about twenty shock treatments in two months while I was there. I didn't find out about any of this stuff until about a year later.

I called the Love Family, . . . I think I mailed a postcard: "Help! This is Consid.," and they sent out *Serious* and *Josiah.* . . . I'm not sure of all the details of how they got there—the plane and that kind of stuff. They stayed in Cleveland two months. They marched around the hospital, and while they were out there Doug Fraimen—his name was *Josiah*—his parents kidnapped him.

I didn't know any of this had taken place at the time . . . I've just heard bits and pieces and haven't really researched it, but I remember, after a couple months of being there, my parents wanted to get me away from what *Serious* and the Family people were doing. So they took me to a hospital in Vermont, to kind of escape.

I was there for two months, and while I was there I was given drugs. I was in a locked ward. This was called The Retreat, in Brattleboro. I remember the doctor trying to show me how wrong the Family was. I learned the *Bible* one way and he would try and show me things, like "Would *God* take away your girl friend from you, like *Love* Israel did, and make her one of his wives? Does that make sense to you?"

I started thinking of these things, but there would always be in the back of my mind, "Well, the Scripture says this and this Scripture says this." This doctor was a psychiatrist. He didn't want to talk religion. So my mind was in two different places. I didn't really know who I was for a long time there. If I go back and these people are *right* out here in the *world,* then what. Also, what if I stay *here* and the Love Family is right?

I can't even describe what that did to me. Living in that type of—this was a matter of life and God vs. the devil. God vs. the devil. You've got to realize that all this took two years and seemed like an eternity to me. . . .

On August 10, 1981, Larry wrote me a still-tortured letter in which he described his torment.

No words could ever describe what happened to me after I was removed, against my will, from the Love Family. It was an eternity of absolute Hell, insanity, and terror, as I knew a thousand eternal deaths and knew what it was to be separated from God forever. Horror and darkness pervaded the depths of my inner being as I, screaming and agonizing, stood in the black abyss, unable to reach and touch the love I desired. No hope, no life, separated from humanity; only I, conscious of eternal Hell. I was there! I was it! Tormented by demons! Deeper than and beyond despair! Fire! Death!

I had to die to who I was in the Family in order to be free. After four mental institutions, in the right moment of my destiny, a destiny connected to all mankind, a Christian man prayed for me, and by the power of Jesus I was set free. "He who the Son sets free is free indeed!" I rose from the dead barely able to comprehend what had happened. I was alive with new life.

It has been only four years since that moment. I now have a beautiful wife and baby girl. I have been growing as a person, struggling and patiently allowing God to have His way with me. I love people and want to give to them. The difference now is I have a direct relationship to the Person of Jesus Christ. Christ is not simply the people around me. He is Himself. I long to know and love Him. I could not see, while in the Family, how *Love* had become my absolute authority instead of God Himself, through His Spirit and Word. I love my friends up there deeply. I have been back to visit them. Although I was drawn to them emotionally in my heart because of the love between us, I knew it would be a lie to what God had shown me to live there again. There are good people there with good hearts, but that is not enough. I cannot accept the error in some of their teachings which I believe are contrary to what has been revealed in the Word of God. For example, the Love Family teaches the spiritual oneness of all mankind. The Bible says only those who accept Jesus Christ and what He did for them on the cross receive of His Holy Spirit and are thereby made one with God and also one with each other. Just because one opens himself up to the spiritual realm and has many visions does not mean what he experiences is from the true source, from God. One needs to be able to discern, and the Bible is one means to do that by. Satan can give visions and plant lies in men's minds.

Oh, how I love the people there and have tried to communicate what I have learned through my sufferings, but they are unable to receive it. I commit their souls to God and trust Him to show them the truth and open their eyes. I don't condemn them. I forgive them and *Love* Israel. It is hard for all human beings to see how we are wrong without the light of God shining on our secret hearts in the depths of our beings. God loves us all and longs with all His Father heart to have a love relationship with us.

Love Family, when you read this and feel that I misunderstood you, please humble your hearts and pray that God would show you of any truth He might want to. You have nothing to lose or fear by praying that.

An important document relevant to the case is the following letter from Seattle's mayor, Wes Uhlman, to his counterpart in Cleveland, Ralph Perk.

April 25, 1975
The Honorable Ralph Perk
Mayor of the City of Cleveland
601 Lakeside Avenue East
Cleveland, Ohio 44114

Dear Ralph:

It has come to my attention that a Seattle resident, *Consideration Israel,* is scheduled to have a hearing Monday, April 28, in Cleveland concerning his possible involuntary commitment as a mental patient.

Attending this hearing will be several representatives of the religious group to which *Consideration Israel* belongs. Leading this delegation will be *Logic Israel.*

I would like to take this opportunity to avert any confusion or misunderstandings which you or your city might have about the Love Israel religious sect and their relationship to Seattle. They reside together in one of the nicer residential neighborhoods of our city, take good care of their property, obey the laws of the city, and are generally regarded as good neighbors. Seattle Police Chief Robert Hanson can vouch for the group as well, and can be contacted at (206) 583-2230. *Logic Israel* has taken the time to personally meet with my staff on several occasions, and we have found him to be a very responsible representative of his group.

I am writing this not to endorse the particular religious beliefs which the Love Israel group holds, nor to comment on the hearing on *Consideration Israel,* but rather to let you know that regardless of their unconventional appearance and life-style, *Logic Israel* and his delegation are good citizens of Seattle, and we hope that they will be treated with courtesy and respect.

Sincerely,
Wes Uhlman
Mayor

But the mayor's fairness was unusual. Because of the public controversy surrounding various Family members, much of the elders' time was concerned with the Love Family's relationships with the outside world. Brian's letters told of their efforts to deal with the Board of Education, with the press when they printed inaccurate stories, with anti-cult groups like FREECOG, with Seattle parents who accused the group of corrupting their children. There was so much bad press that in 1979, when members of the Love Family were interviewed for a local television news feature segment on the group that was more complimentary than usual, Brian was moved to send us a videotape of it, commenting, "Although not 100% accurate, it is a positive statement."

I refer to the responses of *Love* Israel and Brian to reporters' questions during the course of that news feature because of the insights they provide into the Love Family's thinking as the 1970s drew to a close. *Love* Israel was asked if the 300-member group could be described as a cult:

I think any group these days is called a cult; I feel that what we have all seen is that we all have to get together and talk and reason. And it is going to be unusual because you really don't have anything to go by, and you can't believe in a world that you do not believe in. If we believed in the world as it is we would be there. . . .

Everything I read about and talked about always said—if you seek, you shall find, and that you will find your master or that you will find the truth. . . .

So we started looking, and I think that we went through everything, probably, in the sixties that everybody else went through. You know, all the culture, San Francisco, everything. Search and find, until we actually did see it. . . . We saw that everything really is one. And then a lot of us here saw Jesus Christ, and then we came together into one place. . . .

When asked by a reporter about the nature of relationships between men and women in the Love Family and the roles of men as heads of households, with the women in a clearly subservient role, *Love* Israel responded:

Well, you see, if you ran across a man who really was righteous, then you would want to listen to him, and it would be easier and more fun. Then you could put all your energy into making him a success, maybe, and then maybe you would both become successful. . . .

Submission is really happiness. But you want to submit to the truth and submit to righteousness. You do not want to submit to unrighteousness or just that "I'm the boss." You want to submit to the man that you see God in.

In answer to the question of his belief in the sanctity of traditional marriage, *Love* explained:

No, I would say that we were shown that we were all brothers and sisters and that our marriage is in God, so that this is the way we have done it and left it at that.

I figure that any [two] who really loved each other would come together and stay that way. No commitment. People are together because they like each other.

On the role of monogamy within the Love Family community:

Well, it doesn't have to be that way either. I mean it just *can* be that. We want to leave it open. We want everything to happen as it happens. We don't want to be a part of the breaking of any rules or regulations. . . .

He was questioned about his account of revelation from God:

People have seen, and God has shown, that I have seen the overall plan, and so when their vision fits into it and they come and give me a vision it goes—*click*. . . . When I saw that we were all one, really I saw love is the answer. Not to worry or doubt but to just love and love until people have found what they are really looking for. Well, if *life* is a religion, then it's a religion. I think life *is* a religion. . . .

We don't believe in a lot of laws and regulations, so everybody has to know for himself, and if you don't know for yourself, it doesn't work. . . . Even a child has to know. And when it begins to work is when everybody knows. . . . We feel that this is the way to rebuild the world and to make families mean something again. . . . I feel that right at home in my own house is where I have to change the world.

Brian was questioned by the same reporters about his views concerning *Love* Israel and his place in the Love Family:

Some of the things I have seen in *Love*—and I have seen Jesus Christ in *Love*—but that is a very confusing thing. I know that *Love* has seen Jesus Christ in me. I have seen that we are eternal brothers bound together forever, and I see him absolutely as my brother. I also see him as my king, and I have seen him speak representing God for me. He represents my father, *Love,* and represents a king to us. Our family is like a kingdom. If you try to describe what our government is, it is like a royal family.

I am doing everything I can do to drop my old ways of seeing it all, and just to see what real love is left if I am not trying to hold onto anything.

The mother of *Love* Israel's six children, *Honesty,* was questioned as to her perspective on the relationship between men and women within the Family:

I feel that any woman could feel secure here, whether she had a relationship with a man or not. Because this is a place where she can give herself and she can help build a family and raise the children and have plenty of brothers and sisters to relate to.

If someday she falls in love with one of the brothers, then they will work together toward building a family, and that relationship should go on forever. I see no reason why it would stop.

Brian was asked about his relationship with *Love:*

My relationship to *Love* is primary. It is the most important thing I have going. For him and me to totally get to know each other and to know the relationship is beyond any of the things that have ever separated man forever. For no matter what it is—competitions, envy, jealousy, misunderstandings, arguments—we just want to end all conflict.

Elaine Britton, the mother of a Love Family member, who had been coming up to the community for several years to visit her son, had this to say about her impressions of the Love Family:

I think most parents have a distorted idea of what is happening. I think it may be a different situation here from what I read about the other types.

I have never visited any other type of commune, but from what I have read they do have a different atmosphere, I think, and the atmosphere here, ever since I have known them, has always been a very wholesome, well-thought-out atmosphere in maintaining their religious beliefs and trying to live a good life. That is the reason I am satisfied with it.

By this time even the somewhat impartial reader will have perceived the difficulty of arriving at a fair and reasonable judgment about the Love Family. I suggest that it is helpful to avoid making a simple either-or, black-or-white choice. In my view neither total approval nor total disapproval is warranted. No human institution is without faults. Certainly the traditional denominations have much in their history to be ashamed of, not to mention millions of individual adherents who have led sinful or criminal lives. But despite this fact, which is known to most believers, millions still approve of such religious institutions, while reserving the right to disapprove of what they perceive as evil or mistaken in them.

As regards the Love Family, it is clear that its few hundred members believe they are benefiting by certain elements of their experience that, for whatever reasons, they were denied in their earlier lives. The members react favorably to a group sense of order, a sense of self-righteousness, the desire to live a virtuous life, cleanliness, discipline, camaraderie, sense of family unity, etc.

But some of the members, at least, must be deriving more than this from their communal experience. What does Paul Erdman need that he gets from his role as leader? A sense of power, obviously. A perception of self as virtuous, apparently in contrast to his self-assessment in his former life. Perhaps more importantly he—and Brian, too—has a clear-cut role within the Love Family. They are figures of authority, respected by their followers and even by many outside of the Family. Also, they have a sense of responsibility, and the realization that they are living up to it, in attending not only to spiritual but to the daily details of life for which father figures in any traditional family are responsible: providing food, shelter and clothing, and planning for the future.

Even the fact that they are publicly criticized, interviewed by the media, referred to in books, enhances their prestige, though it must wound their sensibilities to be, as they will perceive it, so misunderstood.

CHAPTER 15

The Case of Melinda Loughlin

In late March 1979 I received a strangely accusatory letter from another former Family member—Melinda Loughlin, who had obviously had a difficult time in her Love Family experience. Of the various former Family members I have heard from, she was the only one who seemed totally bitter about her experience, though she would later moderate her criticism.

Melinda had lived in Brian's house, "and though his training was austere, he was then one of the younger, less influential leaders in the group, and his character was much more likable than that of quite a few of the other leaders."

. . . if you knew what the inner workings of the cult was about, I feel you would be as adverse to giving it your approval, as you would Jonestown, or the Manson Family. I helped a wealthy family from Boston try to get their son. When the father flew up to their camp in Homer, Alaska, they held rifles on the father and detectives. They had to wait several months before they went back and took the camp by surprise to get their son. I saw the condition of their son. He was crying, and said "He wished he was their son, but he wasn't. He is *Sure* Israel." To see the grief on that mother's face—I will never forget it.

I know the Family has loosened up; they are not as desperate to hold members there, as they are quite wealthy now. I think since the leaders have now started to father children, that the children are being treated somewhat better. I thank God for that. Last summer I went back to the Family to visit, and see how many people were still there. Quite a few of them were. And I heard sad tales from several of the women I care a lot about. Stillborn children, and one sweet girl had her baby die a "crib death." . . .

I saw your grandson, *Liberty,* at their nudist ranch. I did not know people didn't wear clothes there; I would not have gone to the ranch if I did, and I never went back to the ranch. Each time I saw your grandson, he was not with *Logic* or *Simplicity. Love* doesn't encourage strong individual family ties. And if the men want, they can switch "wives," and have any number *Love* is willing to give them.

. . . The police have been bribed by the Family, . . . turn their heads, ignoring the drug abuse.* HOW COULD TWO MEN DIE FROM SNIFFING GLUE, also called "The Rights of Breathing" and never have the police close the commune down? They don't do the glue anymore that I know of, but when I was there I was told LSD is a sacrament. I also met a young man, who became a Christian, who used to be one of their drug dealers. He said he dealt large quantities of cocaine, LSD, and other drugs to *Love* Israel.*

They might be cleaning up their outward act, but the inner core of leaders don't go from rotten to good; they just become more devious. Did you know that they are trying to organize with other cults (such as the Scientologists)? Their main goal is to someday see the world ruled by *Love;* King *Love* they now call him. It might seem ludicrous, but revolutions and tragedies happen because of an apathetic society. There are over 1,000 cults in the U.S. alone. That includes a figure in the millions of people. I know this is a great country; it has faults because we are human, and I truly appreciate freedom of religion, but I can't condone con-artists. It took many painful, struggling years for me to get back on my feet. I never have been wealthy since I joined the Love Family. My opportunity to complete my education was taken from me. The jewels my mother gave me on her deathbed were taken from me under the pretense of 'we are going to feed the hungry, clothe the naked, and care for elderly people.' This was never done. I was humiliated when I came home and was unable to cope with the normal society for a while. I know of other people who are still under psychiatric care due to the Love Family.

There is a good ending to my story. I finally worked up the nerve to trust God again. I was afraid to for a long time. But God really has done a miracle in me. I now have been healed of my scars and bitterness that I held toward the Love Family. I honestly care to see the people accept Jesus as their Lord. I think the majority of the Family are innocent. But even the ones who aren't, I had to truly

*This seems to me extremely unlikely. S.A.

forgive, and love, so that I can pray effectively for them. And there IS power in prayer and love and faith. I believe we can help these kids. Especially those who want to get out, but feel they have no place to go. Many go into cults because their families don't want them in the first place. I know the adjustment is hard. And I have a vision for a place where people can go and receive spiritual rehabilitation. (It was very hard to rejoin society for me.)

Mr. Allen, I know your son might seem happy; perhaps *Love* treats him well because he hasn't received his inheritance. I pray you never give it to him while he is in the Family. . . . You are a public figure and a respected man; your opinion matters. So either you are going to influence public opinion for them (and perhaps have people think you condone sex and drugs, your grandson at their nude ranch without his parents, being shifted place to place like a nomad—for now it's an adventure, but what about the future?—police bribery, etc. as investigations will get more thorough as time goes on, since Jonestown—or you will take the time to investigate before you give your approval of the cult just because your son seems happy. I've seen happy people in mental hospitals, because they are sincerely deluded. The people in the Love Family think they are JESUS CHRIST. That's what their names represent. They say God broke Himself up into many particles and indwells their temples! [bodies]

People should have freedom of life-style. But what bothers me the most is the religious ripoff going on in the name of Jesus Christ at the Love Family. What bothers me is that the people there are not aware of the underworld connections and how they are being used. I was not aware of it until I got out. It was a very hard thing to admit, because I had given myself so totally to them, and I wanted to believe in the Utopia they were painting. They are creative and industrious, and, as I said, I care about the people.

I know you'd rather hear good reports about the Family, but the truth has to come out. I remained silent for these past years because I had two law suits being processed. . . . My first lawyer is dead; the second became afraid of them and let the statute of limitations run out. It was a half-million-dollar lawsuit, so you can see the influence they have over people. I realize now, educating the people is important, along with prayer. I have been careful not to mention your name in public, as I don't wish you or your family any embarrassment. Again, please know more about the group before you give public approval.

God bless you.

While it appeared that Ms. Loughlin was overstating her case in some particulars, I nevertheless wanted to learn what degree of truth there was in her allegations and therefore sent a copy of the letter to Brian, who responded to its points.

About the Boston father held at rifle-point at the camp in Homer, Alaska, he said,

> . . . detectives posing as Alaska state troopers came in, and actually they were the ones who held the guns on *us,* though I later learned that a member of our Family did have a rifle that he got out of the cabin and held, but only after he saw the guns of the false "state troopers."
>
> . . . *Sure* ran off into the woods, and they were unable to do anything about the situation, so they left. . . .
>
> They came back . . . a few months later. Working with their lawyers, they had convinced an Alaska state judge that we had held *Sure* prisoner in our homestead in Alaska, which, of course, wasn't the case. . . . They came in with actual state troopers, arrested *Sure,* and took him to Anchorage. In Anchorage, without any formal hearing, a judge awarded his parents official custody on the grounds that he was unable to manage his own affairs. Once again *Sure* was taken back to Boston, where he was held prisoner and put through the typical Ted Patrick form of deprogramming. After a while he managed to escape and return to Anchorage.
>
> Fortunately there's a much better relationship now between him and his parents. It seemed that once they resigned themselves to the life-style he'd chosen, things got a lot better. . . . Further on in the letter, Melinda mentions seeing *Liberty* "at their nudist ranch." It's ridiculous to call it a nudist ranch, since we live there in the Northwest throughout the year, including through the snowy months, but in hot weather people do go swimming in the lake without bathing suits. And the kids play by the lake. She mentions always seeing *Liberty* without me or *Simplicity* and implies that we don't live with them.
>
> It mentions that *Love* doesn't encourage strong individual ties, by which I guess she means family ties. Nothing could be further from the truth. The whole intention up there is to build strong family ties. The main difference, of course, is that we don't limit ourselves to family units of one man, one woman and a couple of children. Rather, we look toward the greater family and build our ties to include more and more people.
>
> The next thing Melinda says is that if the men want they can switch

wives and have any number that *Love* is willing to give them. Both assertions create a misleading image of the Love Family. First of all, it's our *hope* that people will dedicate their lives to each other, since history has proven nobody can *force* anyone to do that. And we've had our share of relationships that don't work out, just as the same thing is common in the outside world.

As for the reference to *Love* giving away wives, it's ridiculous. He doesn't own anybody, and it isn't in his power to give people away. . . .

The next allegation is that the police in Seattle had been bribed by the Family. This is an extremely remote possibility. Over the years we've been doing all we can do to build a friendly relationship with the police, since they started out extremely suspicious and doubtful. They didn't operate like our friends on the whole, but we have a pretty good working relationship with them now.

She says here she met a man once who used to be one of our drug dealers. That he dealt large quantities of cocaine and LSD and other drugs to *Love* Israel. I don't know if she's making that up to scare people or whether somebody told that to her and she believed them. But nothing could be further from the truth. One of the things the Love Family stands for is to consciously not have purchased any drugs at all, ever, since the existence of the Family. That's one of the things we're against.

Melinda says that it took her many years to get back on her feet. Well, number one, Melinda came and lived in my house. She seemed to have a lot of troubles. In fact, she gave me more difficulty than anyone I ever lived with, and I often thought ours wasn't the right situation for her and that we weren't doing much good for her at all. But *Love* always encouraged me to just continue to love her and help her out and to try to build a nice relationship with her because he knew she needed friends more than anything.

It seems that much of her bitterness is based on the fact that when people join the Love Family they are asked to give all they possess to the Family to share in common, which *is* one of our main beliefs, which of course we got from the Book of Acts, which is the structure set up by the first churches after Jesus Christ.

As I recall she didn't have much. She had the BMW sports car and some jewelry that her mother had given her. I don't recall if she had any money, but it seems the car and the jewels are what she's still worried about. And they, like everything else, were used however we could to feed the people and to pay the rents and just keep life rolling on in the Family.

One of her last accusations is that people in the Love Family "think they are Jesus Christ. That's what their names represent. They say God broke Himself up into many particles and indwells their temples." That is a misunderstanding of some things we truly believe. We do believe we are particles of the body of Jesus Christ, and our names represent the different aspects of Jesus Christ. And of course we only desire to represent Jesus Christ. As Christians, who else would we want to represent?

And we do believe that Jesus was trying to explain to his Disciples at the Last Supper, when he broke bread with them, that he was going to give himself into each of them. And we believe that Jesus Christ does dwell in us.

I was just reading over the newspaper article [*New Era,* Lancaster County, Pennsylvania, March 19, 1979] based on the interview with Melinda. It seems one of her main beliefs was that while she was in the Family she was being given drugs in her food or something. This, of course, never happened.

These things make me wonder whether she really believes that or whether people convinced her of it after she left the Family. I know that she was involved with deprogrammers, and so many of the things she says, inasmuch as they aren't true, you wonder what she's been basing them on.

Two years later, in Seattle, the Love Family heard again from Melinda. She had a cordial conversation with Brian, after which she wrote a letter "intended to be an open letter," saying that "it was good . . . to be very open and honest about our points of view—our understandings and especially our misunderstandings . . . "

Last night I realized a grave injustice that I have done you and the Love Family—I never called you to get your side of the story, and there were things that ex-members said, or other parents, that I never questioned—and after talking with you I see how easy it is to misunderstand one another *unless* we are honest and communicate.

Another unfairness was: the positive and good side of the Family was always undercut by the press. There were times—numerous ones—that the press exaggerated, lied and printed things without my permission.

For instance, I had to hire a lawyer to stop [name withheld] from putting a chapter in his book from third-hand information that was filled with lies (about my experience). It was for personal gain, and I was sick of people using other people's hurts and fears to make a profit.

I guess what I am trying to say is I came to a realization, after talking with you, that you are an intelligent and dedicated man; you have been with *Love* long enough to know his motives. I can see you are there, along with the rest, under mutual agreement.

You have dispelled my fears that you and the other elders are looking for personal gain by taking personal properties from each member—for that motive.

I admit I went through many phases of hurt, anger and bitterness after I left the Family. It was hard to have gone from a life of financial and material security to poverty. But I must also admit it has built character and forgiveness in my heart.

Hopefully, this letter will touch hearts that were hurt by testimonies made by me. I did not say things with a malicious intent, but in hopes that things I heard were wrong—that they would be changed.

No one denies that the time I lived at the Family was an "austere and severe time."

I see a difference of night and day there now.

The children look happy. Things are down to earth—becoming mothers and fathers has changed things—also acknowledging relatives, such as your own mothers and fathers.

The bottom line is that I think, after ten years of your professing the same thing—"people who want to get together in peace and love and put their trust in God"—is not a sham.

Perhaps all the people who have been hurt, or who have mistrusted and misunderstood motives of the Love Family, could get together and talk things out. I think you can understand and appreciate that the anguish of some parents and ex-members was real—and with this in mind there can be mutual forgiveness and peace.

It might seem a contradiction to say I have held love and deep affection for those I knew at the Family, but it's true.

In the future, if people ask me about the Love Family, they will get a balanced explanation, and I will encourage them to see for themselves and come to their own conclusions.

Hopefully, this letter will be a step toward counteracting a very one-sided view I have held and presented of the Family.

I also hope I can continue dialogue with you, as I still have some questions I would like cleared up. Hearing your viewpoint has really helped me understand things I took the wrong way in the past.

May we continue to strive to swell in the love of Jesus Christ.

CHAPTER 16

David Visits the Love Family

I was not of course the only one who was concerned about Brian. When he was thirteen, Bill, who grew from early adolescence to manhood during Brian's ten years in the Love Family, had written to him, "Please forgive me for not calling you *Logic,* but you have been Brian to me all my life and I love my brother Brian, not *Logic....* I don't know why you've done this. If you don't mind my saying so or even if you do, I feel that you are copping out and are deserting us. I feel you are hiding from reality. ... Your love and understanding that I have always appreciated so much would be of much greater use here."

And Steve, Jr. worried about Brian. When *People* magazine did a story on the Love Family (April 2, 1979), concentrating chiefly on Brian, journalist Cheryl McCall quoted Steve, whom she interviewed by phone. It was easy to see that although several years had passed since Brian had made his decision, Steve was still puzzled and hurt. What Brian had done Steve saw as a rejection of our family. "Maybe we weren't helping him enough."

Steve also pointed to my career as a factor that influenced Brian, saying that he and Brian stood in my shadow, "and it was a long one to climb away from because he was so good at so many things."

In 1979 Brian's mother, Dorothy, got a better understanding of Brian's life by spending a few days with him, his wife, *Simplicity,* and their children, *Purity* and *Liberty;* they were all drawn closer, as letters from Seattle showed. *Simplicity* wrote to Dorothy, announcing that the "queesy-ness" of her third pregnancy had passed, and said, "I've thought about you so many times since your visit. I looked forward to meeting you for so long, and after we did meet, I really got attached to you fast! We all miss you a lot. *Purity* keeps telling me that you shouldn't live so far away!"

150

But her letter was eventually followed by one from Brian, explaining that the baby had come about two months early, living only about five hours; he assured Dorothy that *Simplicity* was doing well and resting. And after the *People* story, he wrote to Dorothy, "Have you heard from Steve, Jr. . . . ? I haven't written him yet. I guess I'm not sure just what to say to him."

On Easter Sunday, 1980, when Brian had been a member of the Love Family for nine years, David flew to Seattle to visit. A creative young man himself, David keeps an ongoing writer's notebook, so he returned from his eight-day visit with a number of notations and observations. He liked most of what he had seen. Here is his journal of the visit.

. . . I was looking forward to visiting with Brian, whom I had not seen in three years, and his wife, *Simplicity*. When we met, they both seemed very happy and healthy. Our communication felt good. I had not yet met their two children, *Purity* and *Liberty,* who were both out at the ranch where we would be driving the next day after a night's rest. Besides living in houses in the city, the group owns a beautiful 300-acre ranch about an hour's drive from Seattle.

Love Israel is still the leader of the group. My brother, now called *Logic,* is second to *Love;* together they run the Family in the name of Jesus Christ. There are approximately 300 Family members. They live in several houses which are next door to each other. They have taken down the walls and fences that once divided the properties, creating a spacious area which has been beautifully landscaped by Family members. There are beautiful flowers and blooming trees and a path leading from house to house with a productive greenhouse nearby, where Family members spend hours working and taking care of the plants and flowers. Two of the San Francisco-type houses were being joined together with a bell tower between them. An outdoor hot tub was in the process of construction. As one stands in this serene garden one can sense that a loving spirit prevails here.

Upon arriving I began to meet many people. Each was very warm and treated me with great respect, partly because I am *Logic*'s brother.

I met nearly 50 people the first night and noticed that everyone was cheerful and healthy-looking. *Logic* gave me a partial tour of the grounds. We stopped at a house in which one of the teachers, a woman named *Understanding,* was working with another teacher, *One*, and a group of children. They were putting on improvisational plays. The theme of the play we walked in on was "Be sure to floss your teeth or you won't have any to floss later in life." They have a school system that is separate from the Seattle city schools. All of the children I spent time with were well-informed Bible students and for the most part seemed to have better-than-average communication skills.

Most members I visited with have had some kind of Christ experience. Many say they have seen or felt Jesus. Several members told me that they wanted to make people feel better and that their purpose is to shine forth the Love and the Light of God. Several people told me about experiencing messages telling them to move to Seattle. There is a great sincerity here and even a magical quality about the group's togetherness and sense of spirituality. I found it inspiring to hear the different ways that people felt moved by the spirit of God and to see how such a large group runs so smoothly and free of many problems that can be observed in other group living situations.

There was a big Sunday celebration going on; some parents were visiting and some visitors were arriving for the upcoming celebration.

After eating a delicious vegetarian meal, we all gathered in a big room. Rock music was played for a while with electric bass, electric guitar, drums and piano. From time to time *Love* would join the group, playing electric bass. Many people danced, and while there were couples, the dancing seemed more like a group of twirling people happy to be together. Celebration is definitely a big part of these people's daily lives.

The next day we packed up for our drive to the ranch, where we would be staying for the next week. The Family consists of many different households of approximately 15 people each. Each household is headed by one man, an elder. Most of the people on the ranch live in tents which have wooden floors, a stove and often running water. Some of the tents are called yurts and are round. We arrived at night as most people were going to bed. From where we parked at the main barn it was about a ten-minute walk around a small lake to *Logic*'s tent. When we got inside the spacious tent, by the light of two or three candles I saw for the first time beautiful little *Purity* and *Liberty* asleep on their mats. They woke up just enough for a hello, and after some whispered conversations (so as not to wake up the others in the tent) we all went to bed. The sound of singing frogs ran through the night until rain came and quieted them. I fell asleep to the pleasant sound of rain landing against the canvas roof of the tent.

There was a visitors' meeting the next day, set up to make sure that the many arriving visitors had somewhere to connect and ask questions. A young woman asked *Logic* about their school for children. He replied, "For our children we believe in the basics . . . reading, writing, math, drama, music. . . . It's all communication."

"Do you use doctors?" another woman asked. *Logic* explained, "If we have to . . . whatever the person needs. Of course if there could be a faith healing, that is desired, but we don't force anything. You can't force fate. We are trying to build our lives by trying not to lose ourselves in too much structure. We try to meet the needs of each situation."

Downstairs in the barn the old beautiful blond mare is about to give birth. She is the mother of four other work horses used here on the ranch.

Excitement is mounting as this is the week leading up to the big Passover dinner and celebration. This is the most important holiday for the Love Family, as in a sense they greatly identify with the Passover story, which includes the story of Moses leading the people out of Egypt. Passover is like New Year's to this group. Visitors are invited to morning Bible classes that explain the Passover story in an effort to unite with the new people.

Family members travel back and forth between the country and the city, but I believe a lot of time in the country is recommended for the children, and many of them spend a great deal of time at the ranch. *Libery* and *Purity* seem to love the ranch; it gives them plenty of sunshine and fresh air and exercise. They learn about wild life and develop self-sufficiency skills. They are both good climbers and runners and know the names and habits of many of the animals on the ranch. I spent one enjoyable afternoon in a canoe with *Purity,* who explained the different moves that an elusive beaver was making.

At dinner *Logic* told a morning messenger to wake the ranch up at 4:00 for a 4:30 morning meeting. These meetings were called to establish group unity, to sing and dance in celebration and organize the day's activities. There was extra work this week in preparation for Passover dinner for over 300 people.

Waking up for the early morning meeting seems like a dream. I remember someone opening the door to our tent and saying, "Good morning. It's going to be a good day." Walking down to the barn in the fog was beautiful; the entire lake was covered. Good coffee and cream was waiting for us at the barn as we gathered to sit on the upstairs wooden barn floor covered by multi-colored carpet squares. Twelve home-made banners and emblems decorate the huge barn interior, and an old piano sits alongside various amplifiers and electric guitars. *Solidity* and *Integrity* are playing the mandolin and guitar as we all look around and smile sleepy good mornings.

Songs were sung telling sweet tales of open doors and open hearts and forgiveness and love and everlasting peace.

"Get Together" was one of the songs we sang. "Come on people now, smile on your brother, everybody get together, try to love one another right now . . . " That is a song I have known for years, but most of the music that the group plays and sings is original and written by different Family members.

Logic then leads a morning prayer. We also chant, and, with eyes closed, we hold hands. After silence fell on the group for a while a strong group closeness was felt. There was a special calmness that I noticed. During this peaceful moment I heard my own thoughts saying, "Jesus, please let me feel Your power." I am not sure why I was saying that right then, but at that precise moment a *huge* gust of wind came up under the barn and seemed nearly to lift the entire barn up. Several people later related religious experiences that had taken place during that meeting. Some people had felt Jesus this morning. Some Family members and some of the visitors shared experiences, and we all agreed that we were feeling the spirit this morning. The events of the coming days were discussed; some more music was played and people danced. I found this a very soulful way to start the day. It was like having a party in the morning instead of at midnight. After a night-time party, people usually just conk out, but after this gathering we would all spend the day together.

I spent part of the day with *Simplicity,* who told me that the group used to own a fishing boat and earned money selling fish. They preferred to just feed themselves and to work toward self-sufficiency. Unfortunately the boat burned and insurance money has not yet been received. A relatively new plan in action now requires most of the men to work and earn at least 100 dollars a month. This will help the group pay debts and survive. They have gone through many very lean years but things seem to be looking up now. After each Passover, each year has a name, and this year will be a year of *Increase* for the Love Family. I also learned that one man and woman are working in town as apprentice weavers and are repairing Oriental rugs.

I joined one of the work crews. We loaded a dump truck with wood chips from a sawmill and laid them down over trails at the ranch to dress them up and make them more walkable. While we were smoothing the chips out with rakes, I noticed that they were walking Blondie, who looked like she was about to give birth at any moment. She is a beautiful horse and seems to enjoy the attention she is getting as an expectant mother.

I remember one day thinking about the differences that people have and the way every Family member seemed to get along with one another. The visitors, too, were harmonious, and I was just hoping that I fit in too. Without my sharing this with a young man named *Certain,* he volunteered the feeling that I seemed to round out the group. I felt welcomed by this comment. In my own good life I enjoy many different types of friends, and I feel glad that they share this approach to people.

Love was still back in the city and would be joining us in a day or two. Besides shining the ranch up for the holiday I sensed that part of the spirit of beautification was for *Love,* who does so much for the Family and is always thinking on their behalf. I remembered yesterday in Seattle, as part of a grace prayer, *Love* had said something like, "Heavenly Father, let us be free with our love, like children." I am touched by *Love*'s ability to be a leader, to be fatherly and to be childlike in a natural way at the same time. He seems to me to be more vulnerable than other leaders of groups I have seen or been around. He is a very loving person and seems sincere and grateful to be living the life he is living in the name of Jesus Christ. I would also say that *Love* is very unselfish and that when he does make decisions on the group's behalf he is very just. He is able to communicate well with everyone, and even in situations in which tension seems close by, his sense of humor always rounds out the scene.

Many of the children have chores on the ranch, and since this week was for the most part a vacation from school, many of them could be seen running around and helping with animals and playing.

The next day began with an early morning meeting and a lukewarm shower in the barn. The barn was a large old structure and was not only a meeting place but a fully functioning barn where horses, goats, and other animals lived. The sun was not yet up when cheery faces started gathering upstairs by candlelight. A few songs were sung. After the meeting, another Passover class was held and more aspects of the Passover story were explained. Someone explained that the Israelites were slaves and Moses was given a vision to lead his people out of Egypt. They were to wear the silver of the Egyptians. The Egyptians were to be the victims of a curse which would kill their first male born. To avoid this certain death God told them to slaughter the lamb and spread the blood on the door and when the Angel of Death came they would be passed over. Of course these lines are not meant to be an account of the story; they are just a few lines I remember hearing.

While walking me around the grounds later in the day, *Simplicity* explained that at one point before *Love* started the Family he had been in the hospital, seriously ill with a bad back. He was due to have back surgery the next day. She said that all of a sudden he realized he had to "have faith, now or never," and that he got up and walked out of the hospital and rented a house in Seattle and not long after that the Family started building. As far as I know *Love* is not troubled with back pain now.

Many members join penniless and are totally welcome, while some have money, and it goes for the whole group. Many new members, however, get rid of their material possessions before entering the Family. And some get rid of all their money before they join.

Today I joined *Imagination* and *Lazarus* and we made festive banners to string on poles which we skinned and put in the ground. We put a 30-foot pole up by *Love*'s tent with pretty colored banners hanging freely in the breeze.

I took a late afternoon nap. Later *Logic* came up to the tent. I woke up and as we were talking we heard a loud and frightening echo coming through the forest. *Logic* realized what it was before I did and at seeming supersonic speed he ran out of the tent and down the hill to catch what turned out to be a runaway cart used for gathering firewood which was pulled by two horses. *Logic* and two other men were able to slow the wildly running horses, and eventually the cart rolled over, causing the horses to stop. Luckily this potentially dangerous situation ended without injury.

I went to the next day's early morning meeting. There was frost this morning, and again thick fog blanketed the entire grounds. There was a close, spiritual feeling again in the meeting. We sang a few songs, and then *Logic* prepared to speak. I let a slight wisecrack out and said, "Well, I'm glad we don't have to stop now for a commercial break." Several people laughed and said they appreciated my comic relief.

After a morning snack of bread and milk and sesame seeds I went for a beautiful walk. The sun was rising and streamed through the trees to the moss below. I took some pictures of the beautiful scenery and sat for a while amongst the ferns, mushrooms and moss. A stream sang close by, and I could see why anyone could enjoy the peace and beauty here. I felt the sun's warm rays filtered by the greenery and enjoyed this special moment.

When I walked back down the hill to the main area of the ranch, I saw people still working and preparing the grounds. There is a lot of sisterly and brotherly love here. I also notice a real lack of selfish behavior and large egos. Today I met *Willing,* who seems seven feet tall and very gentle and accepting. *Hope* is a young man who is perhaps in his late teens. At least fifteen people told me how proud they are of *Hope.* He grew up here.

Love finally came out to the ranch today, and it was an exciting moment. It was a day for celebration and for showing *Love* how good the place was looking for the festive days ahead. Later that night there was a party in the barn, with live music and dancing. *Love* spoke to the crowd and said he felt like a stern of a ship and that we were all parts of the ship. He asked everyone to be open with him and tell him of their needs so he could know more properly how to steer the ship. He also said, "I can't take the you out of me or the me out of you." He is a powerful yet loving speaker.

Finally Passover Day came and with it beautiful sunshine. Most of the days had been quite cloudy and cool, but today was a real out-of-doors type of day. People were juggling in the sunshine, playing ball, playing guitar. A group of women sat together and sang, accompanied by one of the visiting mothers.

. . . This was definitely a holiday, and as each hour went by the mood went higher. By the time we sat down for Passover dinner, the barn had been decorated beautifully, and over 300 of us sat and looked around at the happy crowd. *Logic* was sitting across from me and explaining things to two of the visitors. I heard him saying something interesting . . . "Don't be surprised to feel naked when you sit before God . . . or even some shame. You have done nothing bad, but it is such an intimate feeling, such an exposed moment . . . but it's good."

Love spoke to the group and spoke of their years of struggle as a group and how they were more ready to interact with people. "We're going public now," he said, with a grin that made me want to be there.

The meal was splendid, served with wine. We were all dressed up, and after working all week and seeing everyone up to their elbows in some work project, it felt good to see them all shining in fine clothes they had made themselves. This was definitely a holiday for them to celebrate who they are and what they are doing. And it is easy to see the thankfulness for both God's love that they feel and for the sense of family that they share. I felt glad to be included and glad to share my good feelings with them.

After dinner there was a lot of music and dancing, a Family slide show of past holidays, and some amazing slides taken on recent mountain climbing expeditions. I saw my brother dance and also play the saxophone, two things I've never seen him do before. A lot of people seem to flourish here. . . .

As my week drew to a close I felt some sadness about leaving. I had grown attached to many of the people. I look forward to going back again and know that when I get gack to Los Angeles I will miss people coming up to me excitedly, asking, "Hey, aren't you *Logic*'s brother?"

David and I got together a few days after his return, and, with the tape recorder on the old glass table on our patio, we discussed his feelings about the Love Family. The members of the Family seemed to him to be decent people trying to live a spiritual life.

The group, David reported, bases its religious life on the Passover story from the Old Testament. Passover, to them, is like New Year's. "I went there at Passover time. They don't adhere to any particular calendar. They have their Passover celebration when all of the preparations come together."

"Could that be any time of the year, or is it generally—"

"Generally right around our Easter or the Jewish Passover."

"I mean," I said, "is it at a particular date on the calendar, or don't they pay any attention to that?"

"No, it seems to be a bit different each year. This year they served Passover dinner for three hundred."

"If they plan to do something on what you and I would call January first," I asked, "how would they know when January first is if they don't pay attention to calendars?"

"Oh, they're aware of calendars. And they're aware of the time of day, even though I did not see one clock."

"Or a wristwatch?"

"No," he said. "However, there were three days when we had morning meetings. We had to get up at four and be ready for a four-thirty meeting."

"Then somebody must know when four o'clock is."

"Yes. And someone makes rounds, and says, 'It's a good day. It's time for the morning meeting.' Possibly there's a message, or some nice thought to wake people up with. So there must be someone who's got a clock. Also I saw only two mirrors in the eight days I was there. The people are sort of mirrors for each other. They help each other, dress each other, things like that."

"Do I correctly understand that there is no radio, no television?"

"Yes, but they have access to a television. Brian was aware that you were going to be on "The Big Show." In the past they didn't pay attention to news events, but now they've come to realize that it's important for them to know what's going on in the world since there are so many strange things happening, and they know they have to have some understanding of world events."

The eruption of the Mount St. Helens volcano in May of 1980, David said, had a profound effect on the members of the Family. Some of those who did not know that danger was imminent first thought that some sort of attack on the ranch was being made. The possibility of the outbreak of nuclear war or even "the end of the world" passed through their minds, understandably enough.

"How did Brian seem to be getting along?"

"One of the things that struck me is that I saw my own brother flourishing in certain ways with the Family. For instance, he's a great juggler now, and he teaches the other people juggling. And I saw him run at what seemed like super-speed in an emergency one day. I saw him playing the saxophone, improvising with a jazz group. One night I saw him dancing. These were things that he never used to do."

"I'm glad, too," I said, "that he has the love of *Simplicity*."

Simplicity, *Logic*'s wife, has a sweet, spiritual quality which immediately endears her to everyone fortunate enough to meet her. She is pretty, but not in a flashy, "Charlie's Angel" sort of way. She looks as if she were painted by da Vinci. Or—David thought—Botticelli. Jayne, who writes to her as Mrs. *Logic* Israel, is devoted to her.

Simplicity wrote to David, as she had to Dorothy, describing further volcanic activity from Mount St. Helens and thanking him for the beautiful pictures he had taken and the music he had sent. There were two new "cult experts" around, trying to give the Family a bad name, she reported, but it would all die down as it had before. "Love wins in the end though even if it gets discouraging sometimes." She clearly expressed her affection for David. But the part of the letter that was most charmingly *Simplicity* was the postscript:

Submission had a beautiful Baby Boy last night. Named *Recognition*.
It was a fast, easy birth. 9 lbs.
Honesty had a Boy, too. Named *More*. As in "more love," "more
honesty," "more bliss," "more blessings for all."
Charity had a Boy named *All*.
Radiance had a girl named *Increase*.
Belief had a girl named *Home*.
Gratuity had a girl named *Compatibility*.
Lots in the Springtime. . . .

And Brian wrote,

Dear Dad,
    I had a great visit with David. Thank you for making it possible. It
felt very healing to spend time together, have hours and hours to
talk, and let David have a glimpse into my life.

It remained for Steve, Jr. to visit.

CHAPTER 17

Children of God

Naturally my research compelled me to look beyond the Love Family to the religious commune movement itself. No definitive study has identified a specific starting time or place for what in the late 1960s came to be called the Jesus Movement. The concept of a start is, in itself, ambiguous. Regardless of beginnings, the new trend became a sometimes fanatical, sometimes level-headed revival of far-reaching proportions. That the phonomenon erupted during the social turbulence of the sixties is significant. While adolescence is always a time of personal upheaval, the students of the sixties had grievances. The Vietnam War, the assassinations of John Kennedy, Robert Kennedy and Martin Luther King, the ghetto riots—all led to a lack of faith in leadership and to subsequent rebellion.

In 1966 *Time* carried on its cover the phrase, "God Is Dead." Five years later the same magazine featured Jesus Christ on its cover. During those intervening years an estimated 300,000 people around the world had joined the Jesus Movement—and that figure stands apart from the thousands who newly joined Eastern religions.

But why Jesus? Because during those years young people had become entranced with the notions of peace, love, harmony—basics of Christian doctrine. They were looking for a faith and a leader. Their peer society was floundering. In the midst of social turbulence these young people were seeking a solace from the bloodshed and turmoil.

In 1966 a sailmaker named Ted Wise who had started reading the Bible decided to commit his life to Christ. With a quiet but ferocious energy he and his friends contacted between thirty and fifty thousand others within two years. The new converts attracted still others across the country, then around the globe. Wise is one of the key figures whose work launched the new Jesus Movement, the growth of which proved surprisingly easy.

The movement grew, buoyed by the militancy of the times and the fervor of its new adherents. That some were dropouts, failures, unable to make it in the outside world, is clear. That the fervor of some led to their being called zealots, fanatics and freaks is understandable. In a materialistic and conservative society the sight of these young people in their hippie clothes and flowing hair, some of them drug types, and all calling for peace in a time of war, would inevitably arouse suspicion.

The movement did indeed have its share of oddballs. The Jesus revival was, among other things, a rebellion; and all rebellions, peaceful or not, attract a certain number of weaklings or misfits.

No single organization controlled the movement, which is no more unified than Christianity itself has been for the past two thousand years.

An analysis by Ronald Enroth, Edward Ericson and C. Breckinridge Peters, *The Jesus People,* says: "There is so much diversity within the movement that some elements of it consider others non-Christian, even demonic. Also there is a surprising isolation of groups, so that one group usually knows little about others, especially those separated geographically."

The most aggressive of the early sects was the Children of God (COG). By the date *Time* featured Jesus on its cover, over one hundred COG communes had been founded around the world, even in Vietnam and Israel. Observers who visited some of the communes came away perplexed. Daniel St. Alban Greene, reporting for the *National Observer,* visited a COG group in Detroit. He wrote, "Are these hippie revivalists only what they say they are: an all-volunteer army for Christ, laboring to save us all? Or are they, as more detractors insist, brainwashed, anti-American fanatics, fobbing off revolution and hate as the Gospel?"

In the early seventies Maureen Earl, a reporter for a television network, visited a number of Children of God communes. The response when she requested interviews from the members was confused, defensive and suspicious: "You'll only distort things, like the media always does. . . ." Yet, at odds with themselves, they wanted a chance to show the public that they led Christlike lives of harmony and nonviolence. In each commune she reported a common trait—their seriousness: " . . . so earnest that they appeared almost without humor. Even in their efforts to be friendly they retained a definite distance, especially the women. And in their very welcome I was made to feel, covertly, inferior. In not a single commune was I given a satisfactory answer as to why they had chosen their life-style. A sagelike look would enter their faces and the invariable answer was something along the lines of, 'Because it is Christ's will.'"

Part of the controversy about the new movement grows out of the fact that new members renounce their parents and other family members.

"Is breaking up families anything new with God? God is in the business of breaking up families—little private families! If you have not forsaken your husband and wife for the Lord at some time or other, you have not forsaken all!"

That is a portion of a "Mo-letter"—a proclamation from David Berg, also known as Moses, Mo for short, the founder of the Children of God movement.

Though at first the group seemed to be part of the larger Jesus Movement, the Children of God in time spoke little of love and peace. Instead they stood on street corners preaching that doomsday was upon us, and urging their hearers to renounce all earthly possessions, break family ties. "America is headed for trouble. Doom is around the corner. Armageddon is arriving in the form of the comet Kohoutek. Repent. Repent *now.*"

Repent. Wear sackcloth and ashes.

And give all you own to David Berg.

Repent and chant one of Berg's favorite scriptures. "Think not that I am come to send peace on earth: I come not to send peace but a sword. For I am come to set a man at variance against his father, and the daughter against her mother. . . . And a man's foes shall be they of his own household. He that loveth father or mother more than me is not worthy of me." (Matthew 10:34–37)

I have been a lifelong student of propaganda from various churches and sects. But never have I seen material so disgusting as that published by "Father David." He literally advises his young female adherents to use sex to spread the word of their peculiar religion. His most revolting pamphlet, "My Little Fish," contains pictures of naked children engaged in sexual activity. One picture, for example, shows a boy of about three on top of a girl of about two. Another shows a boy about three and a half lying back, unclothed, while the hand of an unidentified adult, presumably a woman, lubricates his penis. So far as one can judge from such literature, Berg's only concession to conventional morality is that "such sexual freedom must never be indulged in or practiced openly in the presence of visitors, strangers or uninitiated relatives and friends. . . ."

Another revolting pamphlet concerns Berg's adventures with assorted bar-girls and strippers; in it he describes a visit to a club where two erotic dancers named Claire and Monica worked. A small child named Davidito—presumably Berg's son—played on the dance floor, after which the woman named Claire "gave a special little show for David, with all her gyrations and heavy breathing, running her hands over her body, really turning *everybody* on!"

Berg, a Jewish convert to Christianity, first emerged in 1968 in Southern California where he led a group of ex-dope addicts named "Teens for Christ." He soon joined forces with the Reverend Fred Jordan, an aggressive and successful evangelist who did a weekly series of telecasts called "The Church in the Home" and who was looking for a method to expand his operation. He found an effective partner in Berg and "Teens for Christ." Jordan featured Berg's followers on his weekly show, proclaiming that by turning to the Lord they had beaten drugs and alcoholism. Berg, in turn, was acquiring massive free publicity and, with Jordan's money and TV prestige behind him, began recruiting under the banner of Children of God. He changed his name to Moses. Membership grew in a climate of aggressive hysteria where young people, for the most part addicts and dropouts, turned their backs on their parents and society at large.

In a period of social upheaval, the Children of God movement offered a communal home where members found a reason to give up drugs and jobs. Given refuge at Jordan's four-hundred-acre ranch in Texas, Berg's followers studied the Bible for eight hours a day, reading prescribed passages aloud while simultaneously listening to them on tape. New converts were forced to memorize long Bible passages and learn a trade. They were also expected to actively recruit new members.

The movement swelled. By 1971 when Jordan, having become aware of bad publicity, kicked them off his ranch, the Children of God had spread throughout the nation.

By this time the Children were receiving national attention. That most of the publicity was harshly critical did not seem to concern Berg or his followers, whose methods became even more peculiar. They entered churches where, after sitting silently at the back during the sermon, they would stand as one and shout, "Repent!" leaving worshippers shocked. They seldom missed an opportunity to appear at public gatherings. Ericson, Enroth and Peters say: "Imagine the stunning impact when Jerry Rubin came to the campus of the University of California at Santa Barbara to make a speech. In marched a long line of sackcloth-and-ashes garbed youth, staves and signs in hand, who stood stone-faced and silent. At the signal the whole line began to clank their staves and chant, 'Woe, woe, woe, woe, woe!'"

By January 1972 the movement had three thousand members who devoutly espoused Berg's teachings that parents were "rotten, decadent, decrepit, hypocritical, self-righteous, inflexible, affluent, self-satisfied, proud, stubborn, disobedient, blind, bloodthirsty, Godless, dead, selfish, churchy, older generation." The followers were allowed communication with their families only in order to obtain money and possessions, which in turn were passed directly to the organization.

Across the country bewildered parents quite understandably formed groups to oppose the Children of God. Finding little support from the government—which argued that, as a religion, the church was protected by the First Amendment—the parents, fearful that their children had been brainwashed or held captive, now started to kidnap them from communes, even though some were heavily guarded by high fences and watchdogs.

Ted Patrick, deprogrammer, led the first "kidnap" expedition to penetrate a Children of God commune in Woodland Park, Denver, Colorado. "The police and the FBI told me it would be impossible to get inside. . . . The security precautions at Woodland Park were the toughest I'd seen. The colony was way back in the mountains . . . surrounded by a seven-foot-high fence with a locked gate. There were 350 kids living there. The grounds were patrolled by three vicious German shepherds. And one of the buildings was topped by a watchtower so that no one could come up the road without being detected at least five minutes before he reached the gate."

Patrick was successful in that kidnap and deprogramming and, over the following years, became involved in what he says were hundreds of similar sessions. As a result Patrick himself became the subject of legal and moral controversy. Convicted and sentenced to jail several times, he immediately bounced back, continuing his efforts to warn the public and government of the dangers in the growing religious sects. Judges have found the issue perplexing. Some have ruled that youngsters had indeed been brainwashed and consequently should be forcibly returned to their families; others argued that if the members were beyond the age of consent their new religion was their own business.

In Canada, Children of God members stated in a national telecast that they had the right to lie, cheat, steal and even murder, so long as it was for the good of the cause. If Berg ordered them to kill, they said, they would do so.

In 1972 an ex-member testified on NBC television that during her stay in a Children of God commune, she was taught that she would have to commit adultery, theft and murder.

A fourteen-year-old girl testified that she had been repeatedly raped at a Children of God commune. The leaders had told her the forced sex was necessary in order to increase the tribe.

Others told of physical and psychological abuse when caught trying to escape. A young woman said she had been locked in a room for three days while members shouted at her to repent.

While a barrage of such testimony has been presented, a few parents, incredibly enough, took an opposite stand, defending the movement as having saved their children from a world of drugs and prostitution.

Unfavorable publicity continued to pour in; ex-members explained how they had been brainwashed and hypnotized, made weak from malnutrition, exhausted after long days of indoctrination, forced to give up all possessions and to steal from their families, subjected to sexual abuse and, on occasion, encouraged to use prostitution as a form of recruiting potential followers. Says one Mo-letter, "You roll those big eyes at them, and peck them with that pretty little mouth, and you go and flirt all around with them. . . . "

Sarah Berg, Berg's former daughter-in-law, reported that she was forced into sexual intercourse with Berg's son, Paul, whom she was later compelled to marry. Says a report from the office of the New York attorney general, "A year later, after the birth of her first child, David Berg, her father-in-law, wanted to have intercourse with her, stating, 'I see you with Paul's son; why can't you have my son?' On a later occasion, when she refused to have sex with her father-in-law, she was severely beaten, even though she was pregnant at the time." Sarah Berg escaped. Her testimony is amongst the most incriminating yet made public.

The Children of God had—they said—received a message that the comet Kohoutek was bringing imminent destruction to America. In 1973 a group of members, dressed in sackcloth and ashes, stood outside the United Nations building in New York, warning the world of the doom about to strike those who would not repent.

By this time some members were leaving the movement to form splinter groups of their own. Others left out of dissatisfaction. Some leaders and members prepared to leave the U.S. for Europe where communes had already been established. Berg fled ahead of the others, before the report was made public.

In October 1974, New York State Attorney General Louis J. Lefkowitz issued a scathing 65-page document accusing the sect of fraud, tax evasion, brainwashing, imprisoning, and sexual abuse of young converts. Mo-letters were not reproduced in the report. Explained the head of the attorney general's staff investigation team, Herbert Wallenstein, to *Newsweek,* "His letters are blatantly pornographic, complete with sketches and diagrams. We didn't even want to reproduce them in our report."

The report included a list of six common experiences described by former Children of God members:

1) A sudden unexplained decision by a new "convert" to drop out of school.
2) An initial refusal to leave the Children of God commune.
3) A complete personality change, resulting in a bitter hatred of parents.
4) An unexplainable and uncontrollable compulsion of a convert to return to a Children of God commune even despite vicious brutalization while there.
5) An uncharacteristic and self-destructive compulsion to transfer all personal assets to the Children of God.
6) The failure of members to receive monies requested from and forwarded from their parents.

The report was forwarded to the Internal Revenue Service and the U.S. Justice Department. Parents now felt encouraged in their fight against the group. But because the Children of God movement was protected by the First Amendment as a religious organization, no legal action was taken.

Members of the Children of God denounced the report as "totally false" and suggested that the state attorney general was seeking publicity for a forthcoming election.

The argument between anti–Children of God groups and the Justice Department is not yet settled. A 1978 letter from the U.S. Department of Justice to some agitated parents contains this extract: "The conclusion of the Department that 'brainwashing,' 'mind control,' and 'mental kidnapping' do not constitute violations of federal law has not changed. . . . We have also concluded that the possibility of drafting effective federal criminal legislation in this area is unlikely." This letter, it should be noted, came on the heels of the massacres in Jim Jones's Guyana commune, which the Justice Department called "abhorrent to decent-minded people everywhere. . . . "

With public furor mounting in the United States, David Berg, who had taken up residence in London, continued to write Mo-letters to his faithful. He advocated polygamy, incest and even sexual activity for schoolchildren.

Mo-letters began to praise the fanatical President of Libya, Muammar el-Kaddafi, describing him as "the saviour who will ignite the young and rescue them from those twin forces of evil, godless Communism and American materialism." The members started distributing "Kaddafi's Third World," from a reading of which Berg had come to admire the powerful Islamic leader. Kaddafi was adopted as their pro-tem Messiah and, in turn, invited members to visit him in Tripoli. Over Libyan radio he commended the Children of God as fighters for the Third World!

In 1978 the Children of God changed their name to the Family of Love in an effort to court a more favorable public image. They are still known as the Children of God, however. In 1980 Berg moved his headquarters from Rome to Zurich—after banishing his wife Jane ("Mother Eve") and taking "Maria," one of his top aides, as his common-law wife. His Mo-letters with their same ugly messages continue to be distributed throughout the world.

In the 1980s the Children of God have tended to attract less publicity. They lead quieter lives on their communes, no longer stampede public gatherings. But they are still actively recruiting converts. Berg, now in his sixties, continues to write periodic Mo-letters to his followers in the U.S. Meanwhile, secure in their righteous ways, the Children of God say they are an entire new nation, "a whole new society built on the Book of Acts. Praise the Lord!"

It is not the first instance in history in which evil has been based on quotations from Scripture.

CHAPTER 18

Reverend Moon and the Unification Church

There are now more than a thousand cults in the United States, with an estimated combined membership around the two-million mark. The Unification Church of the Reverend Sun Myung Moon claims a national membership of between seven and thirty thousand, depending on one's source. The membership—called "Moonies"—stands, it is claimed, at about two million around the world.

I do not like the word "Moonies," incidentally. The diminutive suffix carries a playful connotation associated with such words as "doggies," "kitties," "puppies," etc. There is nothing the least bit playful about the operations of the Reverend Moon's Unification Church.

What are the beliefs that have attracted so many? The basic document of the Moonies is *The Divine Principle,* a 536-page interpretation of the Bible. It is a complicated book. Many ex-members concede that they never grasped all its teachings. The basic concept of Moon's belief is that God intended Adam and Eve to be completely pure in order to reproduce absolutely pure children. But Satan seduced Eve, causing her to become impure. She, in turn, tainted Adam. Their offspring, and all mankind, were henceforth also impure. God gave man a second chance by sending the Messiah, Jesus Christ, who was to marry and produce pure children.

Jesus was to become the True Parent, and as mankind came to know salvation, there would exist a unified world of the faithful and pure. But God was thwarted once again; Jesus was crucified before He was able to marry or father children. The blood of mankind was left impure until a new saviour, the second Messiah, arrived as the True Parent. Whatever else one may say of such a strange scenario, it is certainly rank heresy within the context of Christian orthodoxy.

In some of his statements Moon does not quite claim to be the present Messiah. But he says that the second Messiah was born in Korea between

1917 and 1930. Moon was born in Korea in 1920. Korea, for political purposes, was chosen by God as the new Israel. Moon claims that he was sixteen years of age when Jesus personally explained to him that God again desired to establish his Kingdom on earth and presented the need for someone to assume this mission.

(If every person who is absolutely convinced that he has had a personal conversation with Jesus Christ in recent years is to be believed, then it would seem that Jesus is sending out more such messages than ever before in history. There would be nothing wrong with that in itself—if it actually occurred. The problem is that a good many of the messages are mutually contradictory. It might be helpful if we could convene all those who believe they have been personally instructed by Christ so that they might thrash out the matter among themselves.)

In an interview with *Newsweek* in 1976, when asked if he considered himself to be the new Messiah, Moon replied: "We are in the new Messianic age. But two thousand years ago Jesus Christ never spoke of himself as a Messiah, knowing that would not serve his purpose. I am not saying 'I am the Messiah.' I am just fulfilling God's instruction."

Moon does, however, declare himself to be the True Parent and, as such, the only one capable of cleansing the world of its sins. (So much for the Pope, Billy Graham, Jerry Falwell and company.) With this aim he stages mass marriages among his followers, who are then to produce "pure" progeny who will be the disciples of God.

Stress is placed on sexual morality. On joining the church Moon's followers must confess and renounce all sexual activity, which is said to be derived from Satan, who lays claim to man's body. Chastity is purity. To obtain this purity the members must work and pray until such time as Moon believes they are eligible to form a pure marriage and have the allotted number of children.

Mystery shrouds the sexual taboos within the church. In 1948 Moon was arrested and jailed in North Korea. It has been alleged that he was imprisoned for practicing ritual sex. Moon neither confirms nor denies such reports. He acknowledges that he was imprisoned.

Particularly during the early 1970s, members were expected to raise large sums of money by selling flowers, candles and candy on the streets. The money, of course, belongs to the church; the member is given only room and board. Barbara Underwood, ex-follower and author of *Hostage to Heaven,* tells of how she and five others made $450,000 over a nine-month period by selling roses seven days a week, sixteen hours a day. Her personal average: $400 daily.

A young ex-member who published her story anonymously in

Seventeen magazine recounts that she would rise with the others at 4:00 A.M. and, after a meager breakfast, sell on the streets until the allotted amount of money she had "vowed" to make had been raised. This usually required her to work past midnight. Only then would she return for a meal and ritual singing and chanting—to drive away evil spirits—before she was permitted to collapse in sleep for a few hours.

As well as earning vast amounts of money, the Unification Church adherents are expected to recruit new members. Fully a third of the cultists leave the church each year. Recruiting new members is therefore perceived as vital. Recruiting has an official name: "love-bombing," a potent and psychologically planned effort to disarm with excessive and warm attention.

Following initial social contact, the potential convert is invited for a weekend at a country place, where, in a friendly environment, he is persuaded to remain longer. If visitors show signs of rejection or skepticism, they are made to feel guilty. Once guilt is acknowledged, the members move in. They convince the newcomer that safety and purpose are within the "family." Made to feel loved, important and secure, the newcomer is encouraged to talk freely about himself. He is smiled at, hugged, listened to attentively.

The Unification Church has an estimated annual income of $60 million in the United States alone. Internationally the cult is worth hundreds of millions. Moon himself lives on a $625,000 estate in Irvington, New York; the Unification Church owns the multimillion-dollar New Yorker Hotel, and is said to have made a bid on the Empire State Building. Among the church's assets are the Training Center in Barrytown—an estate of 225 acres—and land in Alabama, California and Massachusetts, where lucrative fishing industries have been launched.

The members work for very little pay—just enough for food—enabling them to undercut local competition and thus causing bitter rivalry with local businesses. The familiar flower-seller on the street is now disappearing as a result of the financial successes of the fishing industry.

But there have been difficulties in the fishing industry. In Gloucester, a picturesque fishing town in Massachusetts, the bitterness was openly expressed by a young fisherman. "We aren't scared of them; we just hate them."

The local police keep the peace in what is a potentially explosive situation.

One of Gloucester's outraged citizens is the mayor, who said to a "60 Minutes" TV camera crew, "Have you ever heard of a religious guy owning one hundred fifty corporations? And running them? Now what in the hell kind of religion is that? You either pray to God or you pray to the [cash] register."

The movement to Gloucester began quietly in 1979 when a company called International Seafood bought a parcel of land, saying they were planning to build a maritime academy. But International Seafood is a Unification Church company. It bought out the Gloucester Lobster Company, the largest lobstering operation in the area, and Bob's Clam Shack, a well-known restaurant.

A New Hampshire couple who, it was later learned, were Unification followers bought a handsome fourteen-room house and sold it to the church for one dollar. It became a Moon dormitory. But the purchase that most outraged Gloucester was that of a mansion that Boston's Richard Cardinal Cushing had once used as a retreat. It had also been used by the Order of the Daughters of Mary of the Immaculate Conception.

The Catholic Church sold the mansion to an out-of-town businessman for $1,000,000. The man, an agent for Moon, immediately resold it to the Unification Church for $1,100,000.

"It was this sale," said CBS's Morley Safer, "that made Gloucester men and women feel that the Reverend Moon had declared religious and economic war on them."

What worries Gloucester is also of concern in Washington, namely, that tax-exempt money taken in by the church goes into the church's many businesses. Furthermore, most of the people working for the church enterprises are themselves Moonies and are said to give back a large part of their salaries as tax-deductible donations to the church, thus providing a church-run enterprise with almost free labor.

Gloucester City Councilman Gus Splint says, "I myself don't believe that there is such a thing as the Unification Church. I think it's one of the greatest schemes ever to come to the country. And the quicker this country and this faith realizes it, then they can drive Mr. Moon back to where he comes from."

Moon had already founded a branch of his Unification Church in the United States before coming to live here in 1972. Upon his arrival the group immediately stepped up activity and discipline. Unlike the Children of God or the Hare Krishnas, the Moonies were deliberately square in their style of dress and appearance, as if the flowing hippie attire of the sixties had never happened. To those who considered the Children of God preachers of doom and the Hare Krishnas too way-out, the anti-Communist, pro-capitalist Moonies, always smiling, seemed a return to a style of clean-cut honest Christian youth.

Unable to speak English (Moon still delivers his public speeches in

Korean), the leader then organized mass rallies, with much fanfare and publicity. Other religious groups were doing the same, but Moon's hypnotic energy attracted greater publicity and interest from press and public. His "God's Hope for America" speech, which he has delivered many times, struck a note of patriotism: "God has chosen America to receive the coming Messiah. Christianity and the United States combined can unify and save the world."

Moon claims that he loves America, but either he is incapable of consistency or he is lying, because he is fervently opposed to some of the principles proclaimed by the American founding fathers. One of the basic building blocks of our free society, for example, is the clear separation of church and state. As scholars of European history, the founding fathers were well aware of the utter necessity of adhering to such a principle if the new nation was to be free. Moon insists on a worldwide *theocracy,* a world that would abolish separation of church and state and be governed by the immediate direction of God. I urge every concerned person in this connection to read the Report of the Sub-Committee on International Organizations of the Committee on International Relations of the U.S. House of Representatives, released on October 31, 1978. It refers specifically to the long-continued investigation of Korean-American relations and is an essential document to anyone interested in the cult phenomenon generally and the Unification Church specifically. On the question of the separation of church and state, the *Congressional Report* quotes Moon as saying, *"Separation between religion and politics is what Satan likes most."* [Italics supplied.]

If we entertain, for purposes of argument, the scenario that Almighty God did appear personally on earth and assumed direct command of human affairs, certainly no religious believer could object. But Moon has nothing of the sort in mind. What he proposes is the establishment of a unified civilization of the *whole world,* to be centered in Korea. The supreme leader would then be not God, who in any event is not subject to human decision of any sort, but Moon himself.

Nor does Moon believe that he is the only Korean who will rule the world. He urges his members to regard the Republic of Korea—the southern half of the nation—with particular reverence and predicts that in time the Korean language will be spoken all over the world. *"In order to set up one culture, we must unify the languages into one . . . in the ideal world centered upon God, everyone will speak only Korean, so no interpreter will be necessary."* [Italics supplied.]

Many of Moon's statements suggest delusions of grandeur. In March 1974 he said in *Master Speaks,* a Unification Church newsletter:

Someday in the near future, when I walk into the Congressman's or the Senator's offices without notice or appointment, the aides will jump out of their seats and go to get their Senator or Congressman, saying he must see Reverend Moon. The time will come, without my seeking it, that my words will almost serve as law. If I ask a certain thing, it will be done. If I don't want something, it will not be done. If I recommend a certain Ambassador for a certain country, and then visit that country . . . he will greet me with the red carpet treatment.

Moon goes on to say, "Let's say that there are 500 [church members] in each state; then we could control the government."

As one learns more and more about Moon and his incredible financial empire, the image that comes to mind is that of one of those forces of evil sometimes portrayed in James Bond novels and films, for Moon and his vast conglomerate seem too bizarre to be real. But real he is; and his ambitions, incredible as they are, are equally real: "If we can manipulate seven nations at least," he has written, "then we can get hold of the whole world: the United States, England, France, Germany, Soviet Russia and maybe Korea and Japan. On God's side, Korea, Japan, America, England, France, Germany, Italy are the nations I count on in order to gain the whole world."

According to the U.S. *Congressional Report* mentioned earlier, Moon has often told his followers to expect opposition, though he has assured them of ultimate victory. But in a speech in 1974 he noted that up to that time opposition to his movement had gone unpunished. That state of affairs, he stated, would no longer pertain. "So far the world can be against us and nothing happened. Now when they are against us then *they are going to get the punishment. So from this time . . . every people, or every organization, that goes against the Unification Church will gradually come down, or drastically come down and die. Many people will die—those that go against our movement."* [Italics added.]

One of the distinguishing characteristics of Moon's Unification Church, the People's Temple, the Children of God, and various other of the new religions is an astonishing meanness of spirit. I have long felt that in evaluating an individual it is not particularly instructive to judge him in his moments of happiness or satisfaction. We are all pleasant company, are we not, at such times? But the true measure of a man may be taken when he is displeased, when he has been contradicted or frustrated. It is in such situations that a person of character will reveal his mettle. There is certainly a time and place for standing up for principle, for speaking truth to power, insisting on the virtuous course, even for fighting back, by legal and moral means. But there is never any justified place for an excessive, vicious spitefulness. Such retaliatory attitudes are characteristic not of great men and women but of fanatics.

One of the more ominous aspects of the new religious forms is that the enthusiasm of some True Believers seems to turn so easily to murder. The world saw the evidence of Jim Jones's People's Temple group killing in what they viewed as defense of the faith. Two members of Synanon were so outraged by criticism from an attorney that they tried to murder him. A number of the groups—the Children of God, for instance—speak openly of their willingness to murder in the cause of what they see as the truth. Many former members of the Children of God and Scientology live in fear of physical attack or harassment, which inhibits them from speaking publicly, for the record, on the subject of their experiences, though they will often share information in confidence and on a not-for-attribution basis.

The world will never know, because there is no way of ascertaining, the exact amount of evil and destruction wrought by criminals perfectly convinced that they are acting in the name of God. The Old Testament is, of course, a rich source of such instances, but there has been no period of history in which such behavior has not been common. As I dictate these observations I have just finished hearing a radio news announcement about England's multiple murderer, Peter Sutcliffe, the Yorkshire Ripper, who announced, after confessing to a long series of grisly crimes, that he felt no guilt because he had been personally ordered by God to act as he did. He asserted, moreover, that if and when he was freed he would resume serving as an avenging angel. It is instructive to note that little or nothing about the man's customary demeanor betrayed the fact of his religious insanity.

While killings by religious people, for religious reasons, are particularly repulsive, the embarrassing historical reality must nevertheless be faced that such crimes have been part of Christian behavior for almost two thousand years.

Even today there are individual fanatics within the traditional folds. But this is quite different from what we find with some of the new religions when they are opposed, for in these instances it is often not rare, unbalanced extremists who commit crimes and other affronts to decency and sense. It is the leaders themselves who not only countenance but encourage such unedifying behavior. And all—God help us—in the name of religion.

Religious believers often delude themselves that, as regards disagreement about religion, the two chief opposing camps are believers vs.

unbelievers. But except in modern times, in countries which have Communist governments, this has not been the case. And even in those modern instances when officially atheistic regimes have hoped to do away with religion, they have discovered that they are unable to do so. Poland under communism, for example, is as staunchly Catholic as ever. The real problem—and one that it is reasonable to assume will persist throughout human experience—comes from disagreements *among* True Believers.

The Reverend Moon and his Unification Church followers, for example, imagine that their true enemies are the devil, the Communists, atheists in general, "the modern world," etc. But secular humanists are more inclined to simply shrug and turn away from such churches, dismissing their members as the religious fanatics they obviously are. No, the true—and effective—opponents of Moon and other leaders of the new religions are Catholics and Protestants in the traditional churches, the U.S. Congress, the FBI, and the IRS. If Moon imagined that his almost hysterical anticommunism would ingratiate him with Christians and Americans of traditional affiliation, he was very much mistaken, at least in the long run. Initially he did deceive many conservatives and Christians by his fervent conservatism, but his name is now mud among Washington officialdom, despite the fact that he managed to sit in a section reserved for guests of the President, the Vice-President, and Congress during Ronald Reagan's swearing-in ceremony.

But from the many unhappy confrontations among the devout, a striking fact emerges, which is that the average believer accepts a surprisingly small portion of the totality of religious doctrine, opinion and custom, and has, moreover, a hearty contempt for by far the greater part of it. The views of the various religious denominations are, after all, to a considerable extent mutually exclusive. In other words, if the Mormons are right, then the Seventh-Day Adventists are wrong. If the Catholic Church is essentially right, then Luther, Calvin, Knox, Wesley and the other Protestant reformers made a tragic mistake and their followers are deluded as regards a good many specifics.

There is a good deal of unclear thinking about this simple point. One form of fuzzymindedness that obscures the factor of mutual exclusivity among various churches and sects is that expressed in such sayings as: "Well, all churches are basically the same "; "We're all taking different roads to the same destination"; "When you get right down to it, the churches are basically saying the same thing." Since this is nonsense, it ought not to be believed. The Unification Church, fortunately, seems now rarely to be included in such tolerant generalizations. Traditional Christians have come to give it a wide berth.

There is so much important information about the Unification cult that it is frustrating to be able to refer here to even considerably less than the tip of the proverbial iceberg. I urge every concerned person to acquire a copy of the book *Gifts of Deceit: Sun Myung Moon, Tongsun Park and the Korean Scandal* by Robert Boettcher and Gordon L. Freedman.

This thorough study, published by Holt, Rinehart and Winston in 1980, is a damning indictment of what is, in fact, a damnable situation. Even more than the insanity, murders and mass suicide of Jonestown, the case of the Unification group raises the most serious questions about the First Amendment and its protection of religion. Presumably every American, as a matter of principle, is in favor of freedom of religion. But is there literally nothing that a church can do, is there literally no crime or depravity it can commit, which will force the American people and their government to rethink the application of the First Amendment to churches of a new, bizarre and dangerous sort?

Suppose, for example, that an ultra-rightist offshoot of the Nazi party decided to do what a number of other essentially nonreligious organizations have done, simply call themselves a religion for the two common reasons: tax benefits and freedom from official investigation. Suppose further that this new "religion" preached that Jews, Communists, blacks and Catholics were agents of the devil and therefore rightfully prey to the new avengers of God. How many people would have to be killed before the Department of Justice, the FBI, the Congress and other agencies of public order decided that matters had gone too far? As the authors of *Gifts of Deceit* ask:

> Does freedom of religion give Moon the right to violate the Thirteenth Amendment to the Constitution, which outlaws slavery?

> Did freedom of religion give Moon the right to be paid secretly by the KCIA to carry out a plot to throw eggs at the Japanese ambassador and disrupt an official visit of the Prime Minister of Japan?

> Does freedom of religion give Moon the right to smuggle large amounts of money into the United States? . . .

> Did freedom of religion give Moon the right to smuggle hundreds of aliens into this country under the guise of "students" or "religious trainees" so he could put them to work full-time in his businesses? . . .

> Did freedom of religion give Moon's minion, Bo Hi Pak, the right to collect $1 million from Americans under the guise of a "Children's Relief Fund," and then use 93 percent of the money to pay public relations men?

Did freedom of religion give Moon and his cult the right to negotiate, as an unregistered agent of the Korean government, for the manufacture and export of M-16 rifles?

Does freedom of religion give Moon the right to infiltrate the offices of Senators and Congressmen with covert agents who report details of personal lives to the cult for its special card file?

CHAPTER 19

Sunburst

The Brotherhood of the Sun, based in Santa Barbara, is another of the smaller religious groups. Consisting of only a few hundred people but apparently one of the strongest communities financially, the group owns thousands of acres of land in California, as well as a successful network of health food stores and restaurants. Sunburst Farms is one of their commercial names. The founder is Norm Paulsen.

There are two aspects of Sunburst communities. One is a church, incorporated as a nonprofit corporation in California. The other is Sunburst Farms, the natural foods business that has four markets in Santa Barbara and one in Ventura. It also has a wholesale health food distributing company, said to be the largest in the nation.

The headquarters of the community is the Tajiguas Ranch, consisting of five or six thousand acres extending from the ocean up into the mountains. The communal center, it is built on an old Shoomach tribe Indian village. The group also owns a 126-foot schooner, *The Star Pilot,* and runs a horse business featuring both show and western horses.

In the summer of 1980 they started a new venture, Sunburst Publications. The first item issued was Paulsen's autobiography, *Sunburst—Return of the Ancients.*

At seventeen, leader Paulsen entered the monastery of Paramhansa Yogananda, an East Indian adept and founder of the Self-Realization Fellowship in Los Angeles, where he studied religion and the yogic teachings. At this time he reported having extraordinary visions. One was an image of young people working and living together on the land in a beautiful environment. These visions or dreams, Paulsen feels, were centered on the Santa Barbara coastal mountain area. He says he saw a free society of people governed by "the Living, Divine Spirit, the masculine and feminine Creative Force."

Paulsen's church, he asserts, is not a cult. "We are a sect. As defined by *Webster's International Dictionary,* a sect is:

179

1. A way of life, hence a faith in certain precepts for the guidance of life.
2. A religion of faith; those attached to a certain opinion or set of opinions. Those following a particular leader or authority.
3. The believers in a particular creed or upholders of a particular religious practice.
4. In philosophy, the disciples of a particular school."

Of himself, Paulsen says, "I was baptized a minister of the Self-Realization Fellowship, Inc., in 1951 by Paramhansa Yogananda, the founder. I left the organization in 1951 to pursue my calling in Santa Barbara. I am now a practicing minister of Sunburst Communities, a state and federally recognized church incorporated in 1971. I have founded Sunburst on many of the principles, practices and guidelines that were passed on to me by my teacher, the late Paramhansa Yogananda, a Swami [priest] in one of the ancient religious orders of India."

Sunburst emerged as a reality in 1969 in Santa Barbara, where Paulsen was given six months' free rent by the Lyons Realty Company on an old building at 808 East Cota Street on the condition he and his friends rebuild the interior and make it habitable. "This we did," Paulsen says, "and the building now serves as Santa Barbara's Indian Center." At first Paulsen taught young men of his community the skills he had learned as a cement finisher, carpenter and brick and stone mason. His group then began to take on small construction jobs on an hourly basis. As they became experienced, they built residential structures for friends and earned money to cover living expenses.

In the summer of 1968, Paulsen suffered a back injury while laying concrete block at the University of California at Santa Barbara. The injury left him unfit ever again to work in the demanding construction field. In 1970 a settlement for his back injury was used as a down payment on the first Sunburst Farm, where his sect began to grow organic fruit and vegetables. In 1971 he began selling natural foods to the community at large and opened the first Sunburst Market.

The goals of Sunburst, however, are not merely to create an attractive physical environment and grow good, natural food. "Our real goal is to meet the Living God face to face, and bring others to this meeting place. This we have successfully done through the years, as people in our society continue to testify of encounters with the Living Spirit. . . . Many have seen the incredible brilliance of Christ, the Son, manifest within and around themselves. We seek to bring our members to the highest place within themselves, the consciousness of Christ, the Son. When we attain this position within ourselves, the mental and physical dimensions respond to us in harmony."

Since some distraught parents assume that their sons and daughters are kept behind locked doors, or under constant supervision—as are, for example, students in a Catholic boarding school (I speak from experience)—Sunburst commune addresses the question directly. "Our people are free to go. They always have been. Of the people who visit us looking for a spiritual community, only about ten percent decide they would like to stay awhile and try our life-style. Once they make that decision, we do not have a large turnover. Orientation procedures for new members are such that they have as long as two years to decide if they want to share this way of life with us on a permanent basis. Usually, those who feel unable to fit into our life-style leave within the first three months. Occasionally, a senior member decides he or she wants to leave the community, either because their goals have changed or they feel that we, as a group, no longer fill their needs."

Are members free to visit parents, friends or relatives? "Certainly. Many of our people spend the holiday seasons with friends and relatives, who are also encouraged to visit Sunburst and participate in our activities."

To those who fear a commune is only a disguised center for group sex or other forms of immorality, the Sunbursters respond, "We have established spiritual goals, and guidelines to help people achieve them. It is up to the individual to follow the guidelines if he or she so chooses. If someone decides to step beyond them, and people occasionally do, it's that person's responsibility to make the necessary correction if he wants to continue living in our society. We never give up on a person unless he gives up on himself. An old saying states: A saint is a sinner who never gave up.

"As we have grown together, we have found that our policies have evolved and changed. . . . We have used the virtue of chastity as another guideline, encouraging members not to live or sleep together unless they are married. Marriage is a sacred commitment to all of us. It identifies the union of two spirits as helpmates. We feel that chastity in marriage is achieved when desire no longer exists, and sex is used only to create a new vehicle for a spirit to inhabit."

On the question of drugs: "We at Sunburst do not *condone* the use of drugs for recreational purposes, but if someone has a medical problem and is under doctor's care, he or she is free to choose to follow the advice of his physician and to take a prescription medication." Herbal remedies are available within the Sunburst community as an alternate approach to traditional antibiotics. While there is no official ban on the use of prescription medication, there is a taboo placed on the use of marijuana and other drugs for recreational use. In fact, use of such chemicals may be grounds for expulsion from the community, according to one Sunburst member who has been a part of the sect for eleven years.

Four charges have been leveled against the Brotherhood. The first concerns an incident in which Paulsen pulled a gun on two citizens; the second involved Paulsen's arrest for driving with an open bottle of liquor in his car. There was a rumor that the entire community was arming and fortifying itself in preparation for the coming Armageddon; and, lastly, there were reports that large amounts of the group's money had come from outside sources, possibly from the followers of the Reverend Sun Myung Moon.

Sunburst responds that all the charges are ill founded. The gun story is said to be based on the fact that Paulsen witnessed a hard-drug transaction being made, pulled a revolver, which he used for his own protection, and made a citizen's arrest. The issue got confused, and he was charged with assault. In any event, the case was thrown out of court for lack of evidence.

The group's version of the liquor bottle incident is that a friend had been drinking in the car and left the bottle behind the seat. Paulsen didn't know about it.

In June of 1981 a suit was filed against the Sunburst community by as many as seventy of its former members asking monetary damages and compensation in the amount of $1.3 million.

From a membership numbering 340 in 1978 the community had dwindled down to under 150. According to articles in the *Santa Barbara News and Review,* most of the "lost" members were veterans of Sunburst who had helped to build the community into one of the most financially prosperous religious and business-related organizations in the country. The basic complaint of the suit was that members worked without compensation of any kind to profit Paulsen and other Sunburst leaders. This free labor allowed Sunburst to purchase thousands of acres of lucrative Santa Barbara real estate—the Rancho Tajiguas property—lying between the ranches of Ronald Reagan and John Travolta, a 145-acre Gaviota property, and a Milnas Street market property. The Tajiguas land was purchased in 1977 for a reported $3.6 million. As of 1981 it was estimated to be worth over three times that figure.

Allegations surrounding the suit contend that Paulsen maintains his own personal security force, trained in karate and marksmanship and known to carry weapons. A former security team member tells his version of the aforementioned arrest of Paulsen for driving with liquor in his car: Paulsen was pulled over on a highway outside of Santa Barbara by officers one night in 1978. He was "extremely tipsy"; an open bottle of vodka was found in the backseat of his car. Though Paulsen denied he had been drinking, officers roughed him up. Later Paulsen returned to the Sunburst ranch and called together his security team: "He . . . organized the security team, armed to the teeth . . . to raid the sheriff's department and find the deputies who beat him up and kill them." Paulsen allegedly prepared everyone for action, and then at the last moment he canceled his order, declaring it "just a test."

Though Paulsen eventually pleaded no contest to lesser charges in the drunk driving case, his reputation as a spiritual leader had clearly been challenged.

The *Santa Barbara News and Review* papers detailing the above information were stolen from newsstands around the community. When a second run was subsequently distributed, some readers who purchased papers noted that the pages on the Sunburst community were missing.

The stories about arming and preparing for Armageddon have been dismissed by Sunburst spokesman John Stump as sheer fabrication and/or distortion. As for the last charge mentioned above—unknown financial support—Sunburst points out that its businesses are successful and the community self-sufficient. In response to questions regarding the philosophical splits within the organization, Stump maintains that there is actually no schism. People have left, sometimes in fairly large numbers, but have not continued another sect or branch. They have just gone away—usually, Stump claims, because of arguments over the use of alcohol. Paulsen's official position is, "You are free to drink, but not here."

So far, it is clear, the way of life described is clearly far preferable, on a number of grounds, to much of the social behavior that characterizes life in modern America.

If this is substantially all there is to existence in the religious communes, why the controversy? Why the cries of outraged parents? Why the odium that attaches to such "cults"?

In the case of Paulsen and his brotherhood, the average person—even one unprejudiced and prepared to consider such social experiments on their merits—will almost certainly regard Paulsen's philosophical rationale for his work as totally out of touch with reality.

For example, in his book, *Sunburst—Return of the Ancients,* he says, "Five hundred thousand years ago the earth supported a super-civilization. This super race, called The Builders, was invaded by a malignant negative force around *350,000 years ago.* This invasion was fought out in space for a while—from Earth, Mars, and the moons of Jupiter. The enemy first forced a landing in the Euphrates Valley, bringing the war to Earth's surface.

"A devastating attack by the Nephilim destroyed the whole continent of Mu finally and generated the great Biblical flood. This flood made the earth uninhabitable for the invaders as well as most of The Builders. The Builders, *suffering the loss of over sixty million people in one night,* began to load their star ships with survivors from other colonies around the earth. . . . " [Italics added.] It is not necessary to quote more to establish the point.

Not only do rationalists, secular humanists, atheists, and agnostics consider such accounts absurd, unscientific and completely lacking in credibility as history, but traditional Christians, too, regard such beliefs as nonsensical.

This is not, of course, true of all followers of Jesus. There have always been a certain number within the Christian fold who are ready to embrace almost any new theory, however preposterous, as long as it embodies references to the Flood, the Garden of Eden, Adam and Eve, Moses, the Apocalypse, or God-knows-what facets of Christian and/or Jewish belief. Of this all-too-common tendency to accept unlikely theories before subjecting them to even the vaguest rational analysis, I shall have more to say in the concluding chapter of this book.

The *desire* to believe explains Norm Paulsen's deluded sense of historical reality and science. People like Paulsen—and their number is increasing in our time—rarely consider any hypothesis other than that which first occurs to them when they speculate on their dreams. We all have bizarre dreams. Dreams, by their very nature, are no respecters of physical laws. But such random visions are likely to be accepted with reverence only by those who are determined to believe.

Those who *want* to have visions, who want to be perceived as wonder workers and dreamers of great dreams, can, to a large extent, dictate the content of such dreams. To the degree that their visions are harmonious with their conscious interests, they then make the mistake of interpreting such dream material as a form of dictation from the beyond. Practically everyone knows this, but the field of religious belief has never yielded to majority opinion. Tell a man that the whole world regards him as a fool for his religious beliefs and you have made not the slightest impression so far as changing his opinions is concerned. This is one of the tragic and unhappy factors that must be credited to the dark side of religion's ledger.

In times of social turmoil such dreamers will always arise and will have little trouble surrounding themselves with followers. This state of affairs will, I assume, continue literally for as long as there is human experience on the earth, unless world society undertakes a conscious and radical change in its process of education.

CHAPTER 20

Synanon

I include the organization called Synanon in this partial study because, although originally it was not religious, it does have a philosophical rationale, as well as other factors common to the purely religious groups: a communal style of living, the contribution of personal financial holdings to the commonwealth, subservience to a strong leader, rigid rules and regulations, and a sometimes strangely fierce group loyalty.

Since I played a modest role in Synanon's early days in encouraging its program for the rehabilitation of drug addicts, I was saddened recently to read a book called *Escape from Utopia*. The author, William F. Olin, spent ten years in Synanon and knows whereof he speaks. But it is still not clear why such a widely respected therapeutic community went wrong. The reader may form his own opinions.

In 1959 Richard Bock, a recording executive, told me about the place and suggested that I go down to visit it. I set aside an evening to have dinner at the Synanon headquarters on the beach at Santa Monica—in the company of our houseguest of the moment, famed Broadway director-producer Jed Harris—and stayed until after midnight. During a long discussion I offered to form a citizens' committee to attract attention to the organization, particularly among people in the entertainment field. Jed Harris and Ivon Goff, a former president of the Screen Writers' Guild, agreed on the spot to serve on the committee.

It is important to appreciate what Synanon was then accomplishing. Most people in those days—and even at present—thought that the right thing to do with addicts was to arrest them and throw them into jail. I suppose if they all served full-life sentences the streets might be a little cleaner; but of course if the reader's own son, nephew, brother, husband, or father happened to become addicted and was sentenced to life imprisonment for "treatment" for his medical problem, the issue would come into clearer focus.

The problem with sentencing addicts to prison—even to institutions that supposedly rehabilitate them—is that the institutions are, by and large, failures. Synanon's founder, Chuck Dederich, saw the terrible futility of the traditional approach. By way of contrast, Synanon, from the first, produced unprecedented results. Dederich was not, of course, the first to attempt to do something to cure addicts. Narcotics Anonymous, fashioned after Alcoholics Anonymous, was already in operation. But it did not provide a live-in situation for drug victims. That was the totally new factor that Synanon provided. The addiction to hard narcotics is so compelling that Dederich realized that nothing but twenty-four-hour surveillance—during an initial period—would suffice.

I made frequent visits to Synanon headquarters in those days, and there were some amusing moments as well as powerfully emotional experiences. One night I sat in with some jazz musician addicts who were residents. We performed on a small stage in a large room. I later learned that a young junkie right off the street had been led to a comfortable sofa in the room, given personal attention, talked to and encouraged, during which process he either passed out or fell asleep. When he woke up, hours later, he said, "Man, I was in such a confused state last night that at one point I actually thought I saw Steve Allen up on that stage playing the piano."

Synanon was not only cleaning up addicts in those days; it was—literally—saving lives. There were a number of tragic cases in which people came to Synanon, toyed with the idea of staying, but were unable to make the commitment. One of them, a young doctor with a family, applied for help, but when he learned that he would have to live on the premises, he left. Two days later he killed himself with a shotgun. Others who almost came in but drew back were found dead from overdoses.

During the next few years I kept in fairly close touch with my friends at Synanon. Soon people who were not addicts at all but were favorably impressed by the life-style of the members moved in, some with their entire families. For the first time in their lives they had a sense of commitment to a group and dedication to a good social purpose.

It was indeed inspiring then to spend social time with sensible, intelligent people, many of whom had formerly been thieves, prostitutes, con men and hustlers of various kinds simply to support their heroin habit. As novelist Guy Endore said after an early visit, "People come to study Synanon and to ask Chuck Dederich, the director, to help open up a Synanon in their community. But not only will Synanons spread geographically, for the treatment of dope fiends in various localities, but it will spread socially, for the treatment of all manner of character problems.

As an example of the responsible thought that characterized the Synanon approach in the 1960s, consider *The Synanon Prayer:*

Please let me first and always examine myself.
Let me be honest and truthful.
Let me seek and assume responsibility.
Let me understand rather than be understood.
Let me trust and have faith in myself and my fellow man.
Let me love rather than be loved.
Let me give rather than receive.

Now consider the Synanon of the 1970s: Chuck Dederich, dressed in flowing purple robes, sits in the King Freak Chair, expressionless, as he watches about fifty people taking part in The Game. They are dressed in white robes; some wear colored scarves around their heads signifying rank; the Head Shepherd carries a crook; the women wear no makeup or jewelry. Most of the men have shaved heads, as do some of the women. All are completely engrossed as they listen to members psychologically strip themselves bare—revealing their innermost hostilities and anxieties. The Game is the prolonged group-encounter session that, during the sixties, helped thousands in their desperate search for a means to kick drugs, booze or pills, or simply to find a better life-style, one that would make some sense in the face of the general social disorder.

Synanon started as a dream of healing, nonviolence, love and support that would enable addicts to kick their habits and find a useful place in society. Twenty years later the dream—in the opinion of some critics—had become a nightmare of violence, lawsuits, psychological abuse, even attempted murder.

In 1958 Charles Dederich—by his own account—was a falling-down alcoholic, unemployed and living in California after a string of jobs and marriages that had all led to failure. Middle-aged, overweight, alone, Dederich called Alcoholics Anonymous. They sobered him, and a dream was born. With a $33 unemployment check he rented a rundown Santa Monica storefront and turned it into a treatment center of his own. He called it the T.L.C. Club, for Tender Loving Care. Society's rejects came: drug addicts, thieves, alcoholics, pimps, prostitutes, muggers, and a few so troubled they could make no sense with words whatsoever, communicating only with grunts and sounds. Most were homeless; a handful came from psycho wards. A few were rich delinquents in need of direction. These were able and willing to supply needed money to Dederich's early movement.

Culling from his experience with A.A. and his knowledge of Emerson, Freud and Lao-tze, Dederich devised The Game. It was an instant success. The losers exposed their frailties. Chuck, whom they loved, spoke tough, harsh truths. Babying weaklings was not part of Dederich's scheme. At one of these Games an addled junkie confused the words seminar and symposium, blending the two into one: Synanon.

In a few months word was getting out: Synanon was saving lives. Junkies put away their needles, alcoholics went sober, pills were thrown out. Contributions from liberals and some public-minded businessmen flowed in. What had seemed an impossibility was becoming a reality. Discussing Synanon, an ex-member spoke of their goal to transform "the scum of the earth, the dope fiends, the drunks, the criminals, into a movement that would be a model for society that, by its example, would change society itself."

Over the next several years the Synanon empire acquired properties throughout the United States, Europe and Asia. Twenty million dollars was spent in creating meeting houses and communal living centers. Dederich was a cheerful visionary creating a Utopia. But he was also a hard-nosed businessman. That he remained something of an enigma personally was one source of his power. He commanded respect; he charmed. "The left loved him because he was a humanitarian and believed in nonviolence and communal living," said a friend of Dederich's. "The right loved him because he wouldn't take a dime from the government and was getting muggers and junkies off the streets. It was the ultimate coalition. You couldn't touch him." He had, by the early seventies, helped thousands of addicts to straighten out. No applicant was turned away, no matter how hopeless, addicted or troublesome.

Dederich wore farmer's overalls, drew an annual salary of close to $100,000, and drove in a chauffeured Cadillac. "A lot of guys could do this from an old Ford roadster and sit on an orange crate," he said. "They're holy men. I'm not. I need a $17,000 Cadillac."

But hidden from public view were the beginnings of problems within the organization. Defectors, "splittees" in the Synanon jargon, were beginning to talk about what they considered Dederich's megalomania and the corruption that came with his absolute power. There were also tax problems. As a nonprofit charitable organization Synanon was exempt from personal income tax, but as a nonreligious organization it was not exempt from taxation on land holdings. The solution came in July 1974 when Dan Garret, the organization's legal counsel, wrote a lengthy letter to Dederich. "We could very probably achieve near immunity from recurring attempts to license Synanon. If we are a religious community, and we are in the process of living our religion as a life-style, then the state and federal constitutional guarantees of freedom of religion would offer complete protection against such legislative or bureaucratic interference.

It appears there would also be considerable advantages from a tax standpoint. . . . "

The original articles of incorporation were amended to state that Synanon's primary purpose was to operate as "a church for religious purposes." It was explained that Synanon had originally been created with religious intent.

By 1974 Dederich's followers by the thousands had proven their loyalty to him and his organization. The Synanon creed was incorporated into the Ceremonies, and flowing gowns were ordered, thus making adherents resemble members of the Love Family and other new communal groups.

The Synanon religion is described as being "pragmatic and not dependent upon divine revelation or dogma. The Synanon Church seeks the essential truth which underlies all systems of philosophy, science and religion."

Prior to 1974 marriages performed in Synanon involved the witnessing and signature of a minister or rabbi. From that date, however, all state marriages for couples wed in the commune were signed by ministers of the Synanon religion. This changed in 1976, when the "Synanon Marriage" replaced the state marriage contract. This was conceived as a three-year, time-limited "love match." The contract is renewable every three years and is described as being a "sacerdotal/ceremony/function of the Synanon religion."

Although Synanon termed itself a church, it was not until May 1980 that the state granted it official recognition as such. During the intervening years legal and moral problems plagued the group. Life within the organization, however, proceeded largely as if oblivious to outside criticism.

Synanon is a highly controlled environment where obedience is both expected and routine. In 1970, when Dederich stopped smoking, he ruled that everyone else should also stop. They did. He shaved his head; so did the members. He took up whittling; for thirty minutes each evening all members whittled. His wife, Betty—a warm, likable black woman—went on a diet; all members were ordered to curtail their food intake and report to weekly weigh-ins. Chuck took up aerobic exercises; for fifteen minutes each morning members also joined in the "huff and puff." Few argued. But few were prepared for the founder's next move—vasectomies.

In January 1977 Dederich decided that Synanon would care for all "the children of the world." The homeless, the neglected, abused, delinquent. Those who had already arrived, those who had been sent by doctors, parents and authorities, and those yet to arrive. In order to take better care of these troubled or abandoned children, Dederich said it was necessary to sacrifice something. That something was giving up the right to bear one's own children. Within a week some two hundred men had undergone vasectomies performed by Synanon's own team of doctors working around the clock. "A lot of these guys were under obvious emotional duress," said a member of the medical team. "They were being coerced. Some of them were scared to death." Some became splittees. Most complied. One who did not was Dederich himself; "I am not bound by the rules," he said. "I make them."

In April of the same year Betty Dederich died of cancer. For a while Dederich was engulfed by profound sorrow. Finally he snapped out of it and looked for a replacement for Betty; "I sent up a flare, like any monarch of old times would have done," he told reporters. "I let the word out that I was available." Applications began to pour in. He narrowed the list down to six, dated each, then settled on a thirty-one-year-old teacher. Dederich, then in his mid-sixties, had become adroit at what he called "changing my position." But taking a new wife for himself was not enough to satisfy him; he now commanded that a massive divorce and remarriage ceremony take place within Synanon. "Most of these couples were going to be divorced anyway," he explained. "I thought 'Wouldn't it be funny to perform some kind of emotional surgery on couples who were getting along pretty well.'" Within days 230 couples had filed for divorce and, after the appropriate Synanon ceremony, were "love-matched" to new mates, in some cases to virtual strangers, in a procedure resembling an auction. Names were listed on a blackboard. "I have a woman. Who wants her?" rang out. There was a festive atmosphere. But people were unhappy and upset.

Once the "love-match" was completed, the couples were expected to consummate the relationship. In order to ensure this, they were observed. One man claims he was severely reprimanded during The Game for failing to make love to his new wife, while his real wife managed to fake illness to avoid consummation of her new love-match. This couple decided to leave Synanon. Three members—after Dederich said, "Put those people in a pickup truck and throw them into a ditch"—drove them to a vacant field eleven miles from the nearest town, where they were then kicked out of the truck, the wife knocked to the ground and the husband threatened with a gun. "If you ever come back, we'll break your backs," the couple claim they were told.

This incident has special significance because Synanon was founded as nonviolent. In 1973, reacting to harassment, vandalism, trespassers, death and bomb threats, Dederich changed his policy: "Nonviolence was a position. We can change our position anytime we want to."

The group purchased an arsenal of rifles and projectiles. An ex-member reports that the attitude was "It's them against us." Members were now trained in "Syn-do," the Synanon form of martial arts. The most intensive training was given to a small, elite group called "The Imperial Marines." Two of these were Lance Kenton and Joe Musico. Their names would later be connected with a sensational public drama.

New instances of physical brutality and cruelty were reported. An ex-resident, then aged fifteen, said in a sworn deposition, "They were always hitting children. In 1974, September, three boys tried to escape from Tomales Bay. After they were caught they were beaten. Two of them slammed against a metal building over and over. The third boy was punched in the stomach. He screamed that he was hurt real bad, but they punched him again. We were told that this is what would happen to us if we tried to run away."

"To hell with you dope fiends," an ex-member quotes Chuck Dederich saying. "I hate dope fiends. I hate that I've had to kiss your ass to build Synanon." But Dederich had from the first refused to coddle addicts. He wanted to strengthen them.

Publicity and media comment—for years largely complimentary—began to be negative. There were stories of Synanon hit-men threatening "enemies" and splittees. Beatings, muggings, threats, an ex-member's dog found hanging from a rope. Lawsuits became common. The *San Francisco Examiner* carried a two-part article written by an ex-member; Synanon sued and collected $2.6 million. A television station was hit with a $42 million slander suit after it aired a highly critical series. Time, Inc. was sued for $76.75 million when the magazine published an article titled "Life at Synanon Is Swinging." Said Dederich, "Nobody fucks with Synanon and gets away with it."

Dederich went too far when he appeared on a television interview to discuss his action against *Time*. In talking about his problem with *Time* he said: "I don't know what these people [Synanon's friends] might do. I don't know what actions they might take against the people responsible, their wives, their children . . . Bombs could be thrown in very odd places, into the homes of some clowns who occupy high places in the *Time* organization. I would certainly not institute anything like that, but I would have no way of preventing it if it should happen."

Splittees began leaving in droves. Violence increased. Members of the Imperial Marines were sent out to track down people who threatened Dederich's life or to sue Synanon. The members put on caps and removed all identification before going out. They were told that if they were caught, Synanon could not publicly defend them or acknowledge that they were working for the organization.

Dan Garrett, Synanon's lawyer, said that because of Synanon's Open

Door policy, a few of those telling stories about such incidents were literally crazy. One man had arrived at the center claiming he was a wheelbarrow, he said.

In September 1978 an ex-member, Phil Ritter, who had summoned the sheriff during the vasectomies—and who had been fighting to gain custody of his daughter, who remained in Synanon with his ex-wife—was clubbed on the skull. As he lay bleeding and in pain, he was beaten repeatedly until his assailant ran to a getaway car driven by another man. Witnesses described the men as having "close-cropped hair, like a prison cut, or the Marines."

Some defectors began receiving notes: "Did you hear what happened to Phil Ritter?" Some ex-members lived in terror. Some of the remaining nine hundred members also lived in fear because they knew too much. Dederich tape-recorded all the Games.

After long years of being dried out, he was even drinking heavily. And he was taping his threats. "Our new religious posture is this: don't mess with us. You can get killed dead. Physically dead. . . . I'm quite willing to break some lawyer's legs, and then tell him, 'The next time I'm going to break your wife's legs, and then we're going to cut your kid's ear off. Try me. This is only a sample, you son of a bitch! And that's the end of your lawyer."

The voice that speaks here is clearly not that of the strong, wise Chuck Dederich of 1960. It is that of a troubled, angry, frightened man.

In September 1978 attorney Paul Morantz won a $300,000 default judgment against Synanon, representing a couple who had charged false imprisonment, brainwashing and kidnapping. Morantz was well aware that in winning he had earned himself a place on Synanon's "enemies list." He bought a gun, kept his eyes open for any shorn-headed men who might be following him, and asked for protection from the police and the state attorney general's office. Letters came in from people around the country, pleading with him to help them gain custody of loved ones still inside Synanon.

At 5:00 P.M. on October 19, 1978, Morantz reached inside his mailbox; in agony he yanked his hand back. A four-and-one-half-foot diamond-back rattlesnake had embedded its deadly fangs deeply between his fingers. He shook the snake free and rushed inside his house, where he shouted: "It's Synanon! Synanon got me!" and then collapsed. He was rushed to a hospital, where eleven vials of antiserum saved his life.

Neighbors supplied the police with the license plate number of a car which had earlier pulled up at Morantz's house. The car was traced to Synanon's Badger commune, 225 miles north of Los Angeles. There the police arrested Joseph Musico, twenty-eight; and Lance Kenton, twenty, son of Stan Kenton, the orchestra leader. Both were members of Synanon's Imperial Marines. They pleaded no contest to the charge of conspiracy to commit murder and were sentenced to a year in county jail and three years' probation.

All that remained for the law to do was to link the case with Dederich. In December 1978 Dederich was arrested on charges of conspiracy to murder Paul Morantz. But the law was unable to arraign him: he was too drunk. "When we went in," said an arresting officer, "he was in a stupor, staring straight ahead, with an empty bottle of Chivas Regal in front of him." Dederich was ordered to undergo a period of hospital treatment under a bail of $500,000. He eventually entered a plea of *nolo contendere* and was released with five years' probation and a $5,000 fine.

Superior Court Judge William P. Hogoboom said that it was Dederich's deteriorating health that led him to grant probation: "This is the sole reason for not imposing a substantial prison term in this case, because I think it is deserved otherwise," said the judge, who also ordered Dederich to abandon any leadership role in Synanon.

Today the ex-founder lives a reclusive life in the Badger Commune, where, according to an old Chicago high school friend of mine, Jack Harrison, legal assistant to the Synanon Church, he suffers from the same illnesses that plagued him for many years—heart problems, involuntary melancholia, and high blood pressure. His daughter, Jady, is now Chairman of the Board in California; his son, Chuck Dederich, Jr., is Chairman in Arizona.

On April 24, 1981, Harrison and Frank Rehack of Synanon came to my offices to bring certain pro-Synanon materials to my attention. We chatted for about an hour, during which time they played a promotional videotape for me. It told about the Synanon Distribution Network, which acquires nonsellable goods from various business corporations and distributes them to worthy organizations. This aspect of Synanon's activities is clearly virtuous. It disposes of breads, cereals, Italian food products, athletic shoes, frozen food, hardware, canned vegetables and other items, in amounts which, by 1979, were running to seven million dollars per year. Synanon conducts the campaign at no profit to itself. Harrison and Rehack showed me copies of letters on the stationery of the Coca-Cola Company, Carnation, Adidas and other established firms, all expressing thanks for the way in which the Synanon people had disposed of materials that could not be sold.

In light of its recent difficulties, it seems surprising to many that Synanon is still functioning. When my research assistant, Maureen Earl, asked Harrison how Synanon is able to function in spite of critical public opinion, Harrison replied: "I would say it's the rightness of our cause, and the fact that it was always a very weak case against Chuck. Also the case against the two young men [Kenton and Musico] was also trumped up. We don't talk to the press now, rarely. They've proven to be slanted, biased. But we continue our process of helping people. We've not stopped our work."

Membership is down. New members once joined at the rate of a thousand a year. The figure was down to one hundred in mid-1981.

There is no denying that Synanon has saved lives; that in the early days it was a miracle worker, worthy of the high praise it received. Most ex-Synanites who once embraced the entire philosophy are saddened by the events of recent years. In the words of an ex-member: "It's just tragic to think that all that positive energy, all that promise, has turned into something so negative and misguided."

The future of the Synanon Church? To continue helping people, to continue changing the world, say the remaining followers.

CHAPTER 21

The International Society of Krishna Consciousness

Notice to Travelers

Representatives of the Hare Krishna organization (also known as the International Society for Krishna Consciousness Incorporated or ISKCON) are under order of court prohibiting them from:

> touching you without your consent
>
> obstructing your free movement by standing in front of you or blocking your way
>
> stopping or soliciting you within a red safety area at an escalator
>
> repeatedly requesting money from you when you have already declined
>
> misrepresenting the true name or purpose of their organization or the intended use of donations
>
> failing to make change for you after promising to do so
>
> threatening you with physical harm
>
> City of Los Angeles Department of Airports

For centuries the West sent missionaries to the East. Only during the last century did the East begin to send representatives to the West. Their purpose, at first, was not so much to convert as to bring an awareness of Eastern religious philosophies to a society that was, at the time, undergoing radical change and reexamination.

The two schools of thought could exchange ideas, but a true blending of such divergent philosophies was not possible. Western philosophy and life were implicitly scientific, constantly questioning, seeking answers to and from outside matter. The East has always looked inward. The Eastern mind accepts rather than seeks to explain. This patience to accept in a passive rather than active manner is, in my view, the result of the Eastern belief in reincarnation and the hopelessness of radical social reform in India.

Part of the appeal of the Hare Krishna movement derives from the centuries-old power of Hinduism, of which the Krishna branch is a form, just as the Methodist Church is a branch of Christianity. Professor A. L. Basham, a leading authority on the history and religions of India, has said, "If you asked me what, in the scale of history, is the most important thing to have happened in the last hundred years in Hinduism . . . I would answer . . . the most important thing . . . is that, for the first time in over a thousand years, it has begun to make an impact outside India."

Basham takes some exception, however, to the activities of those who are largely responsible for the new popularity of Hinduism. "This," he says, "has largely been due to what I call the 'streamlined swamis' and their successful and often very profitable activities in the West. . . . I am thinking . . . of the doctrines which the gentlemen put forth, in a streamlined kind of Hindu mysticism designed to appeal to modern, jet-aged disciples . . . Hinduism without class, without polytheism, without rigid taboos."

But Basham exempts the Hare Krishna movement from his general criticism of the "streamlined swamis." There is nothing streamlined about [Founder] Prabhupada's doctrine. His efforts were directed not at providing a simplified, easy Hinduism, attractive to Western customers, but something much nearer the traditional model . . . and this, as I see it, is the most impressive feature of the Hare Krishna movement. . . . It doesn't sugar the pill for the Western convert, as most of the streamlined swamis do. The Hare Krishna devotee must live the life of the old-fashioned Bengali Vaishnavite devotee, and it's a hard life to live."

For those Americans—whether Christians, Jews or secular humanists—who simply cannot understand the appeal of Hinduism in any form, a book titled *The Path of the Masters* might be helpful. Its author was Julian Johnston, an American who originally went to India to teach Christianity but in time concluded that the Indian forms of religion were superior in certain respects. Much of what Johnston says will seem perfectly acceptable to those who are members of almost any religion. For example:

> We moderns are so busy studying the external world that we have to a great extent forgotten to study the internal world. We worry about the cure of our aches and pains, our asthma and rheumatism, and take no thought for the cure of our feverish desires and unworthy ambitions.

One of the many interesting chapters in *The Path of the Masters* is titled "Quotations from Prominent Christians," which refers to the mystic experiences of medieval Catholic saints. Johnson quotes, among others, St. Francis Xavier.

> After this prayer, I once found myself inundated with a vivid light; it seemed to me that a veil was lifted up from before my eyes of the spirit, and all the truths of human science, even those that I had not studied, became manifest to me by an infused knowledge. This state of intuition lasted for about twenty-four hours, and then, as if the veil had fallen again, I found myself as ignorant as before. At the same time, an interior voice said to me: "Such is human knowledge; of what use is it? It is I, it is My love, that must be studied."

Other Christians quoted in the chapter are St. Ignatius, St. Benedict and St. Theresa.

Today in the U.S. there are five thousand full-time devotees of this religion, and a further estimate of half a million who retain some form of belief and contact with the movement. Internationally, Hare Krishna temples have ten thousand full-time devotees. In India up to three hundred million worship Krishna.

Krishna worship has been a sect of Hinduism in India since 1486. It was not until 1965 that Swami Bhaktivendanta Prabhupada, guru of the International Society of Krishna Consciousness, arrived in the United States and began making converts. Some of his early recruits came from the hippie culture. In New York's Greenwich Village he set up storefront headquarters. Classes started, followers shaved their heads—leaving only the topknot, known as the Sikha—donned yellow robes, made vows of celibacy and took to the streets, naturally attracting a great deal of interest and considerable criticism. What the critics particularly resented was the aggressive manner of recruiting and begging for money. It was, some argued, like a street scene in Calcutta and not fitting for America.

Though the daily regimen for a Krishna devotee is strict, Krishna Consciousness spread rapidly. Attention was drawn by the involvement of popular Beat figures of the era; Allen Ginsberg, who in the fifties had

advocated Zen-Buddhism, now turned to the Swami for spiritual
guidance. George Harrison of the Beatles wrote a song for the Hare
Krishnas, "My Sweet Lord," which became popular, spreading news of
Krishna worship across the Atlantic to Europe. The entire Western world
was now aware of these strange new American missionaries of an Eastern
religion.

To have a clearer understanding of Krishna worship one must
understand something of the theology of Hinduism. It has no known
founder and no specific creed. Hinduism has its own trinity, three
separate gods: Brahma, the creator; Vishnu, the preserver; and Shiva,
the destroyer. According to the Hindu belief, the god Vishnu has been
reincarnated nine times. It was during his eighth incarnation that he
arrived as the god Krishna. The ninth was as Buddha.

Lord Krishna's story is told in *The Bhagavad Gita,* an eighteen-chapter
Hindu poem which Mahatma Gandhi praised as having helped shape his
spiritual life. The *Gita* is a small part of an epic book of 90,000 double
verses called the *Mahabharata.* In this work Krishna is said to have had
sixteen thousand wives, although he is usually pictured with his mistress,
Radha.

As the reincarnation of the god Vishnu, Krishna generated a new sect
amongst the several branches of Hinduism. Swami Bhaktivendanta
claimed to be a descendant of Krishna himself. Many of his followers
believe he was the actual incarnation of Krishna and, as such, an
incarnation of the god Vishnu.

In 1977, at the age of eighty, the Swami died. Prior to his death he
appointed twenty-four senior disciples to act jointly in governing the
movement within the United States. His death went largely unnoticed.
Indeed, some journalists commenting on the Hare Krishna movement in
America continue to cite Swami Bhaktivendanta as the leader. The
followers of the movement, in any event, worship Krishna himself, not
the Swami. Steven Gelberg, official spokesman at the Denver center,
says: "The concept of God in our religion is very spiritual and very
personal. It is not specific. At each temple the members look to the
leader, who may or may not be a swami; but we worship Krishna, who was
alive five thousand years ago. We also revere the god Rama. The word
'hare' simply means 'the energy of God.' 'Hare Krishna, Hare Rama' is
an ancient chant from India used by many Hindu religions. It is not new
and not exclusive to our movement."

Not all Krishna followers are members of the Hare Krishna
Consciousness Society. Thirty years ago in Southern California there
appeared a Krishna Ventu who declared himself to be the Messiah. I

acquired some information about him from an unlikely source—entertainer Donald O'Connor, who knew the man personally and used to spend social time with him when the leader went to Las Vegas to drink and gamble.

"He was a total phony," O'Connor told me, "but seemed like a nice guy. I used to run into him in Las Vegas a lot. He was usually bombed out of his skull and throwing money around like water. Eventually he got into some sort of a fight with another Hare Krishna leader and he was killed."

Why the man's followers could not perceive that he was a fraud touches a recurring theme in religious history. The church now concedes that the man was a crook. He was also a polygamist. That he was intentionally killed in an explosion of twenty sticks of dynamite is clear. Some say the killers were jealous husbands of women he had seduced. An alternative theory was that the killing was the result of a simple power struggle for control of the church.

There are other Krishna missionaries in America, so many in fact that most of the holy men in India are scornful. Swami Govinda Nanda despairs at the incessant recruiting that occurs in the United States: "The well," he says, "does not go to the thirsty. The thirsty go to the well." Other Hindu holy men who for the most part remain in isolated contemplation also criticize Bhaktivendanta and his followers in America. There is no spirit of renunciation, they say, in the many lavish buildings the Swami has set up, no sense of quiet contemplation in the noisy tribes of young saffron-robed disciples who roam the streets chanting. Modern-day Krishna Consciousness has, according to one holy man, juggled the sacred texts and "sold celibate followers on an erroneous belief in Krishna, a popular rural god with sixteen thousand wives."

The young Americans remain ardent. Members of the Hare Krishna Society are strictly celibate. Even within marriage, sexual intercourse is allowed only for the purpose of producing children. Says Steven Gelberg: "Chastity is very important to us because our basic philosophy is that we are spiritual beings. We deemphasize the body. Only our spiritual beings matter. Sex, which is one of man's greatest physical pleasures, can be sublimated fully and totally. We cannot allow for imperfections in our devotion to Krishna."

Early on in the movement, arranged marriages were performed, as they are in modern-day India. "They were not a success," says Gelberg, who is also known as Subhananda. "One has to make concessions for Western tradition. Now if a member wishes to get married he makes it known to the Temple leader and it is seen to." Often the member is not denied marriage, providing the Swami or director of the Temple oversees the marriage.

The Hare Krishna people dress in a strange-looking fashion by American standards. (It would not seem so, of course, on the dirt roads of Tibet.) The shaving of the men's heads to an either totally bald or "Iroquois" manner of cut adds to their exotic appearance. In public, adherents of the Hare Krishna faith chant, dance, bang drums and beg. Even if the Hare Krishna philosophy were the wisest, most moral in all spiritual history, such forms of public behavior would be alien to most Americans.

The male members shave their heads as a renunciation of pride, a gesture of asceticism, and a measure of their humility. Female members pull their hair back to discourage vanity. Because celibacy is so highly stressed, the sexes are segregated where possible. The women are taught, and accept, that they are inferior to men. "Feminism is a trap," says one woman devotee. "Women need men to protect them." If a married couple bear a child without permission of the Swami, they may be "punished" by the birth of a girl. In their schools the girls are taught less than boys, who follow a rigorous training in Sanskrit. "Girls don't have an inclination toward philosophic exploration," explains a teacher from the lavish $500,000 palace in West Virginia where over a hundred sons and daughters of the Hare Krishna movement are being trained in an austere yet calm and loving atmosphere. These children are the first generation to be raised in America according to ascetic Hindu beliefs. The elders protect the children from outside "contamination." According to their teachers, "These children will be able to handle themselves anywhere."

Christianity teaches that sin is caused by man's innate tendency to do evil, his willfulness; and that salvation comes from outside the self, from God. Eastern religions believe that sin is caused by ignorance, and that ignorance can be removed once the devotee has looked within himself. Given that the East and the West are now learning from each other, given that global contact has eliminated the massive isolation of culture, why do Westerners still tend to regard movements such as Hare Krishna with suspicion?

Says Steven Gelberg: "Historically any new religion, or manifestation of an older religion reemerging, causes fear. It is not mere bigotry; it is fear of the unknown. America is a circumscribed nation. Deep devotion to a religion is seen as unacceptable. Therefore they see us, in our robes and shaven heads, as nonacceptable. We're different and therefore we're suspect. We're involved in full-time devotion to our religion. Americans are scared of our intensity. To most Americans religion is going to church once a week, then forgetting it. Our religion requires full-time devotion, and that's not the American way."

Gelberg is saddened by the bad press the Hare Krishnas continue to attract. "We're accused of being highly aggressive in the selling of our literature. We *are* enthusiastic, and a lot of people tend to be put off by this. But the press makes such a big thing about this. They take a negative attitude about violence, too. We're completely nonviolent, of course, yet the press hears we've bought a gun and they do a whole number on how we're building up an arsenal. Yes, we've bought guns; we've had to. On our farms we've been attacked many times. We'd be crazy not to have some form of self-protection. But we've never used the guns, never. But that is not what is reported. It's sad."

Gelberg, like many of the members, comes from a Jewish family. He joined the Hare Krishnas because he felt there was little emphasis placed on spiritual life within the Jewish religion. At the age of fifteen he turned to Eastern philosophy. At first his parents were perplexed and surprised. They have since come to accept their son's devotion and life. "What happens when parents see their kids join our movement is this," says Gelberg. "Usually the kid has been out of contact with his family for quite a while. Often he's dropped out of college as well. So suddenly the family sees the child and he's changed radically. And they say 'Hey! We invested all that time and effort in this kid and look how strange he's become. Look what they've done to him.' But the fact is that his family already hasn't been in contact with him, and now they decide he's forsaken them and taken up with a weird cult."

Not surprisingly, deprogrammer Ted Patrick sees the Krishna sect as part of the general evil against which he wages war: "This is an international movement. It is rich, powerful and fast-growing. It is militant, inflexible and very harsh. I believe that in Hare Krishna you have essentially another Charles Manson movement—only thousands strong. And gaining more every day."

Despite Gelberg's assurances, Patrick contends, in his book, *Let Our Children Go*, that they have "the divine sanction to kill when necessary." In cases where Krishna followers have been arrested for a felony, it has been argued that the member had left the movement or faced expulsion either prior to or following his crime.

Like any religious believers, the Hare Krishnas do actively seek to recruit and retain their membership. Some families have reported being frightened by the sight of bald young men clustered around the house in an effort to regain a "captured" follower from his parents or a deprogrammer.

For the most part, however, Hare Krishnas live quietly on the large farms they own or in the temples they have built. Although a portion of their funds is obtained through street solicitation, a prime source of income is from "life memberships" and from wealthy upper-class Indian families who share their beliefs.

The sale of incense used by the Indian religious movement is its chief means of support, according to a May 26, 1975, Los Angeles *Times* story by Russell Chandler.

"About 400 Los Angeles area devotees of Lord Krishna begin a rigorous daily schedule at 3:45 A.M. by bathing, chanting and reading Vedic scriptures like the Bhagavad-Gita. But the Krishna Conscious are practical people. In addition to worship, study and ceremony in the Krishna temple at 3764 Watseka Ave., Culver City, they expand the bliss of Krishna through Spiritual Sky Enterprises, the business arm of the movement. With retail sales of $10 million a year, Spiritual Sky is the world's leading manufacturer of incense, according to Guru das Adhikary, 33, chief servant of the Los Angeles temple, who was a sociologist named Roger Siegel before receiving his spiritual name.

"Scented soap, oils, shampoo and incense sticks are produced and shipped from the Los Angeles offices, headquarters of the international society, for the world's 5,000 initiated disciples, and the public profits keep up Krishna's 100 temples and spread the movement."

I find it fascinating that Gelberg, who studies religion, is suspicious of many other cults and sects, in particular the Unification Church of the Reverend Moon, which, he says, is "quite coercive and deceptive. In our Temples we cannot fool anyone. We are wearing robes and have shaved heads; people know who we are. But the Moonies hide a lot. Very often a person is not aware he's with a Moonie group. I spent a weekend, undercover, with them and I found them deceptive."

As regards public opinion about the Hare Krishna Society, Gelberg argues that it all depends on which book you read: "There are books condemning us and books in favor of our movement. One has to study our religion deeply before pronouncing judgment, in order to get the full picture."

For those interested in a further study of Indian religion I recommend Arthur Koestler's *The Lotus and the Robot.* Speaking of the Hindu emphasis on sexual abstinence, Koestler says:

The cause of this is evidently the traditional belief . . . in the vital fluid as a kind of attar distilled from the blood, every loss of which, even for the legitimate purpose of procreation, is an impoverishment

of body and spirit. Hence the extreme value set on continence—
brahmacharya. . . . Ability to retain and assimilate the vital liquid is
a matter of long training. When properly conserved it is transmuted
into matchless energy and strength. . . .

The axiomatic belief that sex is both physically and spiritually
debilitating must of course create open or unconscious resentment
against woman, the temptress, who causes this deplorable expendi-
ture of vital forces. . . .

Once again we are brought face to face with the ancient contradiction
between religion and reason.

(Brian and I visited a Krishna Consciousness center in Culver City, a
suburb of Los Angeles, on Monday, August 31, 1981. We were welcomed
by Michael Grant (Mukunda) and by Robert Grant—no relation—
(Swami Srila Ramesvara), who took us on a fascinating tour of the center,
which consists chiefly of a temple—formerly an Episcopal church—and
several nearby apartment buildings that accommodate abour four
hundred members. The community, in essence an urban monastery,
includes a school for one hundred fifty children. The members, of course,
all wear the long two-piece Indian garment, in this case of a pale peach
color.

Inside the temple it almost seems that one is in India, so completely
authentic is the structure. On the intensely colorful altar a dark-skinned
young devotee was with one hand ringing a bell and with the other making
gestures, with what significance we did not know. Michael, the director of
the temple group—a quick-speaking, highly intelligent young man—explained that he had sensed little spiritual content in his original Jewish
faith.

When I made reference to the various god-figures in Hindu mythology,
he said, "Many people have the impression that the Oriental religions are
pantheistic. But in the case of Hinduism there is the ancient tradition that
there is but one God, but that he may be apprehended under many
manifestations or aspects." Brian and I could not help but notice—to the
left side of the marble-floored room—a remarkably lifelike image of the
founder. "The fellow who created that," said Grant, "used to work at the
Hollywood Wax Museum."

On the two sidewalls were several large gold-framed paintings of
excellent quality. Although the subject matter was drawn from Indian
religious mythology, the style, oddly enough, seemed Italian Renais-
sance. Our host mentioned that some of the group's painters had recently
been studying in Florence.

During lunch Grant again referred to his Jewish origins. "I have met with many rabbis," he said, "and have emphasized to them that Judaism will continue to lose many young people so long as it does not place greater emphasis on spiritual values. If it does not, those who hunger for such values will have to go elsewhere."

The most remarkable part of our tour came when we were taken through a highly professional and impressive display, much like the sort of thing one sees at the better museums or Disneyland displays in which figures from history—actually computerized robots—seem to come to life. Some of the figures in the display were movable; most were not. But the combination of computerized light, sound and statuary was remarkably effective as an educational device. The figures shown were, of course, chiefly those of Hindu mythology—or, as our hosts would have said, history.)

CHAPTER 22

Time Spent with My Son

In 1971 Brian's letter telling us of his religious conversion had suggested that we might never see him again. By early August of 1980 it had long been clear that our original fears on that point were groundless. A few months after David's visit, *Logic,* his wife, *Simplicity,* and their two children, *Purity* and *Liberty,* flew down to spend nine days with us. It was a time of rare happiness. Brian had become more mature, both because of the passage of time and because of his responsibilities as a leader in the Love Family. He was as gentle and lovable as ever, but more adult. It was good to see him so happy with his wife.

As for the children, blond, blue-eyed *Purity* and dark-haired, black-eyed *Liberty,* they are incredibly beautiful, in both senses of the word. Their physical beauty is just the breaks of the genetic game; the more significant thing is that they have a magical, elfin quality. I recalled my observation of five years earlier that an important means by which to evaluate the Love Family environment would be in the effect it had on its children. *Liberty* and *Purity* would have tended to be especially sweet children in any event because of the gentleness and warmth of their mother and father, but communal upbringing has obviously provided other values for them. They are somehow different. It is not because of their simple, communal attire, mostly handmade and strangely reminiscent of both pioneer and early Christian dress. More important, it seems to me, is that they have not been raised in traditional American schools, not brought up on the mean streets of our large cities, not subjected to television, commercial bombardments, polluted air, loud mindless music. They are sweet, free little spirits, though in no way wild or uncontrolled. They laugh readily, have a remarkably well developed sense of humor for children so young, and are well-behaved.

In keeping with the custom in their commune they address all adults—including their parents—by their first names, but always with respect and, if appropriate, with affection. They are, of course, aware that I am their father's father and sometimes refer to me as Grandpa.

They took to our swimming pool like two water-creatures of the wild and spent endless hours laughing and splashing about. Watching Brian teaching little *Liberty* to swim, carrying the older *Purity* on his shoulders, my mind went back to the years when he was their size and we played together in the same way. When the children were instructed to get out and dry off, they obeyed—with a minimum of that "Aw, Dad" complaining to which most children are prone.

Jayne, though a busy professional woman, delighted in bringing in groceries, cooking meals, providing poolside refreshments for our visitors. *Liberty* and *Purity* took to her immediately and she to them. All in all, it was a wonderful time of growing even closer together, for all of us.

I was concerned that so many years had passed without Brian and Steve seeing each other, but as fate would have it they were soon to have a happy reunion. Several months later, Steve's wife, Ann, was scheduled to come to Los Angeles—her hometown—to take part in a conference on education. I arranged for Steve and their two children, Danny and Julie, to come out at the same time. Two speaking engagements in Seattle and Vancouver that same week—May of 1981—afforded me the opportunity to spend more time with Brian, *Simplicity* and their children. Steve, Jr. flew up from Los Angeles the day I was speaking in Vancouver.

On arriving in Seattle I was taken to the Washington Plaza Hotel. The moment I walked into my suite the phone rang. It was Brian. "We're down in the lobby," he said. "Come right up," I said, giving him the room number. A few minutes later I opened the door and heard, down the curved hallway, two familiar little voices. Brian, having accepted an invitation to attend the dinner that evening, had gone to a local store and purchased a handsome, conservative three-piece suit.

He was wearing the costume of my professional world, the sort of clothing he might have worn if he had followed his talent for art. He looked very handsome indeed. That he felt free to do this—as did *Love* Israel, I was later that evening to discover—suggested that the Love Family was no longer as rigid in its customs as it had been a decade earlier.

When it was time for me to report to the dinner, I told *Simplicity* and the children they should call room service for their needs and stay in our suite overnight. Brian and I went off to the dinner at the Seattle Center, at the former World's Fair grounds, where we were met by *Love* and his wife, *Honesty*.

When, at the end of the evening, Brian and I returned to the hotel, our little friends were asleep. Brian was happy. We had had a wonderful few hours together, and he had been introduced as *Logic* Israel, "Steve

Allen's son," by the master of ceremonies. I was proud of him as he stood, smiling, to acknowledge the applause of the audience, mostly Seattle's social leaders and corporate executives and their wives.

After completing my duties in Vancouver I flew back to Seattle, where Brian met me at the airport. Steve, Jr. had flown up from Los Angeles earlier that morning. I wondered what the emotions of the two brothers would be after so long a separation.

"It must have been exciting for you," I said to Brian during the drive, "to see Steve again after ten years."

"Yes," he said. "It was great."

"Was it easy for the two of you to talk?"

"For the first hour it was a little stiff. After that we got more relaxed. He doesn't look much different, except for the mustache."

When we arrived at the Love Family commune in the Queen Anne section of town we were welcomed again by *Love* and a few others. Steve was waiting for us in Brian's house, having just wakened from a much-needed nap.

A woman named Kadmeil, a resident of the same house, greeted us and offered refreshments. *Liberty* and *Purity* smiled up at us all, pleased to be surrounded by adoring adults, including the newly discovered Uncle Steve.

In novels, plays and films, important characters spend almost all of their time talking about the main issue or theme that concerns them. In actual life no such process takes place. Small talk, casual conversation, is almost always part of the communication, even among those who are involved in the most significant dramas—love affairs, separations, divorces, illness, death. In this case, too, what was important to Brian and Steve and to me—if I may read their minds—was simply our being together. Our mutual sense of humor led to much laughter, jokes, and sweet, simple exchanges on, for the most part, less than earth-shattering matters. Steve and I were offered floor-length robes, which we accepted, as I had on my two earlier visits. We three men, united by love, dressed now alike—as Brian and I had been dressed alike in a more conservative mode the day before—luxuriated in a certain kind of closeness that can occur only among members of families. Brian and *Simplicity* showed Steve and me how to comfortably tie the belts that held our warm, colorful robes closed.

Kadmeil, a short, graceful woman apparently in her thirties, answered my questions about how she had joined the group. The women of the Family rarely speak unless spoken to, and at the table see that the men present are served before themselves. Kadmeil told me that before she came to the Family in Seattle she had had some odd psychic experiences that, in her opinion, related to her eventually moving into the Seattle commune. "A psychic I went to," she said, "told me that she saw a black dog coming into my life, a dog that would jump up and put her front paws on me. Later, when I got here to the Love Family, I met a black dog named Logo."

"Logo?" I said.

"Yes," Brian said. "The dog got the name because one of our artists, *Imagination*, had done a logo-design for a local pet shop. The shop owner paid for the artist's services by giving us the dog."

"I also had a dream about a place like this," Kadmeil said, "and when I got here it was just like I'd imagined it." Many of the Family's members have had such experiences, *Logic* later told me.

That night *Logic* told me that he, Steve, *Simplicity* and I would be having dinner next door, in *Love*'s house. At the appointed hour we were shown through the house, a remarkable structure still under construction, built on two smaller houses that had sat side by side.

On the way to dinner I met *Resolve,* the son of Sam Sherman, the attorney from Chicago who had written to me in 1974. With the help of a gifted instrument-maker, *Resolve* had built a beautiful authentic harpsichordlike Mozart piano which I was invited to play. Mrs. Sherman, *Resolve*'s mother, I was told, had recently spent six months with the Family. She had left a few days before my arrival, but was planning to return soon.

Logic told me the Family's jazz group, the Solid Resolve, had improved greatly and was going to provide music for the show scheduled for the after-dinner period. Besides the Shermans' sons, *Solidity* and *Resolve*, *Jubil* and *Logic* sometimes participate. As David had said, *Logic* had learned to play the saxophone. *Love* sometimes sits in on bass.

Logic also told me of another Family member, *Abishai*, a doctor of biochemistry and embryology. "He's building a laboratory here, and he's created a mosquito repellent out of ferns that grow at the ranch." As of 1981, *Abishai* had been with the Family for eight years. He continues his studies at a nearby university, where he works several days a week.

The dinner, in an upstairs room, was served at a low Japanese-style table. *Love* and the other Family members present—all of whom seemed quite limber—have no difficulty sitting comfortably at such tables, whether their legs are extended or in the lotus position. Perhaps in recognition of my age, I was provided with an extra cushion and a sort of low bench or stool on which to lean. Prepared by one of the women, the dinner itself was, quite literally, a banquet; it began with a wonderfully flavored lettuce and tomato salad topped with small fresh shrimp, which was followed by assorted seafood—fried clams, oysters and large shrimps. Apparently the Family had abandoned the custom of not eating shellfish. Fresh cauliflower and asparagus were served, along with tender new potatoes cooked in their skins. The young man who served us poured Washington State wine. Dessert was homemade ice cream with fresh strawberries.

Seated to my left at the dinner table was *Wisdom,* an attractive middle-aged woman with white hair, whom I remembered from an earlier visit. Aware that some of the young women in the Family have had no previous experience with motherhood, and perhaps do not know from their own upbringing how to raise children, she makes it her business to advise them. *Wisdom* is a quiet, competent woman, with the sort of personality one associates with Mothers Superior, doctors, teachers, or other maternal authority figures.

The dinner conversation was by turns animated, thoughtful and amusing. Throughout the hour we were pleasantly entertained by the piano music of *Resolve,* from downstairs.

Afterwards all hands repaired to a large basement meeting room, where an audience of perhaps thirty adults and children were watching a slide show of colorful pictures of happy scenes at the ranch. During the show *Purity* climbed on my lap and whispered, "This party's for you, Steve."

"I know," I said. Special entertainment is often scheduled for visiting parents or other guests.

"We're going to do our play for you, too."

"Wonderful," I said. "I can't wait to see you in it."

Seated near me in the audience in the darkened room was a very old couple, neighbors who were on friendly terms with the Family. The man, I was told, did not have much longer to live.

Won, a professional mime, introduced the show by calling little *Liberty,* the pixie, up to the stage and explaining that they would do a pantomine called "The Great Fisherman." They pretended to throw fishhooks into the audience, reeling the line in, getting it caught on a branch behind them, getting the line and hook caught on their feet, then catching a strong fish which when laboriously pulled in turned out to be about three inches long. *Won* handed it to *Liberty,* who gave the "punch line" by throwing the imaginary fish back into the water.

In the next routine *Won* established by pantomime the trunk of an enormous redwood tree. He then gave *Liberty* an invisible axe and said, "Little man, big tree." *Liberty* shortly gave up on the axe and switched to a power chain saw.

The next mime involved *Won* holding the string of an equally imaginary group of big balloons. He offered one to little *Liberty,* who shook his head no. "I want another one. *That* one." The little boy eventually was given such a big balloon that it lifted him up into the air, aided by *Won,* who then used *Liberty* as if he were a puppet in a variety show, bending him into a comedy bow. The two exited to hearty applause.

Won, formerly a member of Yod's group, as of 1981 had been with the Love Family for about four years.

One sketch was particularly clever. A group of visitors alive in a future century were being conducted through a museum described as "The Far Corners of Your Mind." Various live figures, posed like statues, were described by a guide as relics of a race of people once common on the planet Earth. In contrast to the virtue-names of the Love Family, they had names such as *Greed, Want, Disobedience, War* and *Jealousy.*

The visitors were warned not to come into physical contact with these evil personages, lest their destructive spirits be released. Of course contact was made, as a result of which the formerly virtuous, peaceable, and loving visitors began to act out the negative emotions. Little *Purity* was very effective—and also hilarious—as she acted out disobedience. The moral lesson of the playlet was such that the production could have been presented in any church, synagogue or ethical society in the world.

The next morning, after a deep sleep, I wakened just in time to be served a marvelous breakfast, which was introduced by little *Purity* rapping gently at the bathroom door and saying that she had a glass of fresh orange juice for me. After I had shaved and dressed I joined the others at the breakfast table.

Sitting on the back steps of the house, before a tour of the neighborhood and a long walk to Seattle's famous Space Needle, I had a delightful conversation with *Ease,* a beautiful little blond girl who appeared to be about eight years old. To my surprise, she not only had read one of my books, *Princess Snip-Snip and the Puppykittens,* but reviewed the story in her own words; her version was charming. *Ease's* father is *Courage,* who had visited us with *Cooperation* in 1974. Her mother is *Patience,* who had made the beautiful dress she was wearing.

Among the other children about me as I sat in the morning sunlight was an adorable little blond fellow named *Action* who appeared to be about five.

"Dad," Brian said, "I'm not sure that you remember that *Action* was born the last time you were here. You held him in your arms right after his birth and gave him your blessing." I had not recalled the baby's name. I was glad to see that the little fellow had turned out to be such an appealing, happy child. I shook hands with him and did a few little jokes which made him giggle.

The weather was glorious, the neighborhood brilliant with flowers. Our group, consisting of *Logic, Simplicity,* Steve, Kadmeil, *Liberty, Purity* and myself, started off and passed the public school a block away from the Family's houses in the Queen Anne section. On the grounds a large map of the United States is painted in white on the asphalt. The children from the Family sometimes go there to learn the outlines of the nation's geography by standing on the map, discussing the names of the states—which are not printed in—with the adults. When they learned that their Uncle Steve lived in Elmira, New York, whereas Grandpa Steve lived in Los Angeles, California, they were surprised, since they had assumed that all members of a family would live at the same place.

We were taken to the next corner, where a soon-to-open natural food store run by the Family was under construction. The most dramatic features of it were the beautiful woodwork, wall paneling and display shelves.

We next stopped into the neighborhood Queen Anne Bakeshop. As we were leaving his premises the baker, a middle-aged man, said, "We enjoy your boy up here. He's a real nice boy."

"That's good to hear," I said, and meant it, although I was not surprised that one more person had succumbed to Brian's charm. That reminds me, incidentally, of the occasion—in the early 1970s—when Brian and a few other Family members were in a Seattle courtroom; it may have been in connection with the Vicky Sinunu case. A kindly police official approached Brian during a recess and said, "You know, son, it's not you young people we're concerned about. It's your leaders."

Brian smiled back at him and said, "I'm one of the leaders."

Next door to the bakery is the Front Door Inn, which *Logic* identified as "our free restaurant." Two doors from the inn is a shop also run by the group, called Wood 'N Things. On a display shelf in its front window was a model of one of the yurts, the large tents in which the Family lives at the Arlington ranch. *Logic* and Steve also brought to my attention a remarkable device about six feet long, a sort of erector set. By playing with it the children learn what carpentry was like in earlier centuries before nails were invented. Pieces of wood fit together in ways now rarely seen in Western carpentry and cabinetmaking but sometimes still encountered in the Orient. The set comes in a box about 14 inches wide and 2-½ feet long.

Ceramic items, chiefly cups and candle holders, are made at the ranch. Behind the showroom was a large room in which there were professional work tables and woodcutting equipment. The degree of sophistication of carpentry, woodworking, and cabinetmaking among those members of the Family qualified to do it is remarkable.

A few minutes later we came to a beautiful garden area maintained by the Family. "We're employed by the Seattle Parks Department to maintain three parks in our neighborhood," *Logic* explained. "Our purpose is to keep the parks beautiful. The money we receive goes to support our other gardening efforts."

Steve was obviously favorably impressed by the Family members he had met. "Brian, how do you solve the problem of keeping out the 'flakes'?" he asked at one point as we strolled along.

"That's not very difficult," Brian said. "Two of our customs are that you must keep yourself very clean and you must work. Our example puts some sort of peer pressure on visitors, although we allow new folks a chance to relax, without pressure, while getting to know the Family."

The Family does not, of course, close its doors to those who are troubled or neurotic; it tries to help them. Occasionally, Brian explained, the results are not happy.

"Sometimes," he said, "even a technically accurate statement can be used against us in such a way as to be deliberately misleading. For example, there was one woman, a stranger to all of us, who came in here one night, obviously in a very troubled emotional state. Unfortunately she committed suicide by hanging herself the following morning. There was no way at all that the tragedy was our fault, but of course it was referred to as one more death in the Love Family and that sort of thing."

As our little group strolled along, it occurred to me that one of the distinguishing factors of the Love Family is its smallness. There are hundreds of thousands of Scientologists, millions of followers of Reverend Sun Myung Moon, vast armies of Hare Krishnas. But I doubt if the various Love Family commune groups combined add up to 350. Nor does the Family seem particularly interested in enlarging its membership. Certainly it conducts nothing like the proselytizing and street-conversion of the larger denominations.

Based on my studies of other groups—Scientology, Jim Jones's People's Temple, the Children of God, the Reverend Moon church—I had begun to have a more favorable impression of the Love Family. Although no church—large or small—has ever been tempted to claim perfection, the Family seems far preferable to certain other sects and cults. I had detected in it none of that lust-for-revenge which is so evident in both the statements and the actions of many of the other cults. The Love Family occasionally reacts by issuing a statement on a particular issue, but this usually involves nothing more than mailing a few copies to interested individuals, families or journalists. There have been no incidents such as that which so disgraced Synanon, in which two misguided members put a poisonous snake into a critic's mailbox. So far as I have been able to learn, the reaction of Love Family members and leaders to attack is a sort of sad resignation. It is conceivable that in the future some misguided individual member could take it upon himself to retaliate against harsh criticism, but it seems unlikely. Neither God, Jesus Christ nor the Pope, for example, has ever been able to guarantee virtuous conduct on the part of the world's hundreds of millions of Catholics; nor, for that matter, has any religious leader been able to assure virtue in even one follower. But if a Love Family member ever does commit a formal offense in the defense of his faith, it seems unlikely that he will have done so on instruction from either *Love* Israel or the elders of the group.

(It is significant, in this context, that in interviewing and exchanging correspondence with scores of people over a period of several years, I have frequently heard the Church of Scientology—by way of contrast— singled out as specifically dangerous to critics or even impartial researchers. "Look out for the Scientologists," has been the general warning. "If they perceive you as an enemy, they can really come down hard on you." I leave it to the Scientologists to face the grim question as to how their church has acquired such a reputation.)

Walking that morning in the refreshing air of the seaside city, visiting again with various members of my son's commune, I had seen much evidence of a desire to live a simple, clean, wholesome life. I had seen attractive young men with their long hair and clear eyes working with wood, planting flowers, building houses, preparing meals. I had met the gentle young women of the Family. Though I do not agree that women are inferior to men—they are obviously different, in certain respects, but that is quite another matter—I nevertheless recognize that no woman is kept in the Love Family against her wishes, just as none of the Mormon women who approved of polygamy—and, for that matter, do to the present day—are kept in that church against their wishes.

If this is still not the life I would have chosen for my son, what of that? Such choices are not mine to make. Again, Brian's life must be compared not to some nonexistent representation of perfection but to life in the world as it really is. In our time, in our portion of the planet, that world often presents a depressing, pathetic spectacle. Our prisons and orphanages are full. All manner of crimes and moral outrages increase daily.

Our long stroll of several miles finally brought us to the Space Needle, at the top of which we enjoyed a tasty lunch.

On Friday, May 22, after Steve and I flew back down to Los Angeles, eleven students from the University of Montana were scheduled to spend a few days with the Family. They were doing some research in connection with a study of religious cults and communes in the U.S.

The two-and-one-half-hour flight back to Los Angeles gave Dr. Steve and me time to discuss his reactions to the Family. "I feel better now about Brian," he said, "having been up there. It makes more sense for him than I thought it did."

"I know what you mean," I said. "Somehow seeing it as reality instead of an image constructed purely out of our fears, concerns and rumors makes it at least easier to grasp and to deal with."

I put my head back, closed my eyes and smiled. It was good that my two sons had reestablished contact. Although I am sure he would never express such an opinion, perhaps Steve had felt some degree of shame, years earlier, when he first heard that his dearly loved brother had joined what seemed a far-out, perhaps dangerous religious cult. Now Steve, the responsible, mature physician, had seen that his younger brother had matured, gained more confidence, assumed responsibility for the welfare of other members in the Love Family.

I thought back to an absurd fantasy that I do not believe I have ever mentioned before, except once to a psychologist. There is no dialogue in the scene I envision; it is merely an image of a primitive cave, the floor of which is covered with furs and other animal skins. In the cave I live, surrounded by my loved ones, as men lived hundreds of thousands of years ago. The significant thing about the fantasy is that on the rare occasions when it has crossed my mind I have felt a strange sense of comfort and warmth.

Consequently, when any portion of the vision becomes reality—whenever, for example, I am in the physical presence of my sons and my wife, my grandchildren, when we are all under the same roof—I have a sense of warm contentment.

Now, flying toward Los Angeles at thirty thousand feet, my oldest son beside me, I knew that important family connections had been reestablished. We had not lost Brian.

Relationships between fathers and sons are of a special sort. Although the father may not even be conscious of participating in the creation of a new human self, he must consciously provide for, protect, guide and love it. And yet, in the end, he must set it free. . . .

CHAPTER 23

Some Concluding Thoughts

Part I—The Problem

As the parent of a cult member, I can easily enough define the ideal study of the cult phenomenon in our country: like a doctor, the writer should observe and analyze, diagnose or explain the symptoms, and then produce a remedy. For the sake of parents whose hearts ache for their children and for those children whose lives are damaged by cult participation, I wish I or another student of the situation could provide such a study. But the cult phenomenon is not, alas, the measles.

Nonetheless, in proffering my conclusions, I model myself more on the doctor who wants to help than on the academic scholar who wants only a dispassionate, rigorous description.

The new religions defy easy analysis. It is difficult to generalize about them. There are no simple formulas to explain, for instance, which young people join them. While many critics assume that their membership is comprised of social misfits or failures in personal or professional life, straight-arrow types live alongside the dropouts. Nor do factors like intelligence alone explain the membership. One meets both low and high IQ types in the new tribes. One general observation that seems valid is that the adherents appear to come mainly from middle- to upper-class families. True poverty apparently grants a degree of immunity.

Nor can we pinpoint a universal or general motive for joining. The presence of those with no apparent reason to join is typically "explained" by the suggestion that they fell under the influence of evil cult leaders with hypnotic powers or an awareness of brainwashing techniques. But the real situation is hardly so simple. And what about those for whom a commune represents upward mobility? For those who were in trouble on the streets, were drug abusers or had serious psychological problems; for the rootless, shiftless dropouts, a religious commune is a step up. Instead of loneliness, aimlessness, a sense of self as sinful, a sense of life as pointless, it offers friends, order, a sense of virtue, a view of life as meaningful.

Past religious belief does seem to be a factor. Few articulate atheists, agnostics or secular humanists have been attracted to the new religions. The overwhelming majority were formerly affiliated with the Catholic, Protestant or Jewish faiths. Obviously the traditional religions failed to maintain their allegiance or capture their creative imaginations.

If we cannot find the common denominator that explains all cases, however, we *can* describe the world that gave rise to the commune movement of the sixties. Shortly before the emergence of the movement, leading Protestant theologians, uncomfortably accustomed to the dominance of secular currents in political and moral philosophy, developed the God-is-dead theology, which was misunderstood. Clearly, the phrase is not meant to be interpreted literally; if there is a God, it follows by definition that such an entity could not possibly die. The phrase meant—to put it most simply—that evidence of divine intervention in history, in human affairs, was lacking in the twentieth century, although it had seemed to characterize earlier ages. The people of France, for example, made Joan of Arc a saint as well as a national heroine partly because they believed God had intervened in her military campaigns to guarantee victory.

If God no longer played a part in history, we were alone on earth, completely responsible for ourselves. There was no point in looking heavenward to some kind of father figure. For some people, this view of life was simply too hard. Life lost hope, meaning and order for them. Thus, while theologians, clergy and scholars debated, religious development on the street was taking quite another turn. Not only was there a sudden revival of interest in old-fashioned Fundamentalist belief—the very sort of thing that had earlier been laughed to scorn by such popular American figures as Ralph Ingersoll, Clarence Darrow, H. L. Mencken and other secularists—but religious and philosophical belief of an unashamedly nonrational nature suddenly burgeoned. At the outer fringes of religious fundamentalism Pentacostalists, Seventh-Day Adventists, Jehovah's Witnesses, speakers in strange tongues, workers of mass revivalist frenzy, were heard again in the land. Many Christians might have been contented enough had the phenomena stopped at that point. But of course it did not. That it was enlarged much further became evident from the revival of interest in astrology, witchcraft, demonism, numerology, belief in the magical power of pyramids, tarot cards, séances, levitation and God-knows-what else.

To cite an illustrative parallel, sociologist Peter Berger has pointed out that when the Catholic Church chose to accommodate contemporary life by offering mass in the vernacular instead of in Latin, "a period of convulsive disintegration unparalleled since the sixteenth century" followed. "One of the more piquant consequences of the effort to spare modern Catholics the spiritual difficulties of the Latin mass is that some of them are currently babbling away in *glossolalia* (in growing numbers, apparently), while others are chanting hymns to the Lord Krishna—in Sanskrit."

In other words, the loss of a tradition that could be depended on resulted in disorder.

At a deeper level, Berger offers another clue to the resolution of the mystery which concerns us—or at least describes a condition within which the partly strange religious revival is taking place. There is in the contemporary world, Berger has observed, "a very curious co-presence of modernizing and demodernizing processes." Berger has centered his attention in recent years on what is called the Third World. From his studies he has drawn the unexpected conclusion that there are "resistances to development" in the very portions of our planet where the modern amenities—plumbing systems, clean water systems, roads, automobiles, modern universities, etc.—would seem to be most needed. "What is most interesting is that these 'resistances' (which I prefer to call demodernization) increase rather than decrease as so-called development progresses." Having observed such a phenomenon in more primitive cultures, Berger then realized that it was occurring in the developed world as well.

I submit that the reversion to essentially nonrational forms of belief is part of this same strange process, a resistance to the development of the intelligence. Although some of the new groups are more consciously reasonable, many have in common a closed-minded fanaticism.

Ours is not the first nation, of course, nor is the present moment the first in history, in which such a pattern has emerged. As Isaiah Berlin has observed:

. . . the domination of the philosophical schools of Athens in the Hellenistic period was attended by a noticeable increase in mystery cults and other forms of occultism and emotionalism in which nonrational elements in the human spirit sought an outlet. There was the great Christian revolt against the great organized legal systems, whether of the Jews or the Romans; there were medieval antinomian rebellions against the Scholastic establishment and the authority of the church—movements of this kind from the Cathars to the anabaptists are evidence enough of this; the Reformation was preceded and followed by the rise of powerful mystical and irrationalist currents.

I naturally do not suggest that life is either all intellect or all emotion. Nor do I argue that nonrational equals bad. There is much to life that lies outside of the scope of reason but is nevertheless valuable: the beguiling evidence of the physical senses, the content of dreams, the beauty of nature, the appeal of the arts—music, poetry, painting. Indeed, love and sex are hardly the result of logical decision. But the successful life is one in which the two conflicting modes of thought are maintained in some sort of oscillating equilibrium. There must be balance. Rationalists err if they delude themselves that the affairs of society are fully subject to the control of the reason pure and simple. But to abandon reason is to convert society into a sort of large, unwalled madhouse in which every person is his own authority.

Young people coming of age in the sixties found themselves in an insecure world, one which could literally end at any moment. The Bomb had hung over their adolescence like a question mark. They had seen a President, his brother, and a great civil rights leader assassinated. Theirs was also a world in which humanistic values were overwhelmed by science and technology, by the rapid development of computers and by the space race. They also found themselves in a conflict of values with their elders, whom they considered conservative and materialistic. "You can't trust anyone over thirty," was a motto of the Free Speech Movement at Berkeley in 1964. The fundamental reason was that adults had "sold out." And in a sense the young were right, though they did not understand or sympathize with the sources of their elders' attitudes. The parents' generation worshipped the ideal of education, for instance—not so much for intellectual reasons, alas, but because they saw that in American society schooling was the primary means by which one could ascend the ladder of the social classes. Many in the older generation could remember the suffering, the widespread poverty of the Depression of the 1930s. Others, if they were not old enough to have lived during that period of capitalist collapse, recalled the unanimity of purpose that characterized American attitudes during World War II and after, when the world had to be rebuilt.

But the young saw a world in which there was little to depend on. Even the families from which they came could not be counted on to survive. In the sixties we got used to hearing about marriages of twenty years or more that were suddenly breaking up. This was one element that definitely contributed to the commune movement, the relative collapse of the

American home, a phenomenon recognizable chiefly, though not solely, by divorce statistics.

The divorce explosion in the last twenty-five years was itself created by such factors as: 1) the dramatic shift from rural to urban living in modern America; 2) the increased personal mobility afforded by the train, the automobile, the airplane, the bus, the streetcar, etc., all of which greatly enlarged the individual's opportunities to meet and interact with others, while simultaneously taking him out of the traditional, narrower range where close family and neighborhood influences were dominant; 3) a shift away from traditional religious affiliations; 4) the greatly increased assailing of the consciousness by motion pictures, radio, television, popular music, books, newspapers and magazines which—in the aggregate—tended as much to confuse as to enlighten; 5) the massive social dislocation of World War II, Korea and Vietnam, understood in the context of the fact that war has always had destructive effects on the home society as well as on the battlefield.

Such unrest, taken all together, provided a fertile soil for the growth of dissatisfaction with life and society as they appeared to young people growing up in the sixties. A consideration of such factors, then, makes it easier to understand two developments: first, that certain individuals with innate gifts for leadership or social dominance conceived what they viewed as alternatives superior to the chaos they witnessed; and second, why large numbers of rootless young people so uncritically accepted the social prescriptions of the new self-appointed messiahs.

"Uncritically accepted" are key words here. There is another reason why at present Christianity in its least intellectual aspect—obscure sects and fundamentalism—is undergoing one of its periodic waves of resurgence. Neither we nor our children know how to think, how to reason, how to evaluate logically the arguments of those who want to sell us one bill of goods or another. I believe, in fact, that over the past twenty-five years there has been a steady, demonstrable deterioration of the American intelligence. To me, the proliferation of partly mindless belief can be ascribed in large part to ignorance of relevant information and the inability to think well.

We mentally respond on the basis of our conditioning, but we do not feel comfortable with active, logical thought. Instead of reasoning our way to an hypothesis or conclusion, we let tribal loyalty, bias, prejudice, superstition or self-interest lead us. We too often think with our emotions or our egos rather than our brains. Consider some of the beliefs we hold: "Opposites attract." "Fish is brain food." "There's nothing new under the sun." "The mental health movement is a Communist plot." We are full of such misinformation.

It is no surprise, then, that many of our children listen uncritically to the appeals of cult leaders or the enthusiasm of their peers.

The present rise of nonrational belief results in part from the unhappy confluence of the notoriously weak human mind with that notoriously difficult collection of books—as seminary students across the nation bear witness—the Bible. Most people assume that as regards the great majority of statements, there is an essentially simple interpretation that is the right one; and that, to the extent that other interpretations present themselves, they are likely to be introduced by individuals of low intelligence or ill will. But this is not true. Laws, for obvious reasons, are worded more carefully than any other class of statements, yet an entire legal and judicial profession is concerned with their *interpretation*. Statements found in the Oriental Scriptures, the Koran and the Bible—in sharp contrast to the style of legal language—are often vague, abstract, impenetrable, mysterious. Now if it takes the most brilliant legal minds of a society to interpret laws, it is inevitable that there is far less agreement, even among the best-intentioned Biblical scholars, about the meaning of Scriptural passages.

Every theologian is perfectly aware of this, but the country is full of poorly educated religious fanatics who are convinced that every passage of Scripture has one correct interpretation—their own, needless to say—and that all those who do not accept such divine truth are either sadly misguided or consciously demonic. Of course, not every specific opinion or belief held by religious or political fanatics is itself in error. The most stupid individuals, the most evil, the most ignorant, the least informed, nevertheless are not totally mistaken. Their evil and error are invariably mixed with a certain amount of accurate information or reasonable belief. Unfortunately they hold to the nonsensical part with a fervor equal to—perhaps even surpassing—that which characterizes their more sensible views.

It is crucial here to distinguish between fanaticism and firm belief. The latter can be admirable, even necessary in the context of certain social dramas, but there is nothing admirable in loyalty of the mindless sort, loyalty that is quite prepared to cast aside all ethical and moral considerations so long as the believer can convince himself that the crimes, atrocities, or inanities he commits are performed in the service of the True Faith.

Not only are there irrational elements in the beliefs of various of the new faiths, but also some of their practices tend to discourage independent exercise of reason. For a brief period early in its existence, the Love Family permitted its members to read nothing but the Bible. Whatever benefit the reading of the Scriptures may impart, there is not the slightest doubt that reading literally nothing but the Bible will lead, within a fairly short time, to a remarkable ignorance about matters that mankind has for thousands of years considered of enormous importance. Fortunately, in time the Family realized it could not educate its young without secular books. It now has various texts available, a few of which I have provided myself.

(Concerning some of the beliefs and practices of the Love Family, it is clear that they were not created by Erdman's group but have appeared elsewhere in Christian history. Communal living, concentration on the Bible, living the simple, ungrasping life, putting an emphasis on love, living religion twenty-four hours a day—one may approve or disapprove; one may be skeptical; but few Americans will argue that such attitudes and beliefs are either new or socially destructive.

But there are other aspects of Love Family practice and belief concerning which one can say, with confidence, that they are simply absurd. One example occurs when members of the Family die, from natural or other causes. In February of 1974, for instance, *Marcus* Israel fell to his death from a tree while members of the Family were gathering firewood. Instead of making conventional arrangements for the respectful disposal of his body, the Love Family began a three-day vigil—as they had done earlier in the case of the two members who died from inhaling toluene. The purpose of such vigils is to *pray for the immediate physical resurrection of the dead body*. There are sincere Christians who doubt that this happened even in the case of Christ, though most Christians do have faith in the physical resurrection of Jesus. But it is certainly not going to happen today. It is therefore unreasonable to believe anything so preposterous. The Love Family—like all religions—has, over the decade of its existence, gradually altered certain beliefs and practices. Perhaps when they fully understand how this particular custom makes them look, not only in the eyes of the naturally cynical but even in the opinion of those otherwise sympathetic, they will put such views behind them.)

Part II—Parents

The parents of some cult members are sincere and perhaps devout adherents of a traditional church, and their shock and sadness are especially understandable. It has always been an unpleasant experience for Catholics when their children renounce the Church and join another;

unpleasant for Protestants when their children become Catholics; and even more shocking for devout Jewish families when a son or daughter abandons the faith that has sustained Jews for thousands of years and becomes a Christian.

I have the impression that by 1980 many parents had made either reasonably or totally comfortable adjustments to such wrenching changes, although this usually takes quite some time. But many others have not. Some of these have formed organizations by means of which they share their mutual anguish or outrage. Citizens for Religious Freedom, for example, is one such organization. It takes an outspoken stand on the issue, and its members have frequently resorted to kidnapping as part of what they call a *deprogramming* process. The philosophical rationale for such methods—which are sometimes illegal—runs as follows: My son (or daughter) was enticed into this evil cult against his wishes and certainly against his better judgment. He is being kept a prisoner, brainwashed with pseudoreligious propaganda, made subject to the will of a self-deluded would-be Messiah, and therefore must be taken—by force if necessary—out of such a bizarre setting.

A vitally important factor affecting the decision to resort to such means, of course, is the age of the young person involved. If a boy or girl is only sixteen or seventeen, it is understandable that parents would demand the return of the teenager. If, on the other hand, the new convert is an adult, the situation is quite different, both legally and morally.

Because Brian was a fully self-responsible adult when he became a member of the Love Family, it follows that I had no moral or legal right to force him to conform to my own social standards. Also, the experience with kidnapping and deprogramming, for the most part conducted under the auspices of Ted Patrick, has not been such as to encourage common recourse to this particular method of addressing the problem. I have spoken to a few young people who have been deprogrammed. While some of them have returned to the Love Family—as they have to other religious groups—others have permanently disassociated themselves from the Seattle group. But in most such cases I have the impression that their minds have by no means simply been wiped clean of the experience. Some ex-members who now speak critically of the communes seem, to those who meet them, to be—well, descriptions involve such terms as "odd," "still a little strange somehow," "not entirely with it," "still a religious fanatic," etc. There are exceptions, of course, and the six or seven such cases that have come to my attention by no means constitute a nationwide survey; it would be dangerous to draw conclusions on the basis of so small a sample.

The controversy over deprogramming is additionally confused, not clarified, by virtue of the First Amendment to the Constitution of the United States, which guarantees religious freedom.

The American founding fathers were well aware that if all of us spoke our minds on the subject of religions other than our own, our opinions about most such faiths would be considerably less than flattering. Those to whom church affiliation or attendance is largely a social matter are inclined to be tolerant and compassionate. But to the degree to which a Catholic, Jew or Protestant is fiercely loyal to his own faith and personally convinced that it is the best of all possible religions, his opinion of other philosophies may be conveyed by such adjectives as *superstitious, absurd, dangerous, fanatical, bigoted, antisocial,* etc.

Obviously the law must therefore protect all Americans against encroachments on their religious conscience, since "the people" cannot automatically be depended on to guarantee such freedom.

Distraught parents have also bumped into the First Amendment when they've written to the government to seek federal assistance in dealing with the new sects. Since they perceive at least some of the cults as partially criminal enterprises, they have communicated their concerns to the Justice Department. As one Department official explained in a letter to parents concerned about the Guyana episode, such events

> cannot serve as a catalyst to cause the Department of Justice to investigate a religious group. As you know, the First Amendment's protection of religious freedom is not limited to the traditional and well-established religions. This protection applies to all religions and includes the right to maintain religious beliefs which are rank heresy to followers of traditional faiths.
>
> . . . Any investigation must be based on an allegation of a violation of Federal law. For example, as you are probably aware, the Federal Bureau of Investigation is investigating the murder of Congressman Ryan and other crimes related to the Guyana affair, over which there is Federal jurisdiction.
>
> The conclusion of this Department that "brainwashing," "mind control," and "mental kidnapping" do not constitute violations of Federal law has not changed. . . . We have also concluded that the possibility of drafting effective Federal criminal legislation in this area is unlikely.

It is one of America's proud boasts that it guarantees freedom *of* religion and freedom *from* religion. Our government is prohibited by law—which is to say by the Constitution—from controlling religions as such. But not all the fruits of freedom are admirable, and just as the Constitution protects the religious liberty of the more socially accepted traditional forms of faith, so it protects radical, bizarre and peculiar religions and sects.

But it is not up to parents' organizations alone to address the large problem of parental feelings. The sects, too, to the extent that their members are capable of rationality and thus Christian compassion, must engage in an examination of conscience. Since not only the Love Family but all the Christian communal groups preach love—we may assume quite sincerely—it follows that they are under the moral obligation to direct this virtuous emotion to the whole world, including members' own actual parents, those who brought them into the world and supported them financially, in most cases up to the very moment of their entry into a communal sect.

Such parents, particularly during the early period of their shocking separation from their children, desperately require emotional support. In addition to the simple sense of loss and puzzlement, they will inevitably search their own consciences and—rightly or wrongly—feel guilty.

In the case of some cult groups, the parents' suffering will be even more acute because of the absurd preaching that the parents represent Satanic or otherwise evil, destructive forces. We know, to our sorrow, that there is no shortage of parents in the world who are, in fact, evil and destructive, since the criminal, the violent, the depraved are as likely to become parents as anyone else. It would therefore be perfectly reasonable if a given cult leader said to a new adherent, "We have information that *your* father and mother are evil, sinful individuals and we think you are well out of their home." But to preach criticism of all parents, as an overreaching generality, is itself evil and stupid, particularly when in the next breath cult leaders are preaching love, sweetness and light.

Fortunately, in the Love Family at least, I have seen no evidence of such anti-parent thinking or indoctrination. Even as regards individual mothers and fathers who have made clear their dislike for the group, the only reaction I have seen is a sort of sad, resigned hope that the parents will somehow, in time, perceive the situation in what the members of the sect see as more realistic terms.

Some parents believe that accommodation of a sort is possible with the Love Family but not with the Children of God or the Unification Church, among others. Since no two cult groups are identical, it is reasonable to distinguish among them.

One of the unfortunate, if inevitable, things about controversy is that it leads to a polarization of argument. The young commune members want to view practically all aspects of their experience as noble, uplifting, enriching, spiritual, while critics and angry parents profess to see nothing but evil in the new religious forms. The fact is that there are elements of justice in both arguments.

Some commune members may imagine they are conceding a point to the opposition when they say, "Well, of course what happened in Jonestown was a disaster, and the Manson Family was a criminal and certainly nonreligious operation."

These statements are true enough, but they fall very far short of an honest recognition of the problem. Sect members, are the practices of your group perfect? You know they are not, for there is no perfection in the physical universe. Consider, then, in what sense and to what degree do you fall short of perfection?

Those parents who object to the cults are sometimes guilty of making comparisons between the communal life and existence in the outside world that do not incorporate enough material reality to be meaningful. The commune or cult affiliation may be perceived in totally—or at least largely—critical terms, while the noncommunal alternative may be perceived, and spoken of, in almost ideal terms. Again, had life in the world appealed to these young people, they would not have wanted to reject it.

Part III—Solutions

As regards the "solution" to the problem posed by the proliferation of new religions, what can one say? First of all, that not everyone agrees that there is a problem. We must remember that the social and moral condition of some members is preferable to their preconversion state. And—galling as the fact may be to millions of observers—many individual members of cults seem perfectly content with their lot. If they are ever to return to the world, most will do it on their own terms and in their own good time. Those who are praying for such an outcome will be encouraged by the fact that, historically, philosophical communes in the United States have rarely persisted. They arise, flourish, and then—for a variety of reasons—dissolve.

We must hope that these young people retain some of their critical skills; that they can see, for example, the danger of investing total confidence in a leader who is, after all, another human being. Although it is unfair to compare all religious sects and leaders with Charles Manson and the Reverend Jim Jones and their groups (Manson's group was not religious, in the first place; Jones's was, but it does not follow that because he turned into a monster, other leaders of new small churches are essentially evil), in another sense the comparison is legitimate: such cases teach the danger of investing *total* loyalty in one who is merely another person. Being totally subservient to God, or to one's interpretation of Jesus Christ, is one thing. But paying to a man the same sort of subservience—which is properly part of worship, of adoration—is quite another matter. No Catholic would dream of investing his spiritual loyalties heart and soul in the Pope, however much he might honor and revere whatever gentleman happens to hold the supreme office of his church at any given period. After all, there have been popes who were licentious and murderous. It is reasonable, then—at least within the context of cult members' general assumptions—for them to hold in particularly high respect *Love* Israel, Ron Hubbard, Moses Berg or other leaders. But the wise believer must always protect himself by reserving common sense, so that if a revered leader suddenly orders murder, suicide or any other actual crime, the believer will automatically say to himself, "The leader has gone too far. I am therefore no longer under obligation to follow him."

Nor is it only specific crimes that can serve as warning signals to the adherents of the new faiths. Any obvious offense to traditional morality, reason or even common sense ought immediately to be taken very seriously. Thousands of individual adherents of the new groups do arrive at such points of awareness. As a result their faith in the infallibility of the leader weakens and they simply leave him. But an even greater number seem to have been blinded by the very fact of their faith, so that they are no longer capable of making judgments based on evidence and reason. This is a point to which every True Believer should give the most careful consideration. Neither he nor his leader is protected from criticism simply because his activity is religious.

Three separate factors form part of the equation of most of the new sects. They are *God, Jesus Christ,* and the *Bible.* These three terms—and the concepts they represent—already have a semi-magical power. But they may be attached to almost any corporate, social or religious enterprise. One is perfectly at liberty, for example, to establish a Christian Dogfood Company, a Christian Broadcasting System or a Divine Light Hamburger Stand. Simple incorporation of the magical word or phrase ensures a significant amount of goodwill. Precisely such a process has occurred in the case of all the new and, for that matter, the established religions, Christian or otherwise.

Secondly, a certain protective effect follows from the adoption of such names. If, for example, one establishes something called the New Church of Christ and is subsequently attacked, one may believe that Christ himself is being attacked, which may be construed as a damnable, blasphemous injustice. On purely rational terms, of course, any institution may be criticized on the basis of both belief and practice.

It is utterly unreasonable to claim, in one's defense, that one's work is religious, as if that were all that need be said about the matter. The Inquisition, too, was religious, as were the frequent mass slaughters referred to in the Old Testament. Whatever is negative—in any religion—must be resolutely opposed.

I submit to the reader who is a cult member—with all appropriate respect—that at the time you made your particular religious commitment, it is probable that you were in a state characterized by a willingness to follow any strong-minded leader who promised you direction, hope for the future, and a moral alternative, as well as insights into certain mysteries. It is important for you to grasp that you are unlikely to have made your crucial decision after carefully assessing, let us say, several dozen of the alternatives available. There are, as you know, hundreds of such cult groups and churches at present, though it would be impractical to expect anyone to study so large a number. The fact remains that you almost certainly allied yourself with the first leader who came along, a process which, of course, took place by chance.

That being the case, you cannot possibly know whether, in fact, you would be better off in another group than you are in the one to which you presently owe allegiance.

Whatever capacity for reasoned argument you have retained forces you to doubt whether your present religion is, in fact, the best of all possible, for if it is not, you are under a moral obligation to search for something better.

What can those who are unsympathetic to the commune movement do? Unfortunately, little of an immediate nature. I do not believe that there is any overall means by which the problem of irrational religious behavior can be cured. It can, however, be prevented or discouraged. But it is a social dilemma as complex as the problem of crime. There are short-term measures, such as building more prisons, hiring more police, etc., but all of these together have never solved the problem. To do that would require a massive reorganization of society from the ground up. Just so, our society as presently constituted is likely to perpetuate the cult problem in the short run, rather than resolve it.

Thus, preventive measures are vital. The prevention I urge is that our society undertake a formal commitment to reason. We must inculcate a respect for wisdom rather than attaching credit to blind belief. Man was not put on this earth primarily to buy philosophical merchandise before examining it, just as he was not put here to turn out hit record albums, to be utterly irresistible to the opposite sex, to use cocaine, or to wear the tightest possible jeans.

Do not be deluded that all that is needed is a return to good old-fashioned common sense. No one would deny the shortage of common sense. But we need more than that. Common sense might be compared to playing a musical instrument by ear. It's nice if you can do it, but it's better if you can also read music and know something about the theory behind it. Common sense, after all, for long centuries made man comfortable in his certainty that the earth was flat, that the sun goes around the earth, and that women are inferior, etc. Man starts—if he is fortunate—with common sense, but to it he must add the applied power of reasoning, aided by the observations and methods of science.

We must do a number of things, and as quickly as possible, to encourage respect for reason in our society. We must teach the simple lesson, for instance, that there is a difference between conclusive evidence and consistent evidence. Consistent evidence argues only that we are still on the right track. Conclusive evidence shows we have reached the end of that track. We must, in fact, *add a fourth "R" to our formal process of early education.* The four would be readin', writin', 'rithmetic and reasoning. It might be objected that you cannot introduce a six-year-old child to logical reasoning of a subtle and sophisticated nature. Indeed you cannot. By the same token you cannot introduce a six-year-old child to calculus or advanced geometry. But no one ever uses that fact to argue that we ought not introduce young children to arithmetic.

And we should go back even further than that. We should publicize the findings of groups specializing in infant education, such as the Institutes for the Achievement of Human Potential in Philadelphia. Read their books, such as *How to Teach Your Baby to Read,* by Glenn Dorman. Note that the title is not How to Teach Your *Child* to Read. Specialists have learned that inasmuch as we start learning languages in the crib, just so we can easily learn to read those languages at the same point and with the same remarkable ease.

Read a book entitled *Kindergarten Is Too Late,* by Masaru Ibuka, one of the founders of the Sony Corporation. It has been found—and there seems to be no controversy about the findings—that the children who start learning at the age of two have an enormous head start over those who are not exposed to reading until they are five or six. And it is significant that their lead persists right through to the university. Read *The Right Brain* by Thomas Blakeslee. Society must begin not only to study the findings such books relate but put them to work.

One result of proper early instruction in the methods of rational thought will be to make sudden mindless conversions—to anything—less likely.

Part of the problem at present is that once the untrained mind has made a formal commitment to a religious philosophy—and it does not matter whether that philosophy is generally reasonable and high-minded or utterly bizarre and irrational—the powers of reason are surprisingly ineffective so far as changing the believer's mind is concerned. The uncomfortable reality must first be faced that science, reason and the factual record all taken together are inconsistent with a great part, if by no means all, of religious belief, though not of morality. If we arbitrarily limit our historical research to the last five hundred years and examine the particulars of every argument that pitted the church against science, we find that by and large science has represented the more reasonable and factually correct side of the debate.

But even in personal terms most of us have had experience in trying to "talk sense" to a philosophical opponent and seen that, no matter how reasonable and accurate our statements, they simply do not seem to penetrate the other's consciousness. I recall some years ago having a good-natured argument with a friend—a radio newsman—who was a Christian Scientist. I was defending the Catholic position. At one point during our conversation the fellow said, "I'm firmly convinced that if my faith were strong enough I could drive my car for the rest of my life without ever putting gasoline into it."

I recognized at once that there was no hope of dealing logically or even by means of common sense with such an assertion. I went over the ground once or twice to make sure that I had correctly interpreted what my friend had said, although there was nothing inherently complex in his profession of faith. Indeed he had meant the statement to be taken at face value. The fact that no Christian Scientist in the world has ever been able to drive an internal combustion automobile without gasoline did not seem to him to have any relevance whatever.

But formal instruction in the techniques of reason, beginning at the kindergarten level, is only half the solution. The inability to reason is only half the problem. The other half, as we have seen, is the deterioration of the American family, the soil from which each new generation, individual by individual, grows. I recommend that from the same early point our schools begin to provide instruction on the subject of personal human relationships. We ought to be taught how to love, as well as how to reason. Just as there are millions who do not think very well, so there are millions who do not love well.

We have assumed that the ability to love was naturally nurtured in the home, and the home continues to be the ideal place for that example which is always the best instruction. But the American home is now a partly failed institution.

If you stop to consider it, it is incredible that we train young people for practically everything except for the two most difficult assignments they will ever face. We train them in reading, in mathematics, science; we train them to type, to work machinery, to pull teeth, to perform a remarkable variety of manual and intellectual tasks, as a result of which we produce millions of doctors, lawyers, mechanics, engineers, athletes, scholars, clergymen—accomplished practitioners of all kinds. But for marriage, a complex, troublesome and perplexing business for all its rewards, we prepare them practically not at all.

There are still uncounted millions of young people who approach their twentieth year with only the most confused understanding of the whole area of sex, love, and marriage. To many the three seem merged into one puzzling blur, so that millions still confuse instinctual sexual attraction with love, and then, assuming that one should marry whomever one loves, stumble into marriages, many of which cannot possibly succeed.

Many of today's young people, of course, have different ideas about sex, love, and marriage than did earlier generations, but the majority are obviously still making the historic mistakes.

I am hardly the first to recommend formal courses to help prepare young people for the roles of husband, wife, father and mother. But starting to prepare boys or girls for marriage at fifteen is starting at least ten years too late. Better that late than never, assuredly, but the sooner we can get such courses into our schools and churches, the better.

I would not presume to suggest the specific content of such courses. Specialists know what should be taught; and they have already perceived the wisdom of demanding the support of the church, the support of legislators and educators.

I would suggest that efforts be initiated at once to prepare suitable texts for pre-school-age children. If a four- or five-year-old can be taught to read a book in which he is advised to "see the dog, see the dog chase the ball, see the ball bounce," why could he not learn something about reading and loving at the same time, from a book that would say, "See the dog playing with the little boy. See the dog lick the boy's face. The dog loves the boy. The boy loves the dog. See the boy run with his father. The mother gives the boy a new toy and hugs him because she loves him."

It may be objected that my suggestion is Utopian. No, it isn't. What would be Utopian would be to invest the idea with unrealistic hopes. Just as teaching small children how to think clearly would not automatically return us to the golden age of Greece, where many citizens were practitioners of philosophy, so we ought not to assume that giving every child affectionate counseling and guidance from age five would cause neuroses, mental illness, and unhappiness to vanish.

But one *can* say that our predicament would be far less precarious than it is now.

Thus, certain things can be done to immunize our young against irrational belief. But to do them presupposes the presence of rational, loving parents. And we are faced with the dismaying reality that for many children there simply are no such parents. There may be a divorce, or death, or emotional instability or social irresponsibility, so that the effects of the parents on the children are largely destructive.

Still, in the majority of American homes, it is possible, by consciously starting to address the factors of thinking and loving when children are in the crib, that the societies they live in as children, as teenagers, as young adults, will not seem so unattractive that they will be driven to seek out desperate alternatives. Specifically, we can keep closer to our children, touch them more, spend more time with them, take more interest in their schoolwork, their playtime activities. If we send them to churches, Sunday schools, or synagogues we ought to share these experiences with them. We ought, in addition to being their parents, be their good, understanding friends. We can never speak to them in their own language, obviously; that is a privilege always reserved for one's peers. But most of us can be closer to them than we have been.

Our generation did not speak easily of love. Many of today's young people speak very easily of it. In many cases, I believe, they are telling us of their needs rather than of their gifts.

Finally, a last word about parenthood. We must remember, as the Catholic convert Kahlil Gibran wrote,

Your children are not your children.
They are the sons and daughters of life's longing for itself.
You may give them your love, but not your thoughts, for they have
    their own thoughts.
You may house their bodies but not their souls.
You may strive to be like them but seek not to make them like you.
For life goes not backward nor tarries with yesterday.

APPENDIX

Answers to Questions
Sent to Love Israel

During May 1981, as I was in the last stages of preparing this book for publication, I realized that a number of questions about the Love Family were still unresolved. So I sent them to *Logic* to give the Love Family the opportunity to confront the questions as straightforwardly as possible.

It is interesting that although the questions were addressed specifically to *Love* Israel, *Logic* provided the answers, by tape recording. There were, he later explained, two reasons for this: his father had asked the questions, and he and *Serious* customarily serve as secretaries for *Love*. The three confer, after which *Logic* or *Serious* handles the communication.

It will be apparent that the responses to simple questions of fact are easier to deal with than those which involve opinion or belief, a distinction hardly unexpected since it has troubled students of religion for thousands of years.

Question 1: You believe that the Love Family *is* one of the twelve Biblical tribes of Israel, specifically the tribe of Judah. Obviously you are not the actual tribe of Judah, since that particular group of people lived thousands of years ago. In what sense, then, *do* you believe you are the tribe of Judah?

Answer: First of all, we believe we are Israel; Israel, of course, being the children of God. We see ourselves as *the* children of God in a special sense. The New Testament speaks of spiritual Israel as being the Jew of the heart, and in this sense we feel that we all have one father, God, and therefore we are the children of God and therefore Israel, God's chosen people. Of course the New Testament is filled with statements about Israel and prophecies about Israel, such as the Book of

Revelation, the resurrection of the tribes of Israel and so forth—the placement of the tribes of Israel in heaven. And in this context we believe we are Israel.

Also, many people in the Family have had various dreams and visions of revelations that explain to them in one way or another that they are part of Israel. It is in these dreams and revelations . . . that we've hit upon the tribe of Judah. A lot of people have had some form of revelation that they are connected with the tribe of Judah. I don't necessarily believe that everyone living here in Seattle with us knows for sure whether they're a part of the tribe of Judah—but many people do believe that.

I was just remembering an experience I had where I realized that inside of every man is Jesus Christ—sort of like the king of each man is Jesus Christ. And Judah is the ruling tribe of Israel and, so to speak, the Christ of Israel. And it is Jesus Christ that we identify with, and it is Judah, in this respect, that is the royal kingdom of government of Israel that we identify with, realizing that it's our job to serve, take care of, to host . . .

Question 2: You have often been quoted as saying, "We don't want to get hung up with rules and regulations." And yet those who study your group get the impression that you have just as many rules and regulations as any other religion does.

Can you be specific about that? Exactly what *are* your rules and regulations?

Answer: It is true that we want to build a life that is not based on rules and regulations. Quite simply, our belief is that Jesus Christ represents the New Testament, which is the law of love, and the Golden Rule; as opposed to the Old Testament, which is all these laws and commandments and do's and don't's of the past. Our intention is to develop a life-style which is based on love, respect, and care and consideration for each other, knowing that love (being the opposite of law) will replace all the other laws, which is simply saying that if you have love for each other, then you don't need a law that says "Thou shalt not kill," because obviously if you love each other you're not going to kill each other.

But of course we are growing, evolving. We are always adopting new people, and so, in the formation of our Family, we do need to make certain agreements in order to manage things and keep things together. But it's always our understanding that any rules, so to speak, that we make are subject to change and always open to discussion.

Anybody who's followed our life-style over the years will testify to the fact that those "rules and regulations" have changed dramatically. . . .

But sometimes it seems we're famous for having these nonexistent rules. Every now and then you hear that we have rules like "No one is allowed to go anywhere," or "Women are not allowed to speak," or "Children are not allowed to live with their parents." Frankly, I don't know where a lot of those "rules" came from, because they certainly aren't the way we live.

Specifically, it's hard to answer the question—exactly what are your rules and regulations?—because we aren't structured like that. We don't have a book of rules that people need to learn when they join the Family. Our requirements are simply the New Testament; we ask people to love, honor and respect each other. We naturally do have an order in the Family. We have a system of elders and expect people to listen to and believe in the counsel of those elders. Not because they absolutely have to; if people don't like you, they don't have to listen. And of course it's a total open-door situation.

[Comment] Against the understandable appeal of the uncluttered life, there is another reality, even within the Love Family itself, and it is one that involves a number of rules and regulations. The following are a few that might be cited:

1. Those who come into the Family contribute all of their money and possessions into the common pool.
2. Everyone in the Family must concede that *Love* Israel, formerly Paul Erdman, is supreme.
3. Women must concede their natural inferiority to men.
4. Members do not acknowledge birthdays or ages.
5. Members must take new names.
6. Like those affiliated with other religions, Love Family members wear distinctive attire.

Family members sometimes say, "Well, nobody is forced to do all of these things. They do them only because they want to, because they have already seen the wisdom of them—in many cases—before they even reach our doors. Even some of the saints, for example, were opposed to private property."

No one is absolutely forced to obey the Ten Commandments either. And—alas—millions who profess to accept them break them daily. But the Ten Commandments definitely come under the heading of rules and regulations, and so—in my view—do the various forms and customs designed to maintain an orderly existence within the Love Family.

Question 3: A transcript of a TV news program that I have says that several years ago the members of the Love Family said that they were sixty-six years older than their actual age. Kathy Crampton's voice was heard explaining that she is eighty-five years old, when she is obviously much younger. Can you explain why that practice came about? And can you tell me why it no longer is operative?

Answer: In the early days of the Family we simply took the liberty of playing with time. The thoughts behind that were simply that sixty-six years was an average life span and we looked at it from the point of view that there was a generation of people that lived with Jesus Christ when he walked on the earth, and there is a line from the Bible that says, "This generation shall not pass away."

And then of course Jesus Christ was crucified on the cross and was resurrected. So what does that statement mean: "This generation shall not pass away"? We took it to mean that we are the Family of Jesus Christ and, in one spiritual sense, we are the same family of Jesus Christ that has always existed. And so we just simply played with time, since most of us realized that it isn't as binding as most people think it is. But the concept was not very meaningful to us—it was not super-weighty or a foundation stone of our beliefs. It was difficult for people to understand, and as I said, it wasn't that big a deal for us, so we simply dropped it.

More accurately to us, a lot of us have realized that we are eternal spirits, which is the actual spiritual revelation which was behind taking the liberties with time in the first place, meaning that a lot of us have realized that we're more than just physical bodies, that actually our bodies are vehicles for our spirits, and our spirits are eternal spirits of God.

Question 4: What can you specifically tell us about an orphanage in India that the Love Israel Foundation supports? What is the extent of your support? Do you send them certain amounts of money, clothing?

Answer: One of them is called Father Rego's, St. Joseph's Home, Calangute-Bardez, GOA, India; and the other is Swami Omcar, The Mission of Peace, Sri Shanti Ashram, Shanti Ashram, P.O. Totapolli Hills, (Via) Shankhavaram East Godavari, Dt. A.P. India. What we do is we send them boxes of clothing and food and money when we can. We're just trying to share whatever abundance we have. When we have extra we try to send them some. We've been doing this for several years. We first became aware of these orphanages because of people in the Family who before joining the Family traveled in India. The people who run these two orphanages gave sanctuary to some of our people when they were on the road, and so these people, when they joined the

Family, told us that there were these very good men doing a good service, taking care of orphans in India. So we've been helping support them ever since.

Question 5: Some parents feel that the children of the elders—and your own children—receive better treatment than those of other members of the Family. Why do you think they have this impression?

Answer: I'm not sure. We live so closely there isn't much of a separation between the children of the elders and the children of the rest of the Family. In town we all live in the same houses, and at the ranch we all live in the same ranch. The kids go to the same school; the food comes from the same distribution system. It's hard to say—I don't know who it is that has this impression.

Question 6: In a story published in a newspaper called *New Era* in Lancaster County, Pennsylvania, March 19, 1979, the reporter—on the basis of information given by Melinda Loughlin—says that in one instance a couple of adults stuffed dirty washcloths into a child's mouth until the corner split and began to bleed. She says the child started to turn blue so the adults stopped abusing him, threw him in a laundry basket and shut him in the laundry closet. What can you clarify about the alleged incident?

Answer: I don't know about that particular incident, but I do know that in the growth of our Family, of course, there have been various things of the sort that might happen anywhere in society. Our only stand is just to help people, help them grow, help them mature, help them learn how to understand how to raise their children. And of course our attitude is to forgive and to bless and to really treat everybody like they are our Family, even if people blow it sometimes. Unfortunately anything any one person in the Family has ever done, the Family (and oftentimes *Love* Israel in particular) seems to take the blame.

In a way it's irritating to be constantly judged for rumors and allegations of years and years ago rather than to have people come and take an honest look.

The trouble with an allegation like this is that it implies that somehow we *believe* in child abuse, which couldn't be further from the truth. Anybody who would ever visit or stay with us and see the children, of course, would discover that we love the children, we love to take good care of the children, and the actual conditions of our life are our only defense.

Question 7: There have been reports that the Love Family is rewriting the Bible and developing a document called "Charter." What clarification can you provide on this?

Answer: We have no intention of rewriting the Bible. We do have our charter, which we originally wrote years ago, right at the beginning of the Family, when we first wanted to get our church approved by the State of Washington and learned that notification required a charter stating our basic beliefs.

So we sat down and broke things up into the basic chapters that concerned us—marriage, children, authority, and so forth—the various aspects of our life—and tried to write down our beliefs. Since we're a church we took quotes out of the Bible that were significant to us and in support of our basic beliefs. We never had any intention of using that to replace the Bible, even though it seems to have been printed in some newspaper article long ago that that's what we used *for* the Bible. That's kind of ridiculous.

Question 8: It is said that one of the storefront centers in the Queen Anne section sometimes gives away free food. Is this actually the case? If so, during the average week how much free food is given away, and to whom?

Answer: Yes, we have a table outside of a place called the Front Door Inn—we call it the abundance table—and we put out free food there, which is available to anyone who cares to pick it up. Mostly neighbors pick it up. Whatever we have, whatever food we're providing for the Family, we put out there, and generally, about as much food goes out on the abundance table as would normally go to one of our households of about fifteen or twenty people.

During the summertime, when we have more fresh fruit and produce, we give away quite a bit more than we do during the winter.

Question 9: According to the *New Era* article, the Family "owns a lumberyard, boats, orchards, a cannery." What truth, if any, is there in this assertion?

Answer: We don't own a lumberyard. We do own a small sawmill that we use to cut lumber for our own use sometimes. We did at one time own a commercial fishing boat, but we don't own that anymore. We don't own an orchard, and I don't believe we ever have, but every summer we go pick fruit along with all the migrant farm laborers. As for the cannery—somebody joined the Family whose parents had built a cannery and the person joining the Family operated it. It wasn't a commercial operation; it's what they call a custom cannery where people in the farm area of eastern Washington bring in their own fruit and produce and pack it in the cans themselves, and then the machinery would cook it and can it for them. We took that over and operated it for about two years as a custom cannery and then closed it down. Now what we do there is produce organic juice which we sell in natural food stores and co-ops around the Pacific Northwest.

Question 10: Your critics allege that you have two wives in the Love Family. Since even Ronald Reagan has had two wives this is obviously something our society permits, but the reference is to having two wives *at the same time,* which is considered criminal by American society and referred to by the word *bigamy.* It would seem that your answer on this point must be (a) there is no foundation in fact to this allegation; I have never had more than one wife, or ongoing sexual mate, at one time; or (b) I do indeed regard two separate women as my own helpmate. I consider that this is none of American society's business, that it is justified by references in the Old Testament, etc.

Answer: To answer, let me give you some of our thoughts on the subject, rather than to present gossipy facts of people's private lives.

In our Family we knew we had to approach everything in a new way. Our job was to build a life together where we could live as if we were all One. So we have always looked to build a life that could be run by shared values and customs rather than by laws designed to hold people back from some evil drive within them. Our plan, of course, could work only with true idealists who *knew* that we were One and that the consequences of their private actions would affect those around them.

We have always believed that there wasn't a clear enough example around us to follow for a pattern. We had not seen anything working out perfectly around us or we probably would have joined it. Instead we felt it was up to us to build something new.

In the beginning we all agreed to be celibate. Our purpose was to let the love between us grow in a more brotherly and sisterly way. We were all quite willing to give up anything since we were all gathered together to give and build rather than to seek our own comforts and pleasures.

After a couple of years we began to allow people to have man-woman relationships as long as the people involved seemed well-grounded in their purpose and mature enough to build something good for the whole Family. This of course was a major change that led to having children and all the changes of life that they bring with them. But, rather than have people be married in a traditional way, we felt that we should be married first of all to the church, to something higher than each other, to God. And that we should be living together under agreement rather than a legalistic bond. We didn't want to create more sin and guilt if that relationship changed somehow. We wanted to have something that we were all dedicated to that would remain even if a certain romantic love was lost. That way, if a couple with children did split up, there would still be a way for the parents to respect each other and continue to relate and the children would not have to suffer the all too common pains of divorce, especially divorce with hard feelings.

Our hope is that people will stay together if at all possible, yet we feel that if it just is not working it may be better to accept a change. Once again, by mutual agreement.

In many ways we feel that our life is still taking shape and we want to go easy on each other as we grow, always looking to stay clear and resolved and loving. And as we grow we see the need to put very little restrictions (as a church) on what is right and wrong in a way that will become a law that will only return to haunt us in the future. Instead we leave it up to the people involved to define the limits of their agreements.

Of course, because whatever an individual does affects the rest of us, we regularly talk with and work with each other in a constant effort to understand our relationships.

By keeping our minds open, and always looking to build a life based on love rather than fear, we see that God is bringing down a culture into us that we never could have created by our own design.

So, in the meantime, we are still young, and therefore reluctant to call many things wrong. We have all given our lives to finding a better way to live. In the very beginning we realized that it wasn't any good to complain if we didn't have an alternative. We are building that alternative.

Question 11: What information can you give me about your former connection with the group called the Children of God? For how long were you a member? In what city? For what reasons did you leave the Children of God?

Answer: Neither *Love* nor I ever had any association with the Children of God. I'm not sure what you may have heard that would make you think we did.

Question 12: A former member of the Love Family has reported that in one of the Family's religious ceremonies a group of Family members sat in a circle, holding hands, with one holding a piece of metal that was plugged into an electric outlet.

A book on the subject of religious communes says, "The current was turned on and it ran through our bodies." According to these observers, tolerance to the electric current was a test of faith.

Did such a ceremony or act ever take place, and is it a regular, ongoing procedure? What is its purpose?

Answer: For a while people did things like that, but it was never in the spirit of a test of faith or anything religious. It was just something people did, more like an amusement park trick, just for the fun of it.

Always using enough people to absorb the electric current so that
nobody ever had more than just a light shock, enough to make people
laugh. It had nothing to do with a test of faith.

Question 13: Almost all the published newspaper and magazine articles
I've seen about the Love Family say that you "read nothing but the
Bible." But there are other books on some of your shelves up there.

Obviously there is a discrepancy here, so I'd be indebted to you if
you could explain that.

Answer: I don't know how the rumor got started that we use nothing but
the Bible. [In his first letter Brian had written, "Our only book is the
Bible."] I guess it all started from the fact that we do base our life on the
Bible. But of course we use hundreds of other books besides the Bible,
though none of them have the same authority to us as the Bible does.

Question 14: Back in 1973 someone connected with the Seattle police
said, "The only written material is the Bible, which has been reedited
by *Love* and his name inserted wherever reference to the Diety is
made."

This seems unlikely, since it would take an awful lot of work; but,
in any event, we would be indebted to you for providing us with
whatever comment or explanation you might care to make on the
point.

Answer: This is a ridiculous accusation. It's outrageous. It would involve
a fabulous amount of work, which of course we would never have done.

Question 15: One of the early critics of the Love Family, a Redondo
Beach High School student named David Kugel, wrote . . . "*Love*
Israel believes he is God and has never committed a sin."

No doubt you'll want to comment about that allegation.

Answer: Actually *Love* believes that we are all one with God, and of
course he desires to represent God, as do I and, I hope, all people. And
like most Christians we believe that we have been *forgiven* by Jesus
Christ for everything.

Question 16: An article in the Everett (Washington) *Herald* about you, on
March 9, 1974, says that you claim to draw your own power from a
vision you had while on a Greyhound bus in Texas during a reading of
the Bible. It would be helpful if you could fill in more information
about this particular bus trip, tell what section of the Bible you were
reading, etc.

Answer: That is a true story that *Love* was riding a Greyhound bus
through Texas when he had an experience. . . . He had a vision in
which God showed him a white stone with the name "Love" written on
it and revealed to him that that was his name. But it wasn't until a little
while after that that he actually called himself by that name. At first it

was presumed that it was a spiritual name, not the name that he should actually carry.

Question 17: Some of your [*Love* Israel's] critics refer to your having a police record as Paul Erdman, and even distribute what are said to be copies of it. There are also allegations of sexual contact with teenaged girls.

Answer: So far as I [Brian] know, there is nothing to this. I do know of one case where a man arrested for drunk driving gave his name as Love Israel, but *Love* was with us all that night.

[**Comment**] Either (a) Erdman's critics are lying, or mistaken; (b) Erdman has lied to Brian about the matter; or (c) Brian is not telling the truth.

I trust Brian.